The Dream of Absolutism

The Dream of Absolutism

LOUIS XIV AND THE LOGIC OF MODERNITY

Hall Bjørnstad

The University of Chicago Press CHICAGO AND LONDON

The University of Chicago Press, Chicago 60637
The University of Chicago Press, Ltd., London
© 2021 by The University of Chicago
Published 2021
Printed in the United States of America

30 29 28 27 26 25 24 23 22 21   1 2 3 4 5

ISBN-13: 978-0-226-80366-1 (cloth)
ISBN-13: 978-0-226-80383-8 (paper)
ISBN-13: 978-0-226-80397-5 (e-book)
DOI: https://doi.org/10.7208/chicago/9780226803975.001.0001

Library of Congress Cataloging-in-Publication Data
Names: Bjørnstad, Hall, author.
Title: The dream of absolutism : Louis XIV and
the logic of modernity / Hall Bjørnstad.
Description: Chicago : University of Chicago Press, 2021. |
Includes bibliographical references and index.
Identifiers: LCCN 2021005321 | ISBN 9780226803661 (cloth) |
ISBN 9780226803838 (paperback) | ISBN 9780226803975 (ebook)
Subjects: LCSH: Louis XIV, King of France, 1638–1715. | Louis XIV, King of
France, 1638–1715. Mémoires pour l'instruction du Dauphin. | Louis XIV,
King of France, 1638–1715—Portraits. | Le Brun, Charles, 1619–1690. Le Roi
gouverne par lui-même, 1661. | Louis XIV, King of France, 1638–1715—In
literature. | Despotism—France—History—17th century. | Monarchy—
France—History—17th century. | Power (Social sciences)—France—
History—17th century. | France—Politics and government—1643–1715.
Classification: LCC DC125 .B56 2021 | DDC 944/.033092 [B]—dc23
LC record available at https://lccn.loc.gov/2021005321

♾ This paper meets the requirements of ANSI/NISO Z39.48-1992
(Permanence of Paper).

Contents

Illustrations

On Translations and Spelling

Throughout this book, all translations from the French are mine, unless the name of a translator is indicated. In the interest of consistency, I have modernized the orthography of early modern texts throughout, whether they are quoted from original or modern editions.

Preface

This is *not* a book about Louis XIV. Although I invite the reader to join me in close scrutiny of texts and paintings that focus intently on portraying the king, and whose production is often commissioned and supervised—sometimes even in part effectuated—by the king himself, my goal in doing so is not to offer yet another study of the man monumentalized at Versailles. The inquiry will certainly take us to Versailles, to its symbolic core in Charles Le Brun's paintings on the ceiling of the Hall of Mirrors celebrating the exploits of the king. It will also lead us to the inner secrets of the workings of absolutism as laid out by the king and his team of secretaries in the radically understudied *Mémoires* written for his oldest son, the Dauphin. Furthermore, we will look closely at some written portraits of the king that may seem so excessive, so outlandish, so absurd to modern readers that it has proved next to impossible for scholars not to take them as subversive mockery. They are not. It is in fact a central claim of this book that these seeming absolutist absurdities are driven by the same logic that we find at the heart of absolutism, both in the king's secret *Mémoires* and in its public self-expression in the Hall of Mirrors. Their absurdity, rather than a deviation or failure of the logic of absolutism, is constitutive of political absolutism itself. However, instead of measuring them anachronistically against modern standards of political rationality, I argue that we as modern readers can see them much more meaningfully as different expressions of the same dream. A dream propelled by its own logic, shot through with ideals about glory, exemplarity, and excess. A dream of absolutism that the king, his image-makers, the court, if not the whole nation, dreamt together collectively and that perhaps remains latent in the collective political imaginary today to a larger extent than we would like to think. Rather than about Louis XIV, this book is about that dream.

On the face of it, the project of this book is thus quite straightforward: an exploration of three very different yet complementary windows into the dream and logic of absolutism—namely, the king's *Mémoires* (chapter 1), Le Brun's paintings in the vault of the Hall of Mirrors at Versailles (chapter 2), and two particularly exuberant written portrayals of the king (chapter 3). In this sense, the proof is in the pudding: the import and impact of the project depends mainly on the execution of these analyses and on the pertinence of what they yield. However, as an intervention in the scholarship on the culture of French absolutism widely construed, my enterprise is more controversial, more provocative than this description makes it seem. The book asks us, as modern readers, to suspend for a moment what we think we know not only about absolutism but also about these artifacts and their way of communicating. My premise is that in order to discern the logic of absolutism, we need to analyze closely those cultural expressions that might sit uncomfortably with our modern democratic sensibility. These are cultural artifacts that inevitably strike a post-Romantic observer as lacking in originality and serving as mere propaganda. To our cognitive categories, they register, as if by default, either as expressions of unapologetic subservience or, conversely, as subversive vehicles. But they are neither. Instead, they are witnesses to a still-premodern way of figuring the authority of the monarchical ruler, a *figuring* that needs to be approached as expression and manifestation— what I call here the dream of absolutism—rather than as the more familiar representation, construction, or fabrication.

The first plate of this book takes us directly to the heart of its argument.[1] Seemingly, the inscription under this famous painting by Charles Le Brun captures the essence of absolutism: "Le Roi gouverne par lui-même, 1661" (The King governs on his own, 1661). The image condenses this essence in the gesture of the king's right hand, firmly holding the rudder of the ship of state after the death of Cardinal Mazarin in 1661. It showcases the foundational moment of French absolutism, while itself being a monument of this very moment displayed at the heart of absolutist France: the central detail of the central painting in the vault of the Hall of Mirrors at Versailles. However, as I argue in chapter 2, the simplicity in the message is itself a retroactive projection. It is so, first of all, in the sense that the king's 1661 decision only became decisive in retrospect, while the contemporary sources tell a much more complex story. Designed in the late 1670s and completed in the early 1680s, this painting's imposition of 1661 as an absolute beginning is therefore itself already a dream. A dream about absolutist self-creation dreamt collectively by painter, court, king—reemerging across media in all the other sources this book explores and repeated by modern scholars. But the simplicity of the message is also complicated by the painting itself, and even by its original inscription. The pithy line is another retroactive projection from the following century, while the long-lost original tripartite Latin inscription shifts our attention to the king's attention: his gesture, as condensed in the reach of his left arm and the direction of his gaze, is directed toward what drives him to his foundational action. As he seizes the helm of the state, the king is "burning with love for glory" ("GLORIÆ AMORE INCENDITUR")—entirely consumed by future glory, as figured in the painting by the Roman god of war, Mars, pointing to the female

1. See the color gallery following page 124.

allegory of glory up on the cloud. That cloud itself belongs more properly to the realm of dreams, and the ex nihilo origin of absolutism emerges from this dream, *is* this dream. We join the dream when our retrospective gaze *on* the painting somehow mirrors the king's prospective one *in* the painting, as he looks longingly toward the future, which is the present of the beholder at Versailles (including, as we shall soon see, the present of the king himself)—if not the past, as in our case. The dream of absolutism is, in other words, there from the beginning; it *is* itself the beginning, but at the same time also already ours, in our willingness to dream along.

This first glimpse at the central constellation of Charles Le Brun's iconographic project in the Hall of Mirrors at Versailles is not yet an interpretation or even the beginning of an analysis, which will have to wait until chapter 2. But it already bears the promise of a layered complexity and conceptual richness to be explored. There is a peculiar logic at work here, which I call "the dream of absolutism": a dream that is not only displayed but also enacted, a dream that the painting itself dreams.

But if this is so, why haven't the conceptual complexity and richness at the symbolic center of Versailles already been examined? Indeed, how to explain that none of the artifacts of absolutism analyzed in this book have been taken seriously by the rich scholarship on the culture of absolutism in France?

This book is born from the realization that these questions have a very simple answer: *The material is virtually unexplored because it is almost unthinkable that it has anything pertinent to tell us.* Taken out of context, such a statement could perhaps come off as polemical, controversial, or confrontational, but as formulated here, it serves as a mere observation of fact. And yet, this unthinkability needs to be thought through and understood before turning to the exploration of absolutist artifacts in the later chapters of the book. Therefore, the first half of this introduction proposes something quite different from a traditional survey of the scholarship on absolutism and absolutist culture: rather than situating the project in a wider field, my goal is to uncover habits of thought that foreclose the possibility of submitting this corpus of absolutist artifacts to serious analysis. Less than an introduction proper, doing preliminary groundwork, the aim of the first two sections is a clearing of the ground—in this case the groundwork for a very different kind of approach, presented in the second half of the introduction.

The intervention this book seeks to make is therefore not limited to the outcome of the specific explorations in its three chapters. Beyond the individual conclusions, what is at stake is the status of the artifacts, the methodology used to examine them, and ultimately the concept of absolutism itself. In what follows I start with the latter, making my case for the "problem" of absolutism in the way that the concept is normally deployed, arguing that its analytical application relies on an already modern—and, as I shall demonstrate, therefore contradictory—apprehension of absolute kingship. Paradoxically, this approach has led to an inability to engage seriously with the corpus discussed here and, even more importantly, to an inability to reckon with the phantasmal or dreamlike compulsion that may yet draw us in the twenty-first century toward absolutism even after absolutism. Second, I make a more technical argument about how this misconception positions the modern observer or scholar in relation to the culture of absolutism in a way that will easily lead us to reduce absolutism's artifacts to mere propaganda. As I argue, this reduction to propaganda is so omnipresent that we do it without noticing and without weighing what we thereby exclude from our thinking about absolutist culture. For example, this reduction may take the form of a seemingly innocent application of a modern communication model (analyzing the artifact as the communication of a message), without taking proper consideration of questions of diffusion and intended recipients. This is the surprising case of the Cordouan Lighthouse discussed later in the introduction (19–20) and much of the material in the following chapters.

The two incursions into the concepts of absolutism and propaganda in the first half of the introduction are necessary in order to open a space for thinking differently and non-reductively about what I call *expressions* of absolutism in the second half of the introduction. Importantly, the framework brought forth here is not at all of my own making. Instead, it implies a return to the period's own thinking about kingship through the radically under-explored categories of royal glory and royal exemplarity (section 3) and, finally, the notion of the dream (section 4).

1. *The Problem with Absolutism*

The main problem when discussing absolutism is not so much that modern scholars and observers don't really know what it is about—or better, what it *was* about—but rather that we are so convinced that we do. Absolutism is something of the past, to be sure, but we relate to it as a close and recognizable past. Unlike modes of governing from an unequivocally premodern era or from a non-Western culture, we approach absolutism with the assumption that our modern political conceptual categories are applicable when we make sense of it. It is the past's moment of becoming modern, as characterized in the specific context of absolutism in the age of Louis XIV through a long series of processual nouns, including modernization, secularization, rationalization, instrumentalization, bureaucratization, centralization—if not as a more abrupt transition, as in revolutions in communication, in the management of information, in the control of human life processes, in the waging of war, and so on. All of these processes and developments are certainly well documented and their study important; however, it is my claim that it is not obvious that they promote our understanding of absolutism as such.

What if absolutism were not really the fixed, fetishized moment constructed by these processes (so familiar to us because already carried by a modern rationality)? What if these modernizing constructions in fact impede or preclude our access to what absolutism was? What if absolutism were located in the unfamiliar moment prior to the temporal block constituted by this modernization, driven by a premodern logic from whence all these processes flow?

This series of questions lies at the heart of a central paradox in the scholarship on French absolutism. As modern historians have long noted, the study of the reign of Louis XIV has resulted in "the contradiction of an absolutism that we know incomparably well in its [historical] details but without a good grasp of its [conceptual] totality and coherence."[2] Yet this absent "totality and coherence" will not, *cannot* be found either in the political treatises of the period (there is no theory of absolutism) or through an abstraction from the details on the ground (which do not, in any meaningful way, constitute an archive of absolutism). Absolutism has no room for prehistory; it emerges, as shown in my first brief look at the central painting in the Hall of Mirrors, from a retrospectively constructed point of origin, erasing not only what came before it but also the historicity of its actual process of becoming. As I show repeatedly throughout this book, absolutism writes, paints, dreams its own origin.[3] As an analytical

2. "[O]n en est arrivé à cette contradiction d'un absolutisme qu'on connaît incomparablement dans son détail, sans qu'on en saisisse bien l'ensemble et la coherence." Cosandey and Descimon, *L'absolutisme en France*, 296. For three important contributions to the scholarship on French absolutism from recent years, see Drevillon, *Les rois absolus*; Jouanna, *Le Pouvoir absolu*; and Jouanna, *Le Prince absolu*.

3. This statement does not imply, of course, that French absolutism is not part of a larger history. There is certainly a French theorization of sovereignty in the century before Louis XIV (most importantly by jurists like Jean Bodin and Cardin Le Bret) that can be—and has indeed been—considered to prepare for the advent of absolutism. However, the realization of absolutism with Louis XIV transcends the prior theorization of sovereignty to such an extent that the "totality and coherence" of absolutism need to be sought elsewhere. In other words, the prehistory of absolutism becomes visible as such only through the reign of Louis XIV, whose absolutist "totality and coherence" are, in part, predicated upon the erasure of this prehistory.

tool, therefore, absolutism is useful because it brings into focus the practices of monarchical power's self-representation, rather than because of its indexical value, pointing to a stable definition or sparking discussion on what that definition should be. Indeed, the only place where absolutism incontestably exists is in its manifestations, in the image of itself that royal power projects both outward and inward, in the dream that absolutism is.

What I call "the problem with absolutism" has its origin in a temporal disjunction in the concept of absolutism itself, between what is being observed and the point of observation. Scholars know that the term has always been used retrospectively, since a first attested use by François-René de Chateaubriand in 1797. It later came to prominence in the nineteenth century both in French and English, generally as part of an opposition to what came after it, be it enlightenment, revolution, modernity, or later forms of un-absolute (constitutional) monarchy. It is true that the use of the nominalized form "absolut*ism*" is so close to actual seventeenth-century French political uses of the adjective *absolu* (with *pouvoir absolu* [absolute power] and *roi absolu* [absolute king] attested as early as 1636) that the imposition of the noun might feel like only a very light anachronism, naming a practice of government that was incontestably there at the time. Nevertheless, the specific emergence of the term still bears the risk of reducing the phenomenon observed to a less advanced, less rational, or less modern precursor of what it is opposed to. Confined to its place in prehistory, it is defined mainly by what it is lacking, as compared to more recent modes of governing. This is still the case in the way the term is used today, starting with the nearly identical primary definitions in the *Oxford English Dictionary* (*OED*) and the French *Grand Robert*: "The practice of absolute government; absolute authority, despotism."[4] To our modern sensibility, there is only a comma separating "despotism" and "absolutism." At the same time, any informed observer is of course aware of what is missing here, as spelled out in the much more historically accurate definition of absolutism in the French *Trésor de la langue française* (*TLF*): "System of government where the sovereign holds

---

4. *OED*, "absolutism." The definition in the *Grand Robert* runs as follows: "Système de gouvernement, régime politique où le pouvoir du souverain est absolu, n'est soumis à aucun contrôle." (System of government, political regime where the power of the sovereign is absolute, not subject to any control.) The proximity to despotism is highlighted by a list of cross-references including terms such as "autocracy," "despotism," "dictatorship," "tyranny." *Grand Robert*, "absolutisme." The wider discussion of the conceptual history of the notion of absolutism in this paragraph relies on the sources mentioned in n. 2 above (particularly the introduction in Cosandey and Descimon, *L'absolutisme en France*), in addition to the dictionaries quoted in this and the following note.

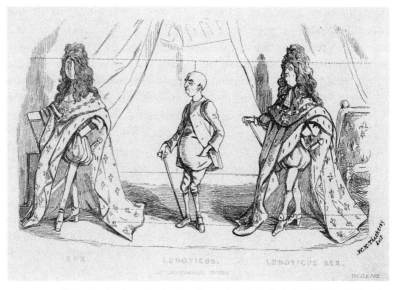

FIGURE 1. "Rex. Ludovicus. Ludovicus Rex: An Historical Study," illustration in William Makepeace Thackeray [Mr. Titmarsh, pseud.], *The Paris Sketch Book*, vol. 2 (London: John Macrone, 1840). The "exact calculation" of absolutism, according to Thackeray. Photograph © The Trustees of the British Museum.

divine-right power without constitutional limits."[5] However, the historical self-evidence of the divine-right paradigm is unavailable to our retrospective gaze: invisible to us, even *unthinkable* to us, yet very much a lived experience for them. Or at least, unthinkable for the concept of absolutism. Indeed, it is as if the concept's temporal disjunction itself served to obfuscate the premodern foundation of the structure it describes, as if the core of the historical phenomenon the term is meant to describe were excluded from its very concept.

The result is a contradiction rendered visible in a well-known drawing by William Makepeace Thackeray (fig. 1). From the vantage point of 1840, Thackeray decomposes a representation of King Louis ("Ludovicus Rex") in all his splendor, clearly inspired by Hyacinthe Rigaud's 1701 iconic painting (fig. 2), into the royal adornment and finery on the one hand ("Rex") and the unadorned old man on the other ("Ludovicus"). The drawing appears in Thackeray's *Paris Sketch Book*, where he comments upon it at length in the essay "Meditations at Versailles" in the following way:

5. "Système de gouvernement où le souverain possède une puissance *de droit divin* et sans limites constitutionnelles." *TLF*, "absolutisme"; my emphasis.

In Louis [XIV], surely, if in any one, the majesty of kinghood is represented.

But a king is not every inch a king, for all the poet may say; and it is
curious to see how much precise majesty there is in that majestic figure of
Ludovicus Rex. In the plate opposite [here, fig. 1], we have endeavoured
to make the exact calculation. The idea of kingly dignity is equally strong

FIGURE 2. Hyacinthe Rigaud, *Louis XIV* (ca. 1701). Oil on canvas. Musée du Louvre,
Paris, France. Photograph: Wikimedia Commons.

in the two outer figures; and you see, at once, that majesty is made out of
the wig, the high-heeled shoes, and cloak, all fleurs-de-lis bespangled. As
for the little, lean, shrivelled, paunchy old man, of five feet two, in a jacket
and breeches, there is no majesty in *him*, at any rate; and yet he has just
stept out of that very suit of clothes. Put the wig and shoes on him, and he
is six feet high;—the other fripperies, and he stands before you majestic,
imperial, and heroic! Thus do barbers and cobblers make the gods that
we worship: for do we not all worship him? Yes; though we all know him
to be stupid, heartless, short, of doubtful personal courage, worship and
admire him we must; and have set up, in our hearts, a grand image of him,
endowed with wit, magnanimity, valour, and enormous heroical stature.[6]

Thackeray's passage further develops the point made so boldly in the drawing through the emphasis placed on "equally strong." The sense of majesty
and dignity associated with the king is not only *supported* by "the wig, the
high-heeled shoes, and cloak, all fleurs-de-lis bespangled"; the trappings
and fripperies of majesty are all there is. His "majestic figure" is *only* figure,
in the archaic sense of external form or shape, without any underlying sub-
stance. By way of decomposition and analysis, the inquiry into "how much
precise majesty" there is in the king's "majestic figure" leaves Thackeray
with the conclusion that "there is no majesty in *him*, at any rate."

But is this really "the exact calculation" of absolutism, as Thackeray
implies? It is, but only *after* the fact, only *after* absolutism. What is missing is the idea—and more than the idea, the lived experience—of the
incarnation of a divinely invested dignity in the king. Thackeray's "exact
calculation" is possible only *after* the loss of faith in a god whose ways
were not so mysterious that absolutist theologians couldn't identify his
will and decipher his hand in history all the way up to Louis XIV. Therefore, while the Rigaud painting depicts what absolutism was, within the
present of its existence, Thackeray's drawing only shows what absolutism
looked like in retrospect, from an external perspective, somewhere between them and us in time.

It is my contention that much of the scholarship on absolutism remains within the mode of Thackeray's "exact calculation," viewing its object of study with a modern demystifying gaze, as if the decomposition
that it performs and that the drawing illustrates so starkly were valid in
Louis XIV's time, as if this truly were all that absolutism was.[7] Such an ap-

6. Thackeray, *The Paris Sketch Book*, 2:281–82.

7. For a similar argument regarding the modern scholarly approach to the Holy Roman Empire, see Stollberg-Rilinger, *The Emperor's Old Clothes*, esp. the introduction.

proach is exactly that: a calculation, and more precisely a calculation that cuts down any element to fit into its model and measurement. If majesty and royal dignity were nothing more than their external trappings, scholars could analyze the whole of absolutist culture in modern terms as an instrument of manipulation, as propaganda. But not so as long as the subjects (and the king) still believed in the divine investment in their king and kingdom; not so in a world where royal dignity was still perceived as a given—or more precisely, a pregiven—truth prior to any legitimizing act or calculation. This, then, is the exact nature of the contradiction central to the enterprise given flesh and form in Thackeray's drawing: it is an attempt at calculating the truth of a time before calculation. The result is certainly a truth, but *our* truth, not *their* truth, about absolutism.

A few precisions are in place at this point. I do not claim, of course, that calculations into the communicative effect of absolutist expressions were absent from the politics of a Colbert or any skillful operator of absolutist politics. On the contrary, they were all accomplished practitioners of the art of rhetoric and persuasion. Nor do I exclude the possibility that the analysis of specific practices or artifacts could fruitfully mobilize a framework relying on concepts like manipulation, instrumentalization, or even propaganda. I do claim, however, that by resorting to such a framework by default, we risk uncritically reiterating the reduction inherent in the concept of absolutism itself, without even considering whether our modern analytical categories are appropriate when making sense of absolutism's premodern logic. As if expressions of absolutism could be nothing but mere propaganda.

Such a reduction to propaganda is somewhat of an unquestioned commonplace in much of the current scholarship on the culture of absolutism, and this default is interrogated in the next section. There is, however, another layer to my argument about the problem with absolutism. I contend that when we let Thackeray's "exact calculation" be our only guiding approach to absolutism, we avoid confronting something that perhaps makes us uncomfortable in its unruly excess, something awkwardly close to the pleasure or joy that propels the dream of absolutism. Yet grasping the "totality and coherence" of absolutism itself requires grappling with that excess and recognizing its alterity.

Interestingly, this last perspective is very much present in the passage from Thackeray, which is in reality richer and less reductive than what a first reading might indicate. There is, in the quoted passage and in the essay to which it belongs, an exuberant *fascination* with all things related to the king and Versailles. Even while disparaging him, the text betrays a very detailed historical knowledge. "[F]or do we not all worship him," despite having performed "the exact calculation," despite knowing the truth that his majesty is consubstantial with its trappings and "fripperies," produced in its entirety by "barbers and cobblers"? "Yes," Thackeray answers, thereby attesting to a continued effectiveness of absolutism after absolutism. It is as if Thackeray were writing—and drawing—to convince himself of what his reason knows very well, but that his heart refuses to accept. Here is the dream of absolutism: "in our hearts, a grand image of him, endowed with wit, magnanimity, valour, and enormous heroical stature." Approached this way, the passage from Thackeray invites the reader to reflect on this post-absolutist admiration and worship of absolutism, then and now, as well as on the nature of the compulsion to give in to it ("worship and admire him we *must*"; my emphasis). A compulsion that, despite the author's demystifying calculation, brings us full circle from the critical "no majesty in *him*, at any rate" (Thackeray's emphasis) back to the final "grand image of *him*" (my emphasis) "in our hearts," an image that, importantly, we ourselves "have set up." Although the materials analyzed here all date from the reign of Louis XIV (with one notable exception), this book aims nonetheless to extend a similar invitation to the reader to reflect on the post-absolutist afterlife of the dream of absolutism.

2. Beyond Mere Propaganda

What does it mean to approach a cultural artifact celebrating the glory of Louis XIV in terms of propaganda? Propaganda certainly is glorification; so why shouldn't glorification be considered propaganda? While circumspect scholars of an earlier generation have voiced their hesitations and qualms in regard to its applicability, the term seems to have imposed itself as a natural part of the current critical vocabulary, in no need of any provisos or reservations. Already in 2000, Pierre Zoberman observed in regards to the age of Louis XIV that "[c]onfronted with the elaboration of a positive image of the King and Monarchy, and with a program for the inscription and diffusion of such an image, the period's historians [i.e., the present-day historians of the period]—whether they concentrate on the Monarchy itself, on mentalities, or on literature—routinely identify this process as propaganda."[8] While the adverb "routinely" is used by the author to stress this identification as something that happens "regularly" or "typically," the routine qualification is nonetheless already marked in the more precise sense of happening "without proper thought" or "unthink-

---

8. Zoberman, "Eloquence and Ideology," 303.

ingly," as the *OED* explains.[9] Today, "propaganda" functions as a critical shorthand, useful because of its seeming clarity and self-evidence. The category is seldom central enough to be thematized or reflected upon. Instead it tends to appear as part of assertive qualifications and striking formulations made in passing, and even more often in blurbs, introductions, conclusions, or section titles. The term's trenchant and pugnacious qualities make it particularly effective for programmatic statements. It is a critical shorthand that will lend a critical edge to a critical juncture. But exactly because of that, it also risks saying more and doing more than what is immediately obvious. Notice the slight unease in the following observation by Ellen Welch at a crucial point of her magisterial 2017 inquiry into the intersection of performance and diplomacy in seventeenth-century France: "In describing the form and content of these entertainments of the height of Louis XIV's reign, *it is difficult to avoid* painting them as displays of force and pieces of effective propaganda."[10] Although Welch's subtle analysis questions the effectiveness of these performances, and at times is close to inquiring whether effectiveness was their purpose in the first place (at least in the current sense of the term), the language of propaganda seems to impose itself, *malgré elle*. It is as if the notion itself exerts the force that it pinpoints.[11] It is against the background of this self-producing force in the concept's routine applications that it becomes important to take a step back and interrogate the meaning of the *gesture* of labeling something as propaganda.[12]

9. All these synonyms are taken from *OED*, "routinely."

10. Welch, *A Theater of Diplomacy*, 148; my emphasis. The example quoted above is one of at least three occasions where Welch registers unease with the "traditional characterization [of practices like these] as propaganda" (85 and 106; 106 for the quotation).

11. This sense of the category of propaganda imposing itself is confirmed by a quick consultation of a select corpus of important books exploring the culture of absolutism published during the last decade or two. In none of these books is the notion of propaganda in any way close to the central argument being made, but the survey still reveals a diffuse yet rather uniform presence of an unquestioned use of the term. Indeed, it is my contention that it is difficult today to write about cultural expressions of absolutism at any length without at some point making the appeal to propaganda.

12. This paragraph has been sharpened by the many stimulating insights in Evonne Levy's reflection on the function of labeling something as propaganda in art history, in the introduction to *Propaganda and the Jesuit Baroque*, 7–10. Otherwise, the project of Levy's book is in many ways the opposite of mine here: a valiant attempt at "mak[ing] propaganda a productive and appropriate tool of art historical analysis" (12), while I seek to demonstrate that the routinely deployed notion of propaganda is an unproductive and inappropriate tool for the material I will look at.

In the context of absolutism, qualifying an artifact as "propaganda" in an open, unqualified sense—which normally means as *"mere* propaganda," *"nothing but* propaganda"—implies diverting the critical attention away from the artistic object in front of us toward the message it is carries: a message that is considered clear-cut and unambiguous, pre-existing the artifact. In other words, it is a way of indicating that the signifier and the signifying gesture that brings it about can both safely be ignored in favor of the pregiven signified. Eminently expected, the message conveyed by the propagandistic object can, by definition, never surprise the modern scholar. It is always a repetition or confirmation of a predetermined meaning. Using the label of propaganda is therefore a way of, if not a *cue* for, closing down the inquiry. It implies the tacit permission to put the artifact safely away, discreetly indicating that it is time to move on to something more worthy of our critical energy. It is always the last word about the artifact, rarely the beginning of a further discussion, and even less the subject of a detailed analysis. As such, it is the not exactly analytical category for that which does not need analysis.

Although much of the scholarship on the cultural production under Louis XIV's personal rule in the past two decades has deployed propaganda as a ready-at-hand, unanalyzed critical term, it wasn't always this way. In preparing the ground for moving beyond the paradigm of propaganda, it is therefore worth attending to the reservations and hesitations of an earlier generation of scholars. The two English-language classics in the field are both interesting for the way in which they betray an attraction to the potency of the concept while also marking a critical distance.

Orest Ranum's monumental study of the career of five different writers who toiled for the seventeenth-century Bourbon kings in *Artisans of Glory* (1980) is particularly important in this regard. Writing in the years following the publication of two more pointed examinations of French absolutist culture in terms of royal propaganda, the concept is certainly on his radar.[13] The fullest formulation of his book's project immediately follows an initial observation regarding the trivial results that an analysis guided by the notion of propaganda will often lead to when applied to a corpus like his:

> Very quickly we realize the impossibility of deciding what is propagandistic and what is not, unless it is possible to discern the conscious acts of a

13. See Solomon, *Public Welfare, Science, and Propaganda*; and Klaits, *Printed Propaganda*; both referred to by Ranum, *Artisans of Glory*, 253n61, and 294 and 315, respectively.

writer who knew he was publishing a work intended to influence public opinion in an ideological way.

Instead of taking this approach, I hope to capture the feelings and expressions of dependency among writers.[14]

Throughout his book, the notion of propaganda occasionally reappears in the discussion of certain aspects of the dependency of the writers in question.[15] But so, too, do Ranum's reservations as to the pertinence of the category widely construed, especially regarding the contributions by Paul Pellisson, Jean Racine, and Nicolas Boileau to the history of Louis XIV.[16] There is thus a deep ambivalence running through the text, since it is not at all obvious that the instances of a more specific analytical use of the term would withstand the broader critique voiced elsewhere. Ranum's methodological qualms and reservations only take on their full meaning when approached in light of the striking endpoint of his own inquiry, which runs as follows:

> The inflated claims by the men of letters may not have seemed so inflated during the long reign of Louis XIV, for they restated French family history in ways that obliged the monarch to carry out politics he could never empirically examine. There was literally no language or conception of kingship or of the state beyond those webs of myths and facts spun by writers, webs that bound the prince to the pursuit of *gloire*.[17]

What looks inflated to us may not have been perceived as such at the time. In a certain sense, this is of course just another reminder of the danger of

---

14. Ranum, *Artisans of Glory*, 22–23.

15. See, for example, Ranum, 149, 253, 260–64, 270, 294.

16. Regarding the case of Pellisson: "It is anachronistic to refer to this literature [the writing of history to the glory of the king]—when its principal subject is the head of state—as propaganda. As a descriptive term, 'propaganda' does not help to define the nature of either historical or other literary genres in the reign of Louis XIV; for in a sense *fidélités*—royal, aristocratic, and parlementaire—encompassed virtually all literary activity." Ranum, 252. And more hard-hitting still, regarding the charges of propaganda and naïveté from modern readers of Racine: "Propaganda his history is, but only in the sense that it conformed to the dominant beliefs and aspirations of the political culture of which he was part. By standing for the principle of recording only the truth, Racine and Boileau sincerely hoped to curb the excessive praise that writers were heaping on the Sun King. Their results, with all the restraints imposed by the *ars historica*, would have been no more and no less propagandistic than histories written by others whose political cultures sustained ideological perspectives on the past." Ranum, 315.

17. Ranum, 337.

anachronism: we cannot necessarily trust the pertinence of our own pre-critical affective reaction to the material at hand from where the charge of propaganda first emerges.[18] But it is only now, at the end of the journey, that the reader fully realizes the extent to which the title of the book, *Artisans of Glory*, points from the outset to something empirically more elusive than what notions such as propaganda can possibly seize. Other tools are needed in order to even start analyzing the stakes of the "webs of myths and facts" structuring the symbolic reality and aspirations of prince and writers alike.

In his seminal study *The Fabrication of Louis XIV* (1992), Peter Burke shares with Ranum the explicit methodological ambivalence toward the concept of propaganda. The concept first occurs in a wider discussion of the dangers and benefits of anachronism, when Burke states that "[a]nother modern way of describing this book would be to call it a study of 'propaganda' for Louis XIV." However, although Burke stresses that "[i]f the term propaganda is defined broadly enough, for example as 'the attempt to transmit social and political values,' it is difficult to object to its use about the seventeenth century," he is quick to stress the risk that such a use can lead to reductionism by "encouraging author [Burke himself] and readers alike to interpret the poems, paintings and statues representing the king as if they were nothing but attempts to persuade." Although Burke concludes that "'[p]ropaganda' is one useful modern concept [among] others," he largely refrains from using it in the rest of the book, adding in his introductory discussion that "[i]t might be more exact to say that the representations of Louis were commissioned to add to his glory."[19] This last remark, reminiscent of Ranum's work, seems to have inspired the choice of title for the 1995 French translation of Burke's book: *Louis XIV: Les stratégies de la gloire* (Louis XIV: the strategies of glory).[20]

However, unlike Ranum, Burke in the end opts resolutely and un-

---

18. In Ranum's stark formulation: "our own repugnance for Ludovician political culture" (24).

19. Burke, *The Fabrication of Louis XIV*, 4–6.

20. Burke, *Louis XIV: Les stratégies de la gloire*. In the 2010 Festschrift for Burke, Nicole Hochner criticizes the title of the French translation in the following way: "The book in French surprisingly became *Louis XIV: les stratégies de la gloire*, wrongly alluding to a warlike tactic of glory and pomp, concealing the fact that Peter Burke had made only a limited case for propaganda." Hochner, "Against Propaganda," 235. This characterization is based on a surprising conflation of glory and propaganda, which is not reflected in Burke's book. Hochner goes on to comment on "the very different connotations of the two titles: the English suggests a process of making, while the French evokes more a propaganda device" (235n22). However, it could be argued that the change of semantic field from fabrication to glory rather brings the

apologetically for an anachronistic approach. He distinguishes between two rival models in the approach to rulers and their images: on the one hand, what he calls a "cynical" view (whose demystifying gaze identifies instrumentalism and manipulation, but at the risk of reductionism), and, on the other, an "innocent" view (taking the royal image seriously at its face value, but at the risk of suppressing actual manipulation, instrumentalism, and dissent).[21] Could there possibly be a third way that would resolve the tensions and oppositions between these two models toward a productive synthesis? Yes, Burke seems to imply, through an approach like the one he is adapting in his book:

> The king and his advisers were well aware of the methods by which people can be manipulated by symbols. After all, most of them had been trained in the art of rhetoric. However, the aims in the service of which they manipulated others were of course chosen from the repertoire offered by the culture of their time. The aims as well as the methods are part of history, and part of the story told in this book.[22]

Their aims and *their* methods were certainly part of history, but Burke's own aims and methods were not. With the final programmatic statement of his introduction, Burke aligns himself with "the analysts of communication in our time," marking as his goal "the attempt to discover who was saying what about Louis to whom, through what channels and codes, in what settings, with what intentions, and with what effects."[23] Therefore, it is not immediately clear how this approach is different from the "cynical" view evoked by Burke himself, except that the execution of the study of manipulation here is carefully, comprehensively, and masterfully historicized.

Unlike Ranum, Burke's choice of title firmly situates the book within the cynical paradigm. It is true that Burke tries to have it both ways in the introduction, by insisting that the word "fabrication" is meant to point to the processual character of image-making across time and media. Yet the need to disclaim other interpretations of the title before making this statement suggests that the natural way to understand it might be different: the word "fabrication" was chosen *not* "to deconstruct or demolish the king" nor "to imply that Louis was artificial while other people are

---

title further away from propaganda, as suggested, for example, by Ranum's analyses in *The Artisans of Glory.*

21. Burke, *The Fabrication of Louis XIV*, 11–13.

22. Burke, 13.

23. Burke, 13.

natural."[24] However, the book tells a slightly different story, starting well before the disclaimers in the introduction. Just after the title page and dedication, on the left page opposite (hence before) the table of contents, the reader encounters Thackeray's drawing discussed above. It appears above the following truncated quotation from Thackeray's text, which takes on the function of a caption: "You see, at once, that majesty is made out of the wig, the high-heeled shoes, and cloak . . . Thus do barbers and cobblers make the gods that we worship." Burke never comments upon this visual and verbal deconstruction of the king, with a function halfway between frontispiece and epigraph, in the main body of the text, despite a second full-page inclusion of the drawing halfway through the book.[25] This is not exactly an omission, since in a certain sense the whole book is a comment on and a working out of what Thackeray called "the exact calculation" of absolutism. At the very least, such is the impact it has had on a generation or two of scholars for whom it has been and still is the main introduction into the making of the image of Louis XIV. Within this framework, the output from the royal image-makers is nothing but communication, nothing but persuasion, *nothing but* propaganda.

What precedes is in no way meant to detract from the synthetic force of the exposition nor from the immense richness of the materials analyzed by Burke. *The Fabrication of Louis XIV* certainly is a summa and a most influential work in the field. Rather, my point here has been to bring attention to the largely unnoticed way in which this force has itself contributed in shaping the field in the following decades through its framework and approach. In many contexts, Burke's unquestioned reliance on the communication model does not make much of a difference, while in some cases the cynical view is certainly warranted and serves to sharpen the analysis. At other points, however, it leads to a slippage, a lack of nuance, to interpretive possibilities being excluded without consideration. Here is one example of such a blind spot from the very last paragraph of the book: "Louis claimed to derive his power from God, not from the people."[26] Is Burke's claim about this being Louis's own claim as unproblematic as this sentence makes it seem? Indeed, doesn't the word "claim" shift the source of Louis's authority from the realm of self-evidence to the realm of persuasion?[27]

24. Burke, 10–11.

25. Namely, Burke, 124, opposite the first page of chapter 9, "The Crisis of Representation."

26. Burke, 203.

27. For a second example of such a blind spot, see the following slippage in a programmatic paragraph from chapter 2, titled "Persuasion": "As for the function of the image [of the king], . . . the aim was to celebrate Louis, to glorify him, *in other words*

But what more, what else could there possibly be? What is it that we do not see when we only see propaganda and persuasion? What is it that may be lost by automatically characterizing the cultural expressions of absolutism as propaganda or even as modern political communication?

To begin answering these questions, I make a quick detour by way of methodological discussions related to the celebration of power in imperial Rome. The prominent French historian of ancient Rome, Paul Veyne, draws attention to the way in which Trajan's Column in Rome poses a radical challenge to the communication model: modern scholars had long interpreted its famous spiral bas-relief, commemorating Trajan's victory in the Dacian Wars, as imperial propaganda, in spite of being for the greater part invisible from the ground. How to make sense of a message without an actual audience? The reason for this radical indifference to the legibility of the monument is simple, Veyne explains, once we liberate ourselves from the blinders of the communication model: "the column is an expression of imperial pomp and not a piece of propagandistic information communicated to the spectator."[28] The same holds for premodern mobilizations of the arts for the celebration of monarchic glory all the way to Versailles, Veyne adds in the following sweeping statement:

> The cult, the incense, the "flattery" that surrounded Elizabeth I or Louis XIV officiated the celebration of their glory [célébraient l'office de leur gloire] without serving to place them on the throne; the palace of Versailles may have made Louis XIV a greater king than the others, but it could not make him more of a king: if it can be said, he was king "always already."[29]

Through this "always already," the king's dignity is never in doubt or at stake: "Pomp is an expression of self that does not seek to make an

---

to persuade viewers, listeners and readers of his greatness." Burke, 19; my emphasis. Does the reduction of glorification to persuasion go without saying?

28. "[L]a colonne est une expression de faste impérial et non une information de propagande communiquée au spectateur." Veyne, "Buts de l'art, propagande et faste monarchique," 389. Burke alludes to an early version of Veyne's argument in *The Fabrication of Louis XIV*: "As the ancient historian Paul Veyne recently suggested, some works of art are created to exist rather than to be seen. The reliefs on Trajan's Column, for example, are invisible from the ground" (5).

29. "Le culte, l'encens, la 'flatterie' qui entouraient Élisabeth d'Angleterre ou Louis XIV célébraient l'office de leur gloire et ne se proposaient pas de les installer sur le trône; le château de Versailles pourra faire de Louis XIV un roi plus grand que les autres, mais non pas le rendre plus roi: il l'était, si l'on peut dire, 'toujours déjà.'" Veyne, "Buts de l'art, propagande et faste monarchique," 412.

impression and that, precisely because of this, makes one, appearing to be a product of royal nature, indifferent, like nature, to the existence of spectators."[30]

Such a gesture can of course still be considered as communication, and nothing stops a modern observer from trying to nail down a message. However, the nature of what is communicated refuses to enter into the framework of the modern "analysts of communication," as invoked by Burke. In effect, what is communicated is in part this refusal itself: a communication that doesn't care about its immediate recipient, a message that declares loudly but without a precise audience in mind, "Because I can."

Two recent revisionary monographs confirm in unexpected ways the pertinence of Veyne's insight for the monarchical culture of seventeenth-century France. Both explore the notion of "visual history" but are otherwise extremely different both in approach and scope. On the one hand, Robert Wellington's *Antiquarianism and the Visual Histories of Louis XIV* (2015) is itself an antiquarian inquiry without any pretension to challenge the way we think about the political dimension of absolutism.[31] Nevertheless it does exactly that through the compelling case it makes for the "visual histories" produced by Louis XIV's image-makers as being intended *not* for a contemporary audience but for posterity. These objects are "artifacts for a future past," as the subtitle of the book puts it. It is not that the production of the king's visual history was not part of a tightly supervised plan, coordinated by Jean-Baptiste Colbert and the Petite Académie; it was, but in a very different way than what our modern tools and categories allow us to seize. On the other hand, in the supremely ambitious *Les rois imaginaires* (2016), Yann Lignereux pursues the role of the imaginary as a constitutive dimension of monarchical French politics from the late fifteenth century through the reign of Louis XIV. In the final synthesizing chapter, the diachronic analysis brings Lignereux to a conclusion along the lines of Wellington's: "The first and true audience of the royal imaginary is posterity."[32] Importantly, however, this is not Lignereux's final word. Rather, it is the point where he radically

30. "Le faste est une expression de soi qui ne cherche pas à faire de l'effet et qui, précisément pour cela, en fait, parce qu'il semble être une production de la nature royale, indifférente, comme l'est la nature, à l'existence de spectateurs." Veyne, 413.

31. "This study looks beyond a self-evident political reading of the iconography of Louis XIV to discover an artistic process deeply entrenched in a sophisticated intellectual and connoisseurial culture." Wellington, *Antiquarianism*, 4.

32. "Le premier et le véritable public de l'imaginaire royal, c'est la postérité." Lignereux, *Les rois imaginaires*, 293.

expands, if not explodes, the framework by reawakening the question of audience in Veyne's reflection while replacing the latter's main point of reference in Trajan's Column in second-century imperial Rome with an underestimated monument of French absolutism itself. Located at the Cordouan plateau four miles into the sea off the mouth of the Gironde estuary, just north of Bordeaux, the Cordouan Lighthouse was built in the late sixteenth and early seventeenth century on the order of Henri III and Henri IV, then carefully maintained through the reigns of Louis XIII and Louis XIV (fig. 3). It is a richly ornamented edifice that in its original design stood nearly forty meters tall, with exterior circular galleries, a sculpted front, and a monumental entrance leading into a lavishly decorated interior, with an "apartment of the king" on the first floor and a vaulted chapel on the second, above which the lighthouse proper sat.[33] Although no French king ever visited the lighthouse, the edifice is a celebration of royal glory, as is legible in the decorative program, from the omnipresence of royal emblems, monograms, and initials to the sculptures of Louis XIV and Louis XV. It was at once a "wonder of the world" and a "monarchical monument."[34]

But—and this is the exact place of Lignereux's intervention—for whom? Who is saying what to whom by way of this monarchical monument whose exterior is inaccessible and whose interior is entirely invisible, to say nothing of the symbolic message inscribed in its details? One could certainly try to make the case that this is a magnificent piece of royal propaganda, expertly diffused by engravings like the one reproduced in figure 3, but only to be left wondering about its rhetorical efficacy. As Lignereux points out, these images "shut the public out from the splendor of its sacrosanct."[35] Sometimes called the "Versailles of the seas," the Cordouan Lighthouse still stands today, less out of sight and reach to us thanks to modern technology than it was back then, and so all the more present as a monumental reminder of the limitations of our modern methods for thinking about royal monuments of the past.

33. This description follows closely the one given by Lignereux (294–96). See also the references given in the next footnote. Most of the structure described here still stands today, but the part above the chapel was radically expanded in the late eighteenth century so that the edifice now measures sixty meters. The lighthouse is still in operation, fully automatized since 2006. For further information and sources, see also the official website of the lighthouse: https://www.phare-de-cordouan.fr.

34. Guillaume, "Le phare de Cordouan." See also Grenet-Delisle, *Louis de Foix*; and Castaner Muñoz, "L'exhaussement du phare de Cordouan."

35. "[. . .] taisent au public la splendeur de son sacro-saint." Lignereux, *Les rois imaginaires*, 297.

FIGURE 3. Mathieu Merian (after a drawing by Claude Chastillon), *The Cordouan Lighthouse* (engraving). From *Topographie française, ou Représentations de plusieurs villes . . .* (Paris: Louys Boussevin, 1655). Photograph: Wikimedia Commons.

There is, however, one sense in which the term "propaganda" is pertinent both for this wider discussion of methodology and for my specific analysis of royal imagery under Louis XIV. In the original etymological meaning of the term as "that which should be propagated," the emphasis remains, importantly, on the entity that is to be propagated, broadcast, diffused, expressed—and not yet on the recipient. But this is not to say that the modern meaning of persuasion and even manipulation is not latent, especially since the term emerged in the very precise institutional setting of the Catholic Counter-Reformation.[36] This more neutral use of the term is still possible today, with an emphasis on the propagating mission as an obligation toward the entity in need of propagation: in the original use, the Christian faith; in the absolutist context, the glory of the king. However, as I have shown, the word resonates today so strongly with the instrumental focus on manipulative impact alone that such a rehabilitated notion would hardly be an adequate conceptual tool. Hence the need to move beyond the traditional framework of propaganda, which can now no longer be more than *mere* propaganda.

3. Approaching Absolutism Differently: Royal Glory and Royal Exemplarity

How to home in on the dream of absolutism, then? How to approach the most extravagant artifacts of absolutism in a less reductive manner than what an approach in terms of propaganda or any modern communication model would entail? How might these artifacts be taken up in a way that allows us to get at the "totality and coherence" of absolutism (per Fanny Cosandey and Robert Descimon)? Indeed, how to start accounting for the force and efficacy of the dream of absolutism, not only in its time but long after it?

The analyses in this book rely on the recuperation of the premodern categories of "royal glory" and "royal exemplarity." Although both these expressions make intuitive sense at a surface level, the conceptual work they refer to may be less than obvious, even to seasoned students of early modernity, due to a systematic neglect in the scholarship. The reason for this scholarly disregard is related to the discussion above. Modern scholars have ignored them for the same reason as the corpus I am studying here, in which they feature prominently: an uncomfortable whiff (to a

---

36. The modern word has its faraway origin in the Sacred Congregation for the Propagation of the Faith, founded in 1622 by Pope Gregory XV in the context of the Catholic Counter-Reformation and often known quite simply as *Propaganda Fide* (from the Latin title: *Sacra Congregatio de Propaganda Fide*). The term wasn't politicized in the precise technical sense of manipulation until the French Revolution. Therefore, it should not be surprising to find the term used by Voltaire in its original meaning of "toute institution qui a pour but la propagation d'une croyance religieuse" (every institution which has as its purpose the propagation of a religious belief). Quoted here from Lignereux, *Les rois imaginaires*, 286n15.

modern nose) of subservience, manipulation, and propaganda. And yet, if we modern readers look more closely, as I will in what follows, it becomes obvious as we move beyond the framework of *mere* propaganda that royal glory and royal exemplarity are of paramount importance in understanding the dynamics of symbolic authority at work in the wider culture. They are central categories in the cultural practices undergirding the strict verticality of the absolutist society's symbolic hierarchy, contributing decisively in the processes that make power real in the person of the king. In short, they are the stuff of which the dream of absolutism is made.

I will tease out the exact function and working of the two categories in the course of the chapters through close scrutiny of central absolutist artifacts across different media. But before turning to the analysis, it is necessary to prepare the ground by introducing the two categories in some depth. In the case of royal exemplarity, this is essential since the concept may seem somewhat abstract and technical at the outset. As for royal glory, the situation is, in a certain sense, the opposite. It seems to speak with a self-evidence fueled by the pomp and splendor of Versailles, but it is in reality a complex and multilayered concept. Although the two categories are not exactly overlapping, they converge incessantly in the material studied here in the exuberant celebration of the glorious royal exemplar.

In light of the discussion above, the notion of royal glory would seem like a promising place to start looking for alternatives to propaganda when discussing artifacts of absolutism. After all, the writers and artists whose work is analyzed in what follows were all "artisans of glory" in the way examined by Orest Ranum, and they were instrumental in redeploying "those webs of myths and facts [. . .] that bound the prince to the pursuit of *gloire*"[37]—webs of examples within a culture of exemplarity, as I shall soon return to. My starting point is a privileged testimony from Louis XIV himself about the extent to which the importance of this pursuit was on his mind from the early years of his personal reign. Here is his often-quoted statement to the members of the Petite Académie in charge of overseeing the production of the royal image across media:

> Vous pouvez, Messieurs, juger de l'estime que je fais de vous, puisque je vous confie la chose du monde qui m'est la plus précieuse, qui est *ma gloire*: je suis sûr que vous ferez des merveilles; je tâcherai de ma part de

37. Ranum, *Artisans of Glory*, 337, as discussed above, 13–14.

vous fournir de la matière qui mérite d'être mise en œuvre par des gens aussi habiles que vous êtes.[38]

(You may, Gentlemen, judge the appreciation I have for you, since I entrust you with the thing in the world which is the most precious to me, namely *my glory*. I am sure you will do marvels; I will try on my side to provide you with matter which deserves to be given form [mise en œuvre] by people as competent as you are.)

This assertion is important not only for its brazen expression of youthful confidence anticipating glorious exploits ahead of him, but also for the place accorded to the arts in this enterprise. In the dichotomy between form and content that the king suggests, there is an implicit promise about artistic glory to come for the academicians: by giving shape to his glorious exploits, they will achieve their own. It could therefore be tempting to read the statement as the recognition of a transactional interdependence; for all practical purposes, couldn't the royal glory at stake here be reduced to the construction and propagation of *reputation* or *renown*? Nothing is less sure. Rather, one could wonder whether the brazenness of the royal utterance is carried by a sense of heaven-sent entitlement. "*Ma gloire*": instead of reputation to be established or fabricated, this would be a preexisting glory to be made visible and given form, to be expressed, externalized, and confirmed by further glorious exploits. It is "the thing in the world which is the most precious to [him]," but that might be so precisely because it is not entirely *of* this world. The glorious matter to be provided by the king calls for the making of "marvels." Although this marvel-making task—which is thus both the king's and the artists'—is formulated in the future tense, the glory of the king exists here, now, in the promise (or the dream) of marvels to come. The scene is thus structurally similar to the one in the central painting in the Hall of Mirrors, evoked in the opening of the introduction, where the king is not looking out in the world but into himself, with a gaze that itself dreams the glorious dream of absolutism.[39]

The concept of royal glory needs to be front and center in any discussion of French absolutism's self-image and processes of self-representation. It

38. The anecdote is reported by Charles Perrault in *Mémoires*, xxv–xxvi; my emphasis. The anecdote is quoted by Ranum, 279.

39. For a further discussion of this anecdote, see chapter 3, 184. It also occurs in passing in chapter 2, 129.

is therefore not at all controversial to speak of the Petite Académie as a "ministry of glory," although, importantly, this does *not* make it a "historical research team for political propaganda," as Jacob Soll would have it.[40] And yet, a synthetic work proposing a thorough exploration of the concept in the context of French absolutism still seems far away. Significant preparatory work has certainly already been done within more widely defined projects, most prominently by Robert Morrissey on the historical side and by Giorgio Agamben in political theology.[41] Olivier Chaline also covers important ground in his landmark biography on Louis XIV (2005).[42] It is a testimony to the difficulty and urgency of the task that the perspectives of Morrissey, Chaline, and Ranum, on the one hand, and of Agamben, on the other, seem incompatible, if not mutually exclusive. If analyzed at all, the early modern logic of royal glory is generally reduced to remnants of aristocratic notions of feudal honor or a nostalgic revival of a Roman culture of renown. The crucial theological impulse behind the pursuit of royal glory—which, as Agamben shows, is much more than (indeed, fully independent of) the moralist denunciation of vainglory—is still largely unaccounted for in the scholarship.

My aim here is hardly one of filling this lacuna. However, the importance of the task and its first outline can be suggested already by a quick incursion into a key resource from late seventeenth-century France— namely, the rich and evocative article on the term in Antoine Furetière's 1690 dictionary. According to Furetière, the first meaning of the word *gloire* is "Majesté de Dieu, la vue de sa puissance, de sa grandeur infinie" (God's majesty, the sight of his power or infinite greatness).[43] This is the theological concept of glory, from the Latin *gloria*, which itself is a translation of the ancient Greek *doxa* (and *kabod* in Hebrew). Notably, Furetière uses a political language here, with terms such as "majesty" and "power." In the context of this discussion of royal glory specifically, I would like to insist on a layer of meaning in the Greek term that remains implicit in the Latin (and thus in the French and also the English) translation but is explicit in the German. The term *Herrlichkeit*'s root, *hehr*, evokes a general idea of highness but is at the same time closely linked

40. Chaline, *Le règne de Louis XIV*, 1:354; Soll, *The Information Master*, 128.

41. Morrissey, *The Economy of Glory*; Agamben, *The Kingdom and the Glory*.

42. Chaline, *Le Règne de Louis XIV*; the first volume of this two-volume work carries the subtitle *Les rayons de la gloire* (The rays of glory). See especially the sections "La gloire du roi" (The glory of the king) and "Les institutions de la gloire" (The institutions of glory) (156–77 and 354–87). See also by Chaline the important article "De la gloire" and the edited volume *La gloire à l'époque moderne*.

43. Furetière, *Dictionaire universel*, "gloire."

to the two substantives *Herr* (master, lord) and *Herrscher* (sovereign), in such a way that (divine) glory literally evokes the manifestation of God's absolute lordliness and sovereignty.[44] In the second definition of the term *gloire*, Furetière evokes man's duty to God: "GLOIRE, se dit aussi de l'honneur qu'on rend à Dieu, des louanges qui lui sont dues." (GLORY is also said about the honor one gives to God, the praise due to him.) This is glory as rendered to God by the faithful in adoration through an act of glorification. Again, the German term *Verherrlichung* serves to make explicit the vertical positioning of this activity: it necessarily happens from an inferior position. It is an act of subjection, the celebration of vertical inferiority.

Furetière's third definition finally reaches the human level and, as the last of a series of examples, royal glory:

> GLOIRE, se dit par emprunt et par participation, de l'honneur mondain, de la louange qu'on donne au mérite, au savoir et à la vertu des hommes. La *gloire* du monde n'est qu'une fumée. Ce Triomphateur est revenu comblé, tout couvert de *gloire*. Cet ouvrage a acquis beaucoup de *gloire* à son Auteur. Ce Prince a tiré beaucoup de *gloire* de cette action de clémence, de justice.[45]

> (GLORY is said, by borrowing and participation, about worldly honor, praise of the worth, knowledge and virtue of men. Worldly *glory* is only smoke. The Victor returned replete with, wholly covered in *glory*. This work has earned much *glory* for its Author. The Prince garnered much *glory* from this act of clemency and justice.)

Here, the primary meaning of the word *gloire* is obviously very close to notions of honor, praise, renown, and reputation. This is certainly the case in the final example from the princely realm. The glory of this exemplary prince is attributed to his virtuous act and to the specific virtues it demonstrates (his clemency and justice). At the same time, the exact formulation of the sentence may appear perplexing in that it seems to invite a suspicion as to his motives. To a modern reader, the verbal locution "tirer gloire" already gives off a whiff of hypocrisy: there seems to be an indication of agency and intention that would risk turning a virtuous act into a mere superficial and virtuoso *show* of virtue. This would be Furetière's fourth definition of *gloire*, which establishes the link to vain-

---

44. Schlüter, "Herrlichkeit. I," 1079–80.
45. Furetière, *Dictionaire universel*, "gloire."

glory and boasting: "GLOIRE, signifie quelquefois, Orgueil, présomption, bonne opinion qu'on a de soi-même. [...] On dit, qu'un homme fait *gloire* d'une chose, lorsqu'il s'en vante, qu'il s'en fait honneur." (GLORY, meaning sometimes Vainglory, presumption, high self-regard. [...] One says that a man *glorifies* himself in a thing when he brags about it or honors himself with it.) However, at the time, "tirer gloire" still tended to qualify the objective outcome of an action rather than its intention. Therefore, the glorious act of the prince in the example is an objective reason for praise and even pride; it is exemplary not only in the trivial sense that it serves as an example in a dictionary, but also with the full moral weight of the term. That said, it should be added that the difference between the positive "tirer gloire de" and the negative "faire gloire de" from the fourth definition was subtle already at the time (while the reflexive form "*se faire gloire de*" didn't appear until the twentieth century). Furthermore, the place of the princely example as the last element in the enumeration, and in that sense closer to the fourth definition than to the third that it serves to exemplify, seems to accentuate the slipperiness of judgment of his action. It is as if this example stages the ambiguity of worldly glory— and also, as I will soon return to, the ambiguity of princely exemplarity as such.

The concept of worldly glory, as it is presented in the definition and examples from Furetière, may seem far removed from the theological sense given as the first meaning of the term. Indeed, there appears to be a rift in the French concept of *gloire*, harking back to a similar tension between theological and pre-Christian moralist layers of meaning in the Latin *gloria*, closer in meaning to the Latin notion of *fama* (itself closer in meaning to the Greek concept of *kleos*) than to the theological concept. Hence a tendency in the scholarship on early modern France in general and on absolutist culture in particular to ignore the theological layer of meaning all together and reduce the discussion of glory to a problem of heroic virtue and renown within—and more precisely, toward the peak of—a social hierarchy. This is certainly a rich and rewarding topic, as demonstrated most recently in Robert Morrissey's magisterial exploration of the cultural and literary history of glory in the long eighteenth century, from Louis XIV to Napoleon, unearthing "the 'economy of glory' Napoleon sought to implement in an attempt to heal the divide between the Old Regime and the Revolution."[46] And yet, as Morrissey himself observes early in his inquiry in relation to Louis XIV, there is another conceptual layer beyond the tradition of glory as *fama* discussed in his

46. The quotation is from the dust jacket of Morrissey, *The Economy of Glory*.

book: "An essential element of this configuration [of court society]: the glory of the king of France is the reflection of that of God."[47] Furetière's article on *gloire* announces this same ontological analogy in the concept of glory itself: human glory signifies "par emprunt et par participation" (by borrowing and participation) from the primary sense of divine glory, a theological *Herrlichkeit* that, as I just have shown, resonates with an otherworldly majesty, lordliness, and sovereignty. Glory as such is thus closely linked at once to the essence of God and the essence of kingship, first in its theological formulation, which is already political, and then a second time in the divine right invested in the French crown. It is therefore not surprising that the most exuberant and excessive celebrations of French absolutism under Louis XIV seem to be carried by a concept of royal glory that sits uneasy with the traditional framework of human glory understood as merely renown (*fama*), as will be shown repeatedly in the close analyses in this book.

At this point, I would like to shift attention to an overlapping concept that better catches the participatory, collective aspect of absolutism and that is of crucial importance in understanding the continued fascination with the dream of absolutism even after absolutism. Again, my starting point is a privileged testimony attributed to the king himself, this time regarding the political importance of exemplarity under absolutism. The following remarkable passage appears in the *Mémoires* that Louis XIV (assisted by his ghostwriters) wrote for the instruction of his oldest son, the Dauphin, in a discussion of the political importance of the royal display of religious humility. It is thus the king who says "je" (I), and the possessive pronoun "notre" (our) that opens the quotation englobes himself and his son:

> Notre soumission pour lui [Dieu] est la règle et l'exemple de celle qui nous est due. Les armées, les conseils, toute l'industrie humaine seraient de faibles moyens pour nous maintenir sur le trône, si chacun y croyait avoir même droit que nous, et ne révérait pas une puissance supérieure, dont la nôtre est une partie. Les respects publics que nous rendons à cette

---

47. Morrissey, 38. The theological perspective opened by this sentence is brought back to the ethical discussion of glory as a heroic ideal of virtue with the observation that this "vision was perfectly compatible with the ideal of the profane hero developed by the Catholic Reformation" (38). Such a delimitation makes sense within the project of Morrissey's book, but it also leaves the question about the deeper politico-theological implications of the reflections of God's glory on to the king's largely unexplored.

puissance invisible, pourraient enfin être nommés justement la première et la plus importante partie de notre politique, s'ils ne devaient avoir un motif plus noble et plus désintéressé.

(Our submission to Him [God] is the rule and the example for that which is due to us. Armies, councils, all human industry would be feeble means for maintaining us on the throne if everyone believed he had as much right to it as we and did not revere a superior power, of which ours is a part. The public respects that we pay to this invisible power could indeed justly be considered the first and most important part of our entire politics if they did not require a more noble and more disinterested motive.)[48]

This paragraph and its context pose arguably the politically most complex yet most significant passage of the whole *Mémoires* and will be analyzed at length in chapter 1. The stakes of the lesson couldn't be higher. As the royal father points out, the stability of the societal hierarchy hinges on the subjects' belief in the king's divine right to his position. Hence the urgency of the visible example of "submission" and "public respects" offered by the king and his son to a higher invisible power: it becomes exemplary of the submission to figures of authority in general. In this sense, exemplarity is "the first and most important part" of absolutist politics insofar as it is the principle that grounds and conserves orderly, hierarchical life in the polis. In other words, the main lesson from father to son is that the force of exemplarity is the glue that holds the ancien régime society together.

The last sentence quoted betrays an unease with the seeming instrumentality in this example of religious humility. Isn't the public royal submission recommended here itself close to propagandistic manipulation in its emphasis on royal self-interest? It is, but as will be demonstrated in the detailed analysis, the king himself here shows an acute awareness of the dangers of what modern readers would call a propagandistic approach and of anything close to Thackeray's "exact calculation." Somewhat surprisingly to a modern reader, according to the royal father, the crucial sincere bottom-up buy-in by the subjects seems to depend on the sincerity of the prior submission of the sovereign. Hence the necessity of

---

48. Louis XIV, *Mémoires, suivis de Manière de montrer les jardins*, 104–5; Louis XIV, *Mémoires for the Instruction of the Dauphin*, 57. Throughout these pages, I have sometimes modified the translation to bring it closer to the original.

"a more noble and more disinterested motive," although even this disinterest remains ambiguous, as I will show in chapter 1.

It is important to stress that my emphasis on royal exemplarity in this book does not at all mean the introduction of a new concept. Rather, it is an attempt at recovering a way of thinking that was ubiquitous and unavoidable at the time but lost to us. According to John D. Lyons, the "period from the fifteenth through the early seventeenth centuries [merits] the appellation 'the age of exemplarity.'"[49] This is certainly true if one looks at elite culture and the ways in which ancient examples were at the heart of the humanist project as a source of political, ethical, and aesthetic models (in the mode of the Ciceronian *historia magistra vitae*). Lyons's scholarship on the topic belongs to a first wave of research exploring early modern exemplarity that revealed the extent to which Renaissance texts by authors such as Montaigne, Erasmus, and Machiavelli not only belong to such a culture of exemplarity, but at the same time profoundly question it. Inside such a framework, the late Renaissance is marked by a "crisis of exemplarity," most prominently voiced by Montaigne, and the end of the period indicated by Lyons coincides with René Descartes's radical rejection of ancient books and examples in *Discours de la méthode*. This model of crisis, however, neglects to note the continued centrality of exemplarity for absolutist political culture of the late seventeenth century. Absolutist culture under Louis XIV was incontestably a culture of exemplarity in the sense that at once political, moral, and artistic choices were still largely justified through reference to the authority of concrete models from the past. Despite scholarly reports about an earlier "Renaissance crisis of exemplarity," the example remained the crucial figure in the cultural construction of authority, the way in which the past is extended into the future through actions in the present. And within this broader culture of exemplarity, the glorious royal exemplar occupied a more central place than ever.[50]

In this light, it is not surprising that many of the most important cultural polemics of the age, known as *Querelles*, can in fact be viewed as

49. Lyons, *Exemplum*, 12.

50. For "the Renaissance crisis of exemplarity," see the special issue of the *Journal of History of Ideas* with that title (59, no. 4), especially the introduction by Rigolot, but also important articles by Cornilliat, Hampton, Lyons, Stierle, and others. See also Hampton, *Writing from History*. For Descartes's position, see Lyons's subtle reading of the new exemplarity of the *Discours* in chapter 4 of *Exemplum* (156–70). See also the more recent collective volume Giavarini, *Construire l'exemplarité*. For the lack of emphasis on royal exemplarity within this rich body of scholarship, see my discussion below.

battles in an ongoing cultural war about the way in which exemplarity is constructed. This is the case for the *Querelles* on theater, monuments, inscriptions, and even the notorious polemics opposing Jesuits and Jansenists. And most of all, it was the case for the most notable one, the "Querelle des Anciens et des Modernes" (the Battle of the Books). Here, the point of contention was precisely the status of the ancient example, not only when it came to the choice of models for artistic creation, but also in terms of authority and legitimacy more broadly construed. Indeed, chapter 3 argues that what was at stake among the learned men of the French Academy and beyond can productively be approached as a polemics about how best to celebrate the royal glory of Louis XIV. I read the *Querelle* as a symptom of a wider cultural unease about exemplarity and argue that for the notion of a "crisis of exemplarity" to be fruitful, it needs to be recast as a crisis of *royal* exemplarity and studied in the most potent self-justifications of absolutism.[51]

These observations are all indications that the logic of exemplarity is under a certain pressure, with a constant need to be renegotiated. They do not mean, however, that the dominant role of exemplarity is diminishing or that the absolutist "siècle de Louis XIV" breaks with an exemplary culture. In a society more and more turned toward the example of the court, behavior and desires were increasingly modeled inside a rigorous hierarchy of curial exemplarity under labels such as etiquette, politeness, and civility.

This brings me back to the above quotation from Louis XIV's *Mémoires* and the position of the initial royal submission as at once the linchpin and the apex of exemplarity's hierarchy. At this point, it is interesting to observe that the logic of exemplarity itself is in fact dependent on a similar structural elevation or exception as the one conserved through the royal example here. In an important sense, all exemplarity is royal, and the logic of exemplarity itself stands in a relation of solidarity with that of kingship.

This solidarity between exemplarity and kingship can first of all be observed in treatises of rhetoric and logic, where the exemplarity of examples (what turns a sample into a model) is likened to the exemplarity of kings. The figure of the great king is omnipresent in theoretical de-

---

51. For the political implications of the "Querelle des Anciens et des Modernes," see the chapter "Modernity and Monarchy," in Norman, *The Shock of the Ancient*, 89–98. For the two other related *Querelles*, see, for example, Vuilleumier Laurens and Laurens, *L'Âge de l'inscription*; and Blanchard, "Ménestrier and the 'Querelle des Monuments.'"

scriptions of the rhetoric of example from Aristotle's *Rhetoric* through Antoine Arnauld and Pierre Nicole's *Logique de Port-Royal* (1662) to Jacques Bénigne Bossuet's *Logique du Dauphin* (1677). In both Aristotle and Bossuet, the king appears as the very first example of how reasoning through example works. Here is the example given by Bossuet after a short initial statement linking example to induction in moral matters, in a sentence that recalls the quotation from the *Mémoires* above:

> [A]insi, pour faire voir à quels désordres l'amour porte les hommes, on représente ce qu'il a fait faire à Samson, à David, à Salomon, comme il a pensé faire périr César dans Alexandrie, comme il a fait périr Antoine, et mille autres événements semblables.[52]

> (Thus, in order to show the types of disorder to which love carries men, one represents what it made Samson, David, and Salomon do, how it nearly made Cesar perish in Alexandria, how it made Anthony perish, and a thousand other similar events.)

The same point could certainly have been conveyed through "mille autres événements semblables"—by a thousand other examples. And yet, the royal example still seems to stand out as more representative, not only for Bossuet, who here writes for the Dauphin, but also for ordinary people, as expressed through the use of the French impersonal subject pronoun "on": *one* turns to Samson, David, and Salomon. Somehow, this series of royal examples seems to communicate more efficiently the general rule, which the reader is made to see (*faire voir*). Therefore, the choice of examples here undermines the conception that examples are mere induction. Rather, it would be tempting to speak of a certain solidarity between kingliness and exemplarity, both implying, as Alexander Gelley has said about the example, "the elevation of a singular to exemplary status."[53] It is as if the exemplarity of examples were most forcefully communicated by analogy with the exemplarity of the great king, just like in the political realm, where the elevation of the king above his subjects is most efficiently justified through exemplarity, as Louis XIV explained to his son.

Whereas early modern exemplarity in general has given rise to an impressive body of scholarship in the last few decades,[54] the question of royal exemplarity as such has remained virtually unexplored. While

---

52. Bossuet, *Logique du Dauphin*, 142.
53. Gelley, *Unruly Examples*, 2. See 32n55 for the relevance of this quotation.
54. By scholars such as Lyons, Hampton, Rigolot, and many others, cf. 29n50.

the scholarship just mentioned has been immensely helpful for a broad understanding of the early modern culture of exemplarity, the insights most important to understanding the logic of *royal* exemplarity can be found in a transhistorical analysis, namely, in Gelley's introduction to a collective volume entitled *Unruly Examples* from the mid-1990s. Gelley's decisive intervention consists in his distinction between two competing impulses in the workings of exemplarity: on the one hand, an Aristotelian impulse, a descriptive, "horizontal" understanding (example as sample or induction); and, on the other hand, a Platonic movement, which elevates a normative, "vertical" dimension (example as the exemplary status of an elevated entity). Gelley's work does not address the political value of exemplarity as such, but to me it is obvious that in an early modern context these two impulses converge in the body of the royal exemplar.[55] In other words, in my reading, the symbolic relationship between kingship and exemplarity maps onto the two impulses of exemplarity studied by Gelley. The king is an individual among many, who through his exemplarity appears as chosen, elevated, *fated*, in a way that erases the traces of contingency, the inductive and the empirical in this selection. The absolutist king is always already exemplary through his elevation. This means that the constructed nature of this royal exemplarity is invisible, unthinkable not only for the king's subjects but also, crucially, for himself (as least as long as the new king follows the advice of his father, as discussed above and in more detail in chapter 1)—an important point that gets lost inside a modern framework where we consider the production of the royal image as nothing but propaganda and conscious manipulation. Through the power of example, the dignity of the king appears as given by nature, or even by God: an evident royal power, the rule of one, instituted by the One.

Royal exemplarity is thus the process through which the sovereign naturally appears as the temporal incarnation of the eternal sovereign principle, or, expressed through the language of another passage from Louis XIV's *Mémoires* to which I will return, as the living image of the almighty, in a way that leads his subjects to spontaneously express that "*Le caractère de la divinité est empreint sur son visage,* etc." ("*The character of*

---

55. The juxtaposition of kingliness and exemplarity is thus mine; in its original context, the quotation from Gelley above only refers to the workings of exemplarity. The juxtaposition could easily be extended to the two sentences following the quotation: "Is the example [or *the king*] merely *one*—a singular, a fruit of circumstance—or *the One*—a paradigm, a paragon? The tactic of exemplarity [or *kingliness*] would seem to be to mingle the singular with the normative, to mark an instance as fated." Gelley, *Unruly Examples*, 2; author's emphasis.

divinity is stamped on his face, etc."), as Blaise Pascal famously observed.[56] And conversely, it is only when exemplarity is reduced to mere induction and representation, without carrying the imprint of divine choice and the aura given by fate—in other words, when the celebration of his royal glory appears as mere pomp and propaganda—that the contingency of the selection becomes visible as such. In this instance, and only in this instance, the subjects can see that the king (or the emperor) has no clothes, in the manner of Thackeray's "exact calculation": that he is a partly exemplary, partly non-exemplary human being like themselves. The French Revolution becomes conceivable once the king's body loses its exemplary glory, once the character of divinity is no longer stamped on his face, and all of a sudden he is one body among many, as a sample or representative, but without the authority of his God-given elevation.

Royal glory and royal exemplarity coincide in the celebration of the glorious royal exemplar and never have they coincided more perfectly than in the case of Louis XIV. But this is also the point where exemplarity threatens to break down. I already discussed how in Louis XIV's *Mémoires* the example of royal submission to the divine was presented as a model for imitation. But what are we to make of depictions of the royal exemplar that are so glorious, so exemplary that he becomes inimitable and incomparable? In the corpus discussed in this book, there is a recurrent emphasis on—and a phantasmal pull toward—the point where the king takes the place of all other examples. Read in sequence, the three chapters trace a progression from center to periphery, from the sublime to the seemingly banal, in their examination of this absolutist obsession. In the first chapter, I analyze closely such a moment in the opening of the king's own *Mémoires*, when he suggests to his son that his book might very well replace all other books in the Dauphin's education. In the second chapter, I explore the choice of decorative program for the vault of the Hall of Mirrors at Versailles, when the plan to portray the king's glorious exploits in the guise of Apollo or Hercules was replaced by a direct depiction of the king himself. In both cases, a direct and literal mirroring of the king in his own (textual or visual) portrait replaces the passage by the tradition of examples from the past (known as "mirrors for princes"). As I shall argue, this new pedagogical mirror structure is actually thematized

56. Pascal, *Pensées*, fragment 59. The italics are introduced by Pascal's modern editor as a way of indicating the presence of a citation or quasi-citation. Pascal's inclusion of the final "etc." is significative, since it suggests that this specific utterance is only one of many similar examples.

at the symbolic center of the Hall of Mirrors, in a surprising—and surprisingly understudied—mirror scene included in the depiction of the birth of absolutism in *Le Roi gouverne par lui-même, 1661*, first mentioned in the opening of this introduction. But it is in the seeming "absolutist absurdities" discussed in chapter 3 that this coincidence is explored the most forcefully. On the one hand, in Claude-Charles Guyonnet de Vertron's 1685 *Parallèle de Louis le Grand avec les princes qui ont été surnommés grands* (Parallel between Louis the Great and the other princes who have been named great), whose curious conclusion runs as follows: "Louis resembles all the Great princes, although none of these Greats resemble him, because only he is similar to himself, and the Great prince par excellence." On the other, in Jean de Préchac's 1698 fairy tale "Sans Parangon" ("Without equal" or "Without example"), which recounts the life of Louis XIV very thinly veiled as that of Prince Sans Parangon, whose actions are dictated by increasingly difficult challenges from an invisible Princess Belle Gloire (Beautiful Glory). These texts may seem so exuberant as to be completely over-the-top, but in their very excess they provide a window to the inner workings of absolutism.

4. The Dream of Absolutism

So far in this introduction, the term "dream" has been used in a loose, intuitive, metaphorical sense. From the outset, the "dream of absolutism" points to a conception that is more capacious and supple than the modern scholarly concept of absolutism. The logic at work in the absolutist expressions analyzed here is dreamlike in that it seems to imply the dimming of certain rational exigencies and allows for the integration of contradictions. Or better, with a tiny twist on a well-known aphorism: like the heart in Pascal's original coinage, the dream, too, has its reasons that reason doesn't know.[57] This rewriting is very much faithful to the meaning of the original, despite the rosy romantic connotations the latter may have for modern readers. Read in context, it is clear that Pascal posits the heart as the site of an extra-rational cognition operating according to a different logic and oriented by a higher principle of love, either divine love or self-love. In the present case, the dream is the site for a similarly larger extra-rational realignment; one where thought and feeling, reason and emotion square off differently; one where bodies move and are moved in a numinous setting, where strong visual manifestations impose

---

57. "Le cœur a ses raisons que la raison ne connaît point." ("The heart has its reasons, which reason does not know.") Pascal, *Pensées*, fragment 680.

themselves as if scripted from the outside and given from above; one where a space is opened for a phantasmagoric sense of truth outside any fixed experience of time. In this sense, the dream carries an extra-rational, premodern knowledge. The dream here stands for the *other* of demystification and of Thackeray's "exact calculation"; the *other* of the modern reduction of absolutist artifacts to mere propaganda.

At the same time, it is important to emphasize that the idea of absolute power is itself dreamlike. *Only* a dream? Putting it that way would disregard the force of imagination and phantasmagoria at work in any conception of politics. Theoretically speaking, the reality of omnipotence is problematic already at the metaphysical level of a divine creator and a contradiction in terms for any creature through its very creatureliness. However, on the practical level of lived experience, it is not. On the contrary, as the king reminds his son in the passage from the *Mémoires* quoted above, there is a generally shared belief about royal participation in an invisible superior power, perceptible as royal glory and upheld through royal exemplarity; an enabling dream without which "[a]rmies, councils, all human industry would be feeble means for maintaining us on the throne."[58]

Within such a framework, the two possible meanings of the genitive construction in the nominal syntagm "the dream of absolutism" come together in a third, richer sense. First of all, the locution will appear to most as an objective genitive, evoking a dream *about* absolutism, a dream that has absolutism as its content, its subject matter, its mental ideation, and that could be dreamt by anybody, any agent. Second, read as a subjective genitive, the construction *assigns* agency, ownership, belonging; it is the dream dreamt *by* absolutism, a phantasmagoric content that belongs to absolutism. The third meaning would maintain both the objective and subjective genitive,[59] denoting absolutism itself as a dream, the one dream that not only belongs to but that *constitutes* absolutism, *the dream that absolutism is.*

While the conceptualizations in the two preceding paragraphs may risk striking some readers as too blatantly anachronistic, it is impor-

58. Louis XIV, *Mémoires for the Instruction of the Dauphin*, 57. Taken out of context, as here, the royal advice may seem to be evoking a purely manipulative dream. As the close analysis of this and the surrounding passages of the *Mémoires* in chapter 1 will show, the situation is much more complicated. For the royal exemplarity to work, the belief needs to be grounded in truth rather than in manipulation. At the very least, that's what the Dauphin needs to believe for the dream to continue working. See 60–66.

59. In a self-contained genitive it would be tempting to call absolute.

tant to stress that the allure of the notion of the dream also resides in its groundedness in the period itself. In important respects, an ambitious conceptual deployment of the notion of the dream would be more easily acceptable to them than to us. The culture of the late seventeenth century was a premodern dream culture, most often closer to a remote past than to modern staunchly demystified ways of thinking about dreaming.[60]

I will end this introduction by taking a close look at an example from this dream culture, at its explicit intersection with absolutism. The first decades of Louis XIV's personal reign coincided with the publication in France of a dozen texts relating to arts and letters called *Songe* (Dream).[61] The framework of the dream here serves to recast both heated polemics of the day and theoretical discussions, while also inviting reflections on the metapoetic status of the dream. In the specific context of my discussion here, one of these dreams stands out: *Le Songe de Philomathe* (The dream of Philomathe) by André Félibien, published in 1683.[62] Félibien is today above all known as an early practitioner of academic art history, but this text is as much a reflection of his charge as royal historiographer of buildings, paintings, sculptures, tapestries, and festivals. In fact, while the larger part of the *Songe* comprises a debate between painting and poetry represented by two female allegories, in the mold of a traditional *paragone* with an allegorical figure of Love as the judge, the dream is set in the gardens of Versailles, and the conclusion of both the debate and the dream itself hinges on no other than Louis XIV. The *Songe* pertains to my discussion here in at least two important ways. First of all, it is significant that although the king is clearly outside the dream, the text doesn't pit wakeful absolutism against dreamlike marvels. Rather, there is a blurring of the line between reality and dream, both on the way into and out of the dream. This is in part because the reality outside of the dream is itself so marvelous. Furthermore, there is a contiguity and confusion both of places and characters. The king himself has an important part at the end of the dream, not only in relation to the major artistic task of the arts

60. The main reference on the topic remains Dumora, *L'Œuvre nocturne*. See also, for the wider premodern context, Kruger, *Dreaming in the Middle Ages*.

61. For a detailed discussion of "this disjointed formal tradition that the history of the genre *songe* is" ("cette tradition formelle discontinue qu'est l'histoire du genre songe"), including its roots in sixteenth-century Italy (starting with *Il Sogno di Parnaso* de Ludovico Dolce [1532]) and early seventeenth-century Spain (especially the *Sueños* de Francisco de Quevedo, originally published in 1627 and in French translation in 1632), see Dumora, *L'Œuvre nocturne*, 471–520 (quote from 472).

62. For Dumora's perceptive discussion of this text, see *L'Œuvre nocturne*, 490–92.

(see below), but even as the source of the movement out of the dream, when the narrator asks the allegory of Love for the following favor: "je te prie, Amour, de vouloir faire connaître à ce grand Prince que tu m'as trouvé dans ces lieux méditant sur les belles actions de sa vie" (I beg you, Love, to deign to make known to this great Prince that you found me here meditating on the beautiful acts of his life) (502–3). Here are the final lines of the *Songe* when the narrator wakes up from his dream, in a scene where the allegoric figure of Love from within the dream and the real-life Louis are nearly superimposed:

> L'Amour m'ayant écouté me fit signe de le suivre: et comme pour lui obéir je voulais sortir du lieu où j'étais, j'entendis un grand bruit qui me fit tourner la tête d'un autre côté.
>
> Il est vrai qu'alors j'ouvris à demi les yeux; et voyant dans l'allée la plus proche de l'endroit où je m'étais endormi, toute la Cour qui suivait le Roi, je fus extrêmement surpris. Cependant me trouvant encore possédé de l'erreur de mon songe, je cherchais à joindre le faux et le vrai. Il me semble que je regardais si l'Amour ne s'approchait point du Roi pour me rendre quelque bon office, et même je fermai plusieurs fois les yeux pour ne me pas détromper sitôt, et goûter plus longtemps la douceur d'une si agréable rêverie.

> (Love, having listened to me, made a sign for me to follow: and in obedience I sought to leave where I was, when I heard a great noise that made me cock my head.
>
> It's true that I then half opened my eyes; and seeing on the path closest to the place where I had fallen asleep, the entire Court following the King, I was astonished. Finding myself nonetheless still in the error of my dream, I tried to join the true and false. It seemed that I watched to see if Love didn't engage the King in order to do me some kindness, and I even closed my eyes repeatedly so as to not break the spell too soon, and to taste a while longer the sweetness of a dream so lovely.)[63]

What exactly is it that brings the narrator back from the dream to reality? The decisive factor seems to be the "grand bruit" (great noise) from the court following the king, but it is important to notice that this is only after he already "voulai[t] sortir du lieu où [il] étai[t]" (sought to leave

---

63. Félibien, *Le Songe de Philomathe*, 503–4. Here and in what follows, my translation from this text draws on the partial translation provided in Lichtenstein, *The Eloquence of Color*, 119–26.

where [he] was), in order to follow Love toward the king. He is at once heading and pulled toward the royal reality outside the dream.

My second observation brings me to the most important passage for my discussion, which can be found a couple of pages earlier, within the dream, in the final words pronounced by Love, in lieu of a verdict in the *paragone* between painting and poetry. This is done by stressing their different tasks in the joint enterprise of celebrating the glory of Louis XIV:

> Si l'une [= la peinture] raconte les grandes vertus de ce Prince incomparable [Louis XIV], et fait une image des beautés de son âme, c'est à l'autre [= la poésie] à bien exprimer ses actions héroïques, et tant de choses mémorables qui sont l'admiration de toute la terre. Songez seulement à représenter fidèlement ce que vous voyez, afin que les siècles à venir puissent encore le voir dans l'état où il paraît aujourd'hui à tout l'Univers.[64]

(While the first [= painting] tells of this incomparable Prince's great virtues and evokes an image of his soul's beauty, the other [= poetry] has as her task to express his heroic actions, which are the object of the whole world's admiration. Think only of faithfully representing what you see, to allow the coming centuries still to see him as he appears today before the entire universe.)

As Jacqueline Lichtenstein demonstrates in her forceful reading of *Le Songe de Philomathe* in her important *La couleur éloquente* (*The Eloquence of Color*), this is not exactly a truce that places painting and poetry on the same level. The final verdict certainly closes the debate by assigning both parties a crucial role in the same noble enterprise of celebrating, but the emphasis on the incomparability of the prince subtly tilts the balance in favor of painting. For while comparison is necessarily discursive, only visual representation can possibly capture the incomparable: "To represent the absolute is, necessarily, to paint it."[65] Within the logic of the *Songe*, this conclusion only confirms a latent supremacy from earlier in the exchange, based on mythological and theoretical arguments. As it turns out, poetry always arrives *after* painting, words *after* images, always already in debt to prior dreams and imagination. The point is rubbed in by the fact that although it is necessarily formulated in words, the truce between poetry and painting happens only within a dream by the sleep-

64. Félibien, *Le Songe de Philomathe*, 501.
65. Lichtenstein, *The Eloquence of Color*, 127.

ing narrator, a dream that reaches us through a verbal account, but published under the title *Songe*, emphasizing its visionary quality.

And yet, there seems to be an additional central insight to be gleaned from the very last sentence pronounced by the allegory of Love to painting and poetry: "Songez seulement à représenter fidèlement ce que vous voyez [. . .]." There is no doubt about the meaning here. The joint task of the two female allegorical figures is to *think* only about faithfully representing what they see, whether in a visual rendition of the prince's beautiful soul or in a verbal description of his heroic exploits. However, Félibien doesn't say "*Pensez* seulement à [. . .]" but instead uses the verb *songer*, which is hardly an innocent choice in a conclusive passage of a text itself named *Songe*. What is at stake here? First of all, this choice of word seems to tilt the balance in the *paragone* a tiny step back in favor of poetry. The word performs something painting can't: movement, displacement, metaphoricity. But in so doing, the delineation of the realm of the dream seems to change, as if the faithful representation that is requested already were a dream of sorts. Rereading the passage, it becomes clear that the universal admiration preexists the faithful representation. Rather than the arts contributing to a fabrication or construction of royal glory, they are carried by a gaze of admiration, of marvel, of wonder, already shared by "the whole world," indeed by "the entire universe." Further, the critical sentence is not about "faithful representation" (as I just indicated a bit too quickly), but rather about "faithfully representing" ("représenter fidèlement"); about verbal action, thus, rather than about the mere output and endpoint of the action; about action filled by faith (as in the Latin root *fides* of the French *fidèlement*) and fueled by admiration. *Songez!* Dream on! The imperative uttered by Love, whom the narrator-dreamer will soon momentarily confuse with the king himself, brings the reader back to the blurry line between absolutism's reality, dreamlike and marvelous, and the dream proper, but to the wake of that divide, that is to say, to a collective dream dreamt with eyes wide open.

The chapters that follow will explore the landscape laid out in the last block quotation above: the "faithfully representing" of the glorious royal exemplar in word and image in a select corpus of absolutist artifacts. Again, I insist on the gerund "represent*ing*." The dream of absolutism is more about expression and manifestation than about representation, let alone the communication of a certain message.[66] The dream character

---

66. This is why there are surprisingly few points of intersection between my project in this book and the project of Louis Marin in *Le portrait du roi* (*Portrait of the King*). It is also worth noticing that the corpus considered is entirely different. It is

is foregrounded throughout the chapters by attending to the expressive (and often excessive) force of the artifacts as well as to traces of a reflection on this expressivity (and excess), as inscribed in the artifact itself.

What happens to that expressivity and excess, what happens to the dream of absolutism after absolutism? While in the following chapters the objects of analysis emerge from within the absolutist culture of the reign of Louis XIV (with one notable exception in the framing of chapter 2), the question about the pertinence and persistence of the dream of absolutism in the early twenty-first century is an underlying, motivating concern of the book. Throughout the chapters, this concern remains implicit as an invitation to the reader to reflect on the unquestioned presence of the dream of absolutism in our collective political imaginary today. It becomes explicit in the conclusion, which advances the exploration at the conceptual core of the project into "Seven Theses on the Dream of Absolutism."

---

surprising that Marin did not include Louis XIV's *Mémoires* or the decoration of the Hall of Mirrors at Versailles in his corpus in this book or elsewhere, but I have not found any traces of such an engagement either in his publications or in his *Nachlaß*. This is all the more puzzling in the case of the *Mémoires*, since Marin lectured on this text toward the end of his life.

CHAPTER 1

The Grammar of Absolutism

1. Introduction: The Dream of a Book Like No Other

What *was* absolutism and how was it transmitted? In this chapter, I look for an answer to the first question (the "what?") by homing in on the second (the "how?") through a close analysis of Louis XIV's *Mémoires* for the instruction of his oldest son, the Dauphin. Historiography on both Louis XIV and absolutism has completely marginalized this document, for reasons that will be discussed—and rejected—shortly. The text of the *Mémoires* is driven by the same questions just asked, answering the "how" of absolutism through an inward-facing series of examples and counsel for the future king, geared toward the inner cultivation of an absolutist will. Already on the second page, the reader encounters a startling sentence that envisions the Dauphin's use of this very book, and this is the starting point of my inquiry into the heart of absolutism:

> Je me suis aussi quelquefois flatté de cette pensée, que, si les occupations, les plaisirs et le commerce du monde, comme il n'arrive que trop souvent, vous dérobaient quelque jour à celui des livres et des histoires, le seul toutefois où les jeunes princes trouvent mille vérités sans nul mélange de flatterie, la lecture de ces Mémoires pourrait suppléer en quelque sorte à toutes les autres lectures, conservant toujours son goût et sa distinction pour vous, par l'amitié et par le respect que vous conserveriez pour moi.

> (I have also sometimes been flattered by the thought that if the occupations, the pleasures, and the affairs of this world should, as all too often happens, take you away from books and from histories, where alone, however, princes find a thousand truths unmixed with flattery, the reading of these *mémoires* might somehow compensate [suppléer] for all the other

readings, always preserving its taste and its quality for you through the friendship and the respect that you would preserve for me.)[1]

What *is* absolutism and how can it be learned? The sentence above may sound like an answer to these two essential questions from the sovereign father to his future successor: his book, *this* book, is all that his son will ever need. But the form of the sentence is too convoluted for it actually to read like a promise. The statement is presented somewhat more hesitantly as a recurrent thought, with the envisioned impact of the reading simply brought up as an idea rather than with the performative force of a promise, as if in quotation marks (one could imagine the following inelegant reformulation: "sometimes I had this thought: 'the reading of these *mémoires* . . .'"). It reads as the account of a pleasant dream occasionally had by the father about the book's potential impact. Stranger still, while the main argument presented to the Dauphin for turning to his father's text is that it would be advice free of flattery, the reflection itself is introduced by the king as a flattering thought. At the same time, the flattering thought at the core of that dream has nothing hesitant about it. Not only does it channel the paternal desire to effectively prepare his son for life in the world without him, but it also stages the royal absolutist desire to control the one element that *by definition* escapes the control of even the most absolute sovereign: the future beyond his own reign.

What comes after, what could possibly come after the sun? More sun? The moon? The deluge? Absolutism does not decline easily in the future tense. The sentence above attests to this absence through its use of the conditional mode, its hesitant, vacillating "pourrait [. . .] en quelque sorte" ("might somehow"). As argued later in the chapter, this is the dominant mode of the whole pedagogical enterprise, every paragraph of the book containing an unspoken *if*: *if*, my son, I should die before you, *then* I would want you to know that. . . . These *mémoires* are designed to come after the sun, prolonging somehow—but only somehow—its brilliance, but not, alas, with any certainty. Later, this initial inquiry into the peculiar grammar of absolutism will bring us to consider the tense linguists may call the *futur du destin* ("future of fate," constructed with the French verb *devoir*)—"celui qui doit régner après nous" ("he who shall reign af-

1. Louis XIV, *Mémoires, suivis de Manière de montrer les jardins*, 50; Louis XIV, *Mémoires for the Instruction of the Dauphin*, 22. In this chapter the reference to these two editions—Joël Cornette's French edition and Paul Sonnino's English translation—will be given parenthetically in the text.

ter us") (section 3)—and, intriguingly, the *futur antérieur*—"ceux qui auront régné" ("those who would have reigned")[2] (section 4)—alongside
considerations of the inception of sovereignty through the *passé simple*
of the royal decision (section 3) and the practical initiation to such decisions, the becoming-absolute of the sovereign (section 5), before the
exploration of the allegorical language of the Hall of Mirrors of Versailles
in chapter 2 leads to absolutism as a permanent present. Throughout,
Louis XIV's concerns about royal succession force the absolute monarch
to consider the limits of royal authority and agency, starting with the delicate intersection between his royal self and that of his son in the sentence
above. And more important still, he starts with the power of his own example, as documented in the *Mémoires*.

Hence the importance of the quotation as an entry point for the discussion of royal exemplarity in this chapter. As argued in detail below,
the tension between a certain reserve in its enunciation ("quelque fois
flatté"; "pourrait [. . .] en quelque sorte" ["sometimes been flattered";
"might somehow"]) and the force of its sweeping claim (*"toutes* les autres
lectures" [*"all* the other readings"]) points to the ambiguity of the central
verb *suppléer*. The text presents itself as a supplement whose meaning for
a moment straddles the line between complement and replacement, and
in doing so reflects a similar ambiguity in the period's conception of royal
exemplarity in general. By falling on the side of replacement, *this* text,
the example of *this* king, comes to take the place of a whole tradition of
royal exemplars. This absolutism, the whole project of power, is characterized by the same perplexing concurrence of ambition and reticence
that I identified above and will continue to underscore throughout my
reading of the *Mémoires*.

My gambit in this chapter is that much is to be gained by giving this text's
particularity our full attention, from its grammatical details to the larger
theoretical-historical work it does in constituting a particular image of
absolutism. Generally ignoring if not plainly rejecting it as a source worthy of serious consideration, scholars at best approach the *Mémoires* as a
source of quotable quips and bons mots and at worst as a compilation of
self-indulgent niceties whose complacency demonstrates why they don't
deserve any further attention. The scholarly editors of the text's modern
editions don't go that far, but even they, I contend, fail to see the value
and pertinence of the text they are introducing. The reasons for the mar-

2. This translation may seem puzzling, rather than "will have . . . ," but it will make
sense when the expression appears in its context below, 67–68.

ginalization of this incontestably central early modern text are complex, rooted partly in a misunderstanding of its status as an expression of the king's actual voice (related to the provenance of the text), partly in a misjudgment of the nature of the document as a historical source (its possible value as a source beyond its relation to empirical facts and what it would actually mean to take it seriously), partly in the discomfort provoked by a document that is still taken *too* seriously by present-day royalist readers.

For that reason, I start this chapter with a reflection on the need and justification for taking the *Mémoires* seriously as a historical source and, most importantly, on what it would mean to do so (section 2). Therefore, this section builds on the methodological considerations expressed in the introduction, making the case for us, as modern readers, to take a new approach to a wider set of early modern texts: a more humble, more open, more attentive approach, without necessarily assuming that we know ahead of time what the early modern text in front of us is about, what it has to tell us, and what its wider context is. It may seem puzzling to adopt such a stance of hermeneutic humility to a text that is not always itself an expression of humility (to say the least). Do the text and its author really deserve our respectful consideration? No, but we owe it to ourselves, in order to better understand the past and the world.

This initial inquiry into the composition and material support of the *Mémoires*, with the ultimate goal of reflecting on what it would mean to take them seriously, sets the stage for my close readings of the grammar of absolutism in the rest of the chapter. First (in section 3), I pay careful attention to the general image of absolutism (its structure and its foundation) conveyed to the Dauphin from the very opening of the text and beyond. Absolutism explained to a child, as it were. Obviously, this is not necessarily the full truth about the French monarchy at the time, possibly quite far from it, but it is still surprising that such an analysis of the self-image of absolutism as conveyed to the next person in line to become king has never really been done before. Formulated in polemical terms: the *Mémoires* certainly present the reader with a highly complacent and partial image of French absolutism, but, importantly, that complacency and partiality are consubstantial with absolutism itself. Interestingly, Louis XIV gives a prominent place to exemplarity, describing it as "the first and most important part of our politics." The remaining sections explore this exemplarity at the textual level in the *Mémoires*. First in the way it presents and justifies itself and its own example, which returns me to the quotation discussed above (section 4). Then, finally, through the rhetoric the text deploys in its didactic effort, and the way the pedagogical focus of Louis XIV's lessons in kingship oscillates between the minute labor of statecraft and the lofty enchantment of royal mastery, between expert analysis and God-given intuition, between (modern) instrumentalism and a (premodern) logic of royal glory (section 5). The actual readings are therefore the most important argument for the need to take the *Mémoires* seriously. What the king sets out to teach his son is the paradoxical art of enlightened absolutism, and the paradoxical nature of this enterprise—and thereby the constitutive tensions of absolutism itself—is legible throughout the *Mémoires*.

First of all, however, since many readers will not be familiar with this text that the king in the paragraph quoted above calls "ces Mémoires," some words are needed about its content and structure—and about what it is *not*. It is not a political treatise, nor advice literature in any traditional sense (e.g., a mirror for princes), nor the retrospective reflections of an elder statesman. The material covered by the *Mémoires* corresponds to five early years in the personal reign of Louis XIV, written strictly from the king's perspective (although not necessarily by the king himself). The text frequently uses the royal "I" and generously attributes royal agency. The king organizes his instruction throughout the *Mémoires* according to a principle articulated in the second sentence of the text. There, Louis XIV ascertains that kings are not "dispensés de l'obligation commune des pères [. . .] d'instruire leurs enfants par l'exemple et par le conseil" ("dispensed from the common and natural obligation of fathers to instruct their children by example and by counsel") (49/21). The order of the two terms is significant: first by *example*, then by *counsel*. This is in fact the way the king proceeds through the whole book, first retelling the principal actions and events from his reign, and then presenting concrete advice extracted from each episode in a didactic tone that often borders on pedantic, cordial at times, and self-aggrandizing by default. The ambition of the text, then, is not only to convey specific pieces of political advice, but above all to lead its only intended reader, the Dauphin, next in line to the crown, to adopt, embrace, and uphold the sole perspective that is properly political under absolutism: that of the king.

2. Taking Louis XIV's Mémoires Seriously

It is a remarkable yet widely ignored fact that in the late 1660s and early 1670s amidst glorious exploits abroad and splendid endeavors at home, Louis XIV devoted a considerable amount of time to preparing his *Mémoires* based on the early years of his personal reign for the instruction of his oldest son, the Dauphin. Specialists of French absolutism are, of course, aware of the existence of the king's *Mémoires*, but it is a testimony to the marginal status of the text that the general public and even colleagues working on other aspects of early modern French culture—or on issues related to kingship in other national traditions—often have not heard about it at all. The text is certainly available to modern readers: there is an excellent English translation from 1970—which also doubles as the best-researched scholarly edition—by the American historian Paul Sonnino. More recently, two eminent French historians, Pierre Goubert and Joël Cornette, published new scholarly editions of the French text, in 1992 and 2007, respectively.[3] Critical attention has, however, remained minimal, and it is still possible to read most of the scholarship on the *Mémoires* from the last fifty years in the course of a long afternoon. This lack of critical interest in Louis XIV's representation of himself is all the more surprising since there has been such rich work over the last few decades focusing on the representation of this very king in the social, political, and artistic system surrounding him. In the words of Ran Halévi, who has written one of the few seminal articles on the subject, the scholarship has "preferred to decipher the political portrait of the prince in the court system, in the iconographic programs of Versailles and in the imagery of royal greatness brought forth by the Petite Académie."[4]

How, then, to explain the lack of scholarly interest in a text that we

3. The critical edition of the *Mémoires* that presents the full extent of editorial choices is Dreyss's 1860 edition. It has, however, been proven faulty on many accounts, above all by Sonnino, "The Dating and Authorship of Louis XIV's *Mémoires*," in addition to being "critical" to the point of risking to dissolve the object of study.

4. "[. . .] en préférant décrypter le portrait politique du prince dans le système de la Cour, les programmes iconographiques de Versailles et l'imagerie de la grandeur royale fabriquée par la Petite Académie." Halévi, "Le sens caché des *Mémoires*," 456. In addition to Halévi's article, the major contributions include the introduction to the three editions of the *Mémoires* already mentioned, by Sonnino, Goubert, and Cornette, respectively, and the critical *mise au point* by Perez in "Les brouillons de l'absolutisme." See also Ackerman, "De l'histoire à la première personne"; Canova-Green, "On ne naît pas roi"; Ganim, "Views of Kingship"; Hoffmann, "Sun-Eye and Medusa-Head"; Kleber, "Louis XIV mémorialiste"; Lockwood, "The 'I' of History"; McClure, "The Absolute Author"; and Sonnino, "The Dating and Authorship of Louis XIV's *Mémoires*." All of these contributions are important for understanding the *Mémoires*, but I would like to draw special attention to the texts by Lockwood and McClure as models of what it could mean to take the text seriously. My approach in this chapter takes up their attentiveness to the wording and nuances of the *Mémoires*, although my overall project is quite different from theirs. For five of the major attempts to decipher the political portrait of Louis XIV without serious consideration of the *Mémoires*, see Apostolidès, *Le roi-machine*; Burke, *The Fabrication of Louis XIV*; Marin, *Le portrait du roi*; Sabatier, *Versailles ou la disgrâce d'Apollon*; and Sabatier, *Versailles, ou la figure du roi*.

could have expected to be central, if not canonical? First of all, it is important to acknowledge the presence of a certain unease among modern academics, especially in France, in their encounter with a text that they may feel other readers take *too* seriously. It is not surprising that the *Mémoires* were mobilized for royalist purposes in the nineteenth century. For example, the earliest publications of the text enter into projects aiming to (re)construct the image of a glorious philosopher-king, as in the multivolume *Œuvres de Louis XIV* from 1806, and, even more intriguingly, several competing editions in the 1820s of the *Pensées de Louis XIV*, based on highlights from the *Mémoires* (at once shaped by and named after the *Pensées* of Pascal).[5] But still today there are readers whose cultic veneration of the *Mémoires* risks making certain other readers uncomfortable with, if not suspicious of, even a detached academic approach to the text. For example, a royalist like Daniel Hamiche ends his preface to a 2001 edition of the *Mémoires* with the following impassioned peroration: "this elegance of thought and style, this clarity of reflection [...], this lofty sentiment of the dignity, the sovereignty and the grandeur of the State [...] can induce, in all Frenchmen worthy of the name, nothing but admiration for the work and respect for the Prince who embodied it."[6] Basically, what Hamiche asks from the modern reader is the same devotion to the image held forth by the text as the *Mémoires* themselves hoped to instill in their only intended reader, the Dauphin.

There are, however, other philologically more tangible factors that complicate scholars' approach to and assessment of the text. The first question is whether it is legitimate to speak of "*the* text" using the definite article, implying that the identity of the noun is known to the reader. Second, and somewhat linked to the first, is the question of in whose voice the text speaks or, in other words, whether the first-person singular pronoun "I" can rightly be identified as the king's. French historian Stanis Perez, in one of the most recent articles to tackle these questions head-on, masterfully demonstrated the instability of both the textual support and the authorial voice. My methodological argument in what follows is twofold: First, in agreement *with Perez*, that in order to justify their editorial enterprise, the three modern scholarly editors posit a more stable tex-

5. See the bibliography for further information. For the fullest recent assessment, see Perez, "Les brouillons de l'absolutisme."

6. "[C]ette élégance de la pensée et du style, cette justesse de réflexion [...], ce sentiment élevé de la dignité, de la souveraineté et de la grandeur de l'État [...] ne peuvent entraîner, chez tout Français digne de ce nom, qu'admiration pour l'œuvre et respect pour le Prince qui sut l'incarner." Louis XIV, *Mémoires et réflexions*, 9.

tual basis and the presence of a more authentic royal voice, presenting a more original political message, than the material strictly speaking allows (thus downplaying the methodological reasons for the marginalization of the text, but at the risk of transforming the text into what Hamiche wants to see in it); second, *against Perez*, that the editors in so doing ask for a much higher degree of material and authorial stability than what is necessary for the *Mémoires* to constitute an important historical document (thereby furthering the marginalization of the text). My point is thus that not only scholarly and royalist editors, but also Perez in his critique of them, hold the text up to a standard of authenticity and originality that is at best irrelevant and at worst may lead readers to embrace or reject it for the wrong reasons. Hence the unease among its readers and the marginalization of the text.

Rather than existing as something that needs to be transcended in order to somehow save the text or highlighted in order to reject it, this instability can be traced and analyzed as an entry point to discussing a vacillation, uncertainty, or hesitation constitutive of absolutism itself, as I will do later in this chapter. However, in order to better make the case for this "third way" as the most fruitful methodological approach to the *Mémoires*, between the positions represented by the modern editors and Perez respectively, a few words are needed about the text's unorthodox composition and uncertain provenance.

Louis XIV's personal reign is inaugurated by the death of Cardinal Mazarin in March 1661 and followed by the birth of his first son, the Dauphin, the same year. The young king—he was only twenty-two years old at the time—had made arrangements to chronicle his actions and decisions from the very beginning of his personal reign, but the project of developing this documentation into a text that would serve as instruction to his successor was not systematically pursued until 1666, at the earliest. The year 1666 is also significant since it is the moment when the political situation finally allowed Louis to turn his attention from internal to foreign affairs, with the French intervention in the Second Anglo-Dutch War. Now the greatest of all kings, who had already adopted the sun disk as his emblem in 1662, could prove his glory through heroic victories on the battlefield. And from this moment on, the king himself started making brief notes for his *Mémoires*, notes that a team of secretaries and writers—most prominently Octave de Périgny until his death in 1670, and then Paul Pellisson—further developed in collaboration with the king.

Although the *Mémoires* readers encounter today respond well to expectations regarding the length of a book, measuring between 220 and 280 pages in the three modern editions, they cover less than five years of a fifty-five-year reign—more precisely the years 1661, 1666, and 1667, with incomplete accounts of 1662 and 1668. The king seems to have abandoned his project in 1672, although he continued chronicling his military campaigns through 1678. In any case, it seems clear enough that the *Mémoires* were never used for their intended purpose. In fact, it is likely that the Dauphin—who never became king, dying four years before his father in 1711—never even read them.

Two observations from the early history of the transmission and reception of the *Mémoires* help shed light on the text's peculiar status, already back then and perhaps even still today. First a scene from 1714 when the aging king starts burning the papers of the long-abandoned *Mémoires*, only to be convinced by the Duke of Noailles to let him conserve the manuscript, which the latter eventually handed over to the Royal Library in 1749. The royal gesture is here twofold, and it is difficult to decide whether the stronger symbolism resides in the decision to let the flames consume the most systematic attempt at fabricating a royal self-portrait in words during the long reign of the now-aging king, after the death of the text's only intended reader, or rather in the way in which his less-than-absolute intention to destroy these documents was (apparently quite easily) swayed by the duke.[7] The same hesitation between keeping and revealing secrets is strangely evident in the text's own self-presentation. Although the text is written only for his son, the royal author would not be unhappy, he explains to the Dauphin in the opening pages, "que vous ayez ici de quoi redresser l'histoire, si elle vient à s'écarter ou à se méprendre, faute de rapporter fidèlement ou d'avoir bien pénétré mes projets et leurs motifs" ("for you to have here the means to correct history if it should go astray and misunderstand, from not having fully penetrated into my plans and into my motives") (50/22). Is the burning of the manuscript a renunciation of this ambition to help future historians give a faithful account of his reign, or is his giving up on the destruction of the text rather the persistence of his focus on his own posterity?

The second observation further complicates the obscurity of the *Mémoires*, by pointing to the puzzling fact that although the specific content was a well-kept state secret, the existence of the text was not. After Pellisson first mentions the project publicly in a 1671 panegyric of the king in the French Academy, it must have become somewhat of a hot topic. In 1677, for instance, the same academy offered the following prompt to the public for its annual poetry prize: "De l'éducation du Dauphin et du soin

---

7. This gesture was less definitive than it may seem, since this manuscript was not the only extant copy.

que prend le Roi de dresser lui-même les Mémoires de son règne pour servir d'instruction à ce jeune prince" (On the education of his royal highness the Dauphin, and the care taken by the King in writing himself the *Mémoires* of his reign, to serve as instruction for this young prince). As Perez points out, the curiosity of the prompt resides largely in the fact that the participants are asked to "exercise their imagination regarding a text which they have not read, which is not addressed to them and which, above all, they will never read."[8] This paradox did not, however, stop the hopeful poets of France from taking on the challenge. Indeed, of the five submissions printed at the time, both the winner and first runner-up were future members of the French Academy: most notable from the perspective of posterity is certainly the philosopher Bernard Le Bovier de Fontenelle, but in this context he was a clear second behind Bernard de La Monnoye.[9]

The link between these texts and the *Mémoires* themselves is not easy to define, and even the term "reception" is not entirely appropriate since they constitute a celebratory anticipation of a radically unavailable text. At the same time, however, the poems by both Fontenelle and La Monnoye demonstrate an acute awareness of the challenges and paradoxes of the enterprise.[10] Furthermore, the *Mémoires* themselves and their early "reception," in the particular sense discussed here, present an interesting challenge to the traditional mode of modern scholarship that approaches the cultural production under Louis XIV as mere propaganda.[11]

Be that as it may, the first serious reader of the actual text of the *Mémoires* may very well have been Voltaire, who got access to the work

8. "[. . .] d'exercer leur inspiration à propos d'un texte qu'ils n'ont pas lu, qui ne leur est pas destiné et que, surtout, ils ne liront jamais!" Perez, "Les brouillons de l'absolutisme," 44. For Pellisson's panegyric, see the modern edition in *Les panégyriques du roi*, ed. Zoberman, 97–104, esp. 103. For the topic proposed to the public for the poetry prize awarded by the French Academy in 1677, see the contemporary resources referenced in 50n9.

9. In addition to the official *Recueil de plusieurs pieces d'eloquence*, see the coverage in *Le Nouveau Mercure galant*, August 1677 and September 1677. The decision about the winner seems to have been almost unanimous; cf. the discussion of the qualities of the two strongest poems in *Le Nouveau Mercure galant*, September 1677, 152–53. For two modern discussions, see McClure, "The Absolute Author," 68–77; and Perez, "Les brouillons de l'absolutisme," 43–45. The most accurate documentation of the 1670s reception of the text still appears to be chapter XII of Dreyss's 1860 "Étude sur la composition des Mémoires de Louis XIV" (CLXXXIV–CXCIV), which traces three more mentions of the *Mémoires* beyond the poetry prize of the Académie.

10. See the discussion in section 4, 70–72.

11. See in this regard section 2 of the introduction.

between the first and second editions of his monumental *Le siècle de Louis XIV* (1751, 1756), into which he subsequently integrated long excerpts from "this precious and hitherto unknown monument."[12] The manuscripts of the *Mémoires*, various manuscripts from different stages of the project, arrive through a complex trajectory and present the editors with important challenges. And yet, the text printed in the two recent scholarly French editions is the same.[13]

If the instability of the text's material support is thus under relative control, the same is not the case for the text's authorship. In a literal sense, it is problematic to speak of the "royal author," as I have done here. For the king did *not* himself actually write his *Mémoires*. However, he made sketches; he prepared and supervised their writing; he corrected and rewrote; he closely directed the rewriting effectuated by what we would call today his "ghostwriters." Therefore, although the royal "I" that runs through the text does not necessarily emerge from the king's own pen, it always bears witness to his collaboration and has been approved by him. Indeed, through a careful examination of the different versions of the manuscript, Ellen McClure has traced a "struggle to identify the monarch's proper voice [. . .] throughout the text's composition," with the conclusion that "the care that obviously went into choosing the correct phrasing of the memoir's final version amply justifies [the] decision to treat the text as the king's own voice and to read each sentence quite closely."[14]

What to conclude from this discussion? Modern scholarly editors of the *Mémoires* first hesitate as if ready to deny the historical pertinence

12. "[. . .] ce monument si précieux, et jusqu'à présent inconnu." Voltaire, *Le siècle de Louis XIV*, chapter XXVIII, quoted here from Cornette, introduction to *Mémoires*, 28.

13. Although most of the editorial puzzles were solved by Dreyss ("Étude sur la composition des Mémoires de Louis XIV") and Sonnino (cf. especially "The Dating and Authorship of Louis XIV's *Mémoires*"), the modern editors do not yet fully agree on which version of the text to use. While Goubert and Cornette both use, for each of the five years covered, the last version of the manuscript reviewed by the king, Sonnino presents a plausible argument for diverting from this practice for the year 1666; cf. p. 17 of his edition. There are also some differences for the years 1661 and 1662, since Sonnino follows the Grouvelle edition from 1806, which relies on copies and revisions that are now lost, while the modern French editions rely on the last versions of the extant manuscripts. Furthermore, as Perez has argued, it is not obvious why the military *mémoires* from the 1672–78 period are not included in the corpus, since they must have been conceived as an important element in the education of a future warrior king (cf. Perez, "Les brouillons de l'absolutisme," 28–29).

14. McClure, "The Absolute Author," 93.

of the document they are editing, before often jumping to conclusions implying a surprising level of royal authorial control as if there were no problems at all in the first place. The position of Cornette in the introduction to his edition of the *Mémoires* is symptomatic in this regard. He has to recognize the philological facts—"the *Mémoires* appear as a composite, partial, and collective work"—but then, only nine pages later, after observing striking similarities between the *Mémoires* and the four-page instructions the king wrote for his grandson the Duke of Anjou in 1700 as the latter was leaving to become Philip V of Spain, he concludes about the *Mémoires*: "Louis XIV is indeed their only author."[15] A similar movement takes place in the introduction to Goubert's edition: although "it is firmly established that the king did not himself write his *Mémoires*, [. . .] the inspiration, the gaze and the hand of the king are discernible everywhere."[16] As Halévi explains, inspired by an argument first made by Charles Augustin Sainte-Beuve, the recognition of "the impeccable work of the writer, [. . .] always with the ease and naturalness with which one associates the 'manner' of Louis XIV" is just a question of taste, and not even of a lot of taste.[17] The strength of the argument obviously depends on whether the reader feels included in the personal pronoun "one" (in French: *on*), among those whose taste allows them to recognize the royal "manner" in the *Mémoires*. The degree to which this argument speaks to those who are already convinced of the royal provenance of the text is highlighted by the fact that it stems from qualities of the king himself, as seen in a discussion of the "spirit of the master" to which I will return shortly: "[O]n remarque presque toujours quelque différence entre les lettres particulières, que nous nous donnons la peine d'écrire nous-mêmes, et celles que nos secrétaires les plus habiles écrivent pour nous, découvrant en ces dernières je ne sais quoi de moins naturel, et l'inquiétude d'une plume qui craint éternellement d'en faire trop ou trop peu." ("[O]ne almost always notes a difference between the letters that we go through the trouble of writing personally and those that our most able secretaries write for us,

---

15. "Les *Mémoires* de Louis XIV se présentent comme une œuvre composite, partielle, collective"; "c'est bien Louis XIV qui en est le seul auteur." Cornette, introduction to *Mémoires*, 34, 43.

16. "Il est fermement établi que le Roi n'a pas rédigé lui-même ses *Mémoires*, [. . .] l'inspiration, l'œil et la main du Roi sont partout décelables." Goubert, introduction to *Mémoires*, 7–8.

17. "[. . .] l'impeccable travail de l'écrivain, [. . .] toujours avec l'aisance et le naturel qu'on associe à la 'manière' de Louis XIV." Halévi, "Le sens caché des *Mémoires*," 460.

detecting in the latter a certain lack of naturalness and the concern of a pen in perpetual fear of including too much or too little") (75/38).[18]

How to understand, then, the resounding silence with which these attempts at rehabilitating the *Mémoires* have been received? One could certainly claim that the reason for its marginalization is the slightly impressionistic, if not circular aspect of the arguments just invoked. They are simply not convincing enough to counter the assessment from the other side (which might be equally impressionistic and circular): the authorial presence of the king feels too insignificant and the rhetorical register of the text too conventional for it to have any intrinsic interest. In other words: the *Mémoires* could still be a legitimate object of study, but only if driven by an *extrinsic* interest, for example, as part of a wider analysis focusing on sociopolitical relations, power strategies, or literary careers.[19]

This is the exact point, I claim, where the unease evoked above becomes important. The modern editors of the *Mémoires* inevitably end up using affect to highlight the text's effect: they transition from affirming the presence of an authentic royal voice to celebrating the royal message conveyed by this voice, an argument that seems to require an equal investment in style and content, an equal celebration of royal authorship and originality. The correspondence between this royal affect and the royalist affect of somebody like Hamiche goes a long way in explaining the negative affective energy with which the opposing camp rejects the *Mémoires*. Perez's article, published in the main French-language journal in the field, *XVIIᵉ siècle*, is a case in point: he carefully and convincingly explains that this voice, which doesn't really belong to the king, in fact doesn't really have anything original to say. Notice the pleasure with which he rubs the point in: "the reflections attributed to the king bring together a list of commonplaces on how to govern"; they are "in no way original"; "in no way an innovation" but rather "old and very common"; "the king's *Mémoires* say nothing that any other person could not learn by reading treatises on education, government and morality"; they consti-

---

18. The passage is quoted by Sainte-Beuve (*Causeries du lundi*, January 19, 1852), as quoted by Halévi, "Le sens caché des *Mémoires*," 460. For the discussion of the "spirit of the master," see section 3 (57–59) and also section 5 (81–84), where the quotation is discussed within its broader context.

19. For two examples, see the way the case of Pellisson's writing for Louis XIV is mobilized in two very different explorations of seventeenth-century relations of writers to power by Ranum, *Artisans of Glory*; and Jouhaud, *Les Pouvoirs de la littérature*.

tute, as Perez notes in his conclusion, "a rich compilation of political and moral banalities gathered here and there."[20]

All of this may very well be true, but it is at the same time completely irrelevant for assessing the *Mémoires*. The critique of the old idea of Louis XIV as a philosopher-king—whose main achievement was not only his reign but also the original philosophical treatise he handed down to us—is of course pertinent. It is, however, also important to notice the anachronism inherent in this critique (as well as in what is criticized), which judges the work on the basis of its philosophical originality and not its rhetorical efficacy.

This point can be formulated both generally and specifically. At a general level, the *Mémoires* belong to a pre-Romantic poetics of imitation where novelty and innovation emerged through the skillful appropriation of traditional commonplaces. It is true that the rhetorical tradition was under pressure at the time of Louis XIV; the cultural production intended to enhance the glory of the king was in fact an important arena for the unfolding of the "Querelle des Anciens et des Modernes," as discussed in the introduction and especially chapter 3 of this book. This strain on traditional forms of both artistic and moral authority should, however, be addressed from within the poetics of imitation and the wider culture of exemplarity whence it emerged and not through a post-Romantic ideal of originality.

The demand for philosophical originality becomes even less relevant in the concrete case of the *Mémoires*, since it completely disregards the specificity of the text, including its place of enunciation. This is a practical or, rather, a pragmatic text. It does not aim to represent an ideal of power for a wide audience of readers, but to efficiently communicate and transmit Louis XIV's power to his successor in the real world. I argue, then, that the principal interest of the *Mémoires* emerges from the relation between the enunciative source and its sole intended recipient or, more precisely, from the complex *gesture* it performs. Put bluntly, the project of the *Mémoires* is to explain absolutism to a child, but not just any child, and with higher real-world stakes than for any book of philosophy. Not only the legacy of this absolute monarch but even the survival of

20. Perez, "Les brouillons de l'absolutisme": "les pensées qu'on attribue au roi ne recouvre qu'un florilège de lieux communs sur la manière de gouverner" (35); "en rien originale" (34); "en rien une innovation" (36); "vieille[s] [. . .] [et] très commune[s]" (37n60); "[l]es mémoires du roi ne disent rien que tout un chacun ne puisse apprendre à la lecture des traités d'éducation, de gouvernement et de morale" (41); "une riche compilation d'évidences politiques et morales puisées ici ou là" (49–50).

absolutism will depend on the success of the enterprise. Therefore, taking the *Mémoires* seriously means carefully exploring the text while attending to questions such as: What self-image does absolutism present in its effort to prolong its reign beyond the present absolute monarch? How can the execution of sovereignty be taught? What example should the young Dauphin follow in order to learn to become absolute and thus to be without example? Or again, mobilizing the etymology of the word "absolute" (as that which is not bound): How to lead him to cross the boundary between bound and unbound without transgressing the line into tyranny? It is with these high stakes in mind that I now, finally, turn to the text and the way it presents itself to the reader.

3. Absolutism, Explained to a Child: "The first and most important part of our entire politics"

The *Mémoires* are ordered chronologically, starting with the year 1661—the first year of Louis XIV's personal reign and also the birth year of the Dauphin. Given the high stakes of the enterprise, it should come as no surprise that the historical account is preceded by an ample introduction (4–5 pages in the French edition quoted from here), which from the outset seeks to establish a relation of friendly authority with its sole intended reader. In fact, the king emphasizes the global project and the reasons he took it on in the very first paragraph of the text:

> Mon fils, beaucoup de raisons, et toutes fort importantes, m'ont fait résoudre à vous laisser, avec assez de travail pour moi, parmi mes occupations les plus grandes, ces Mémoires de mon règne et de mes principales actions. Je n'ai jamais cru que les rois, sentant, comme ils font, en eux toutes les tendresses paternelles, fussent dispensés de l'obligation commune des pères, qui est d'instruire leurs enfants par l'exemple et par le conseil. Au contraire, il m'a semblé qu'en ce haut rang où nous sommes, vous et moi, un devoir public se joignait au devoir de particulier, et qu'enfin tous les respects qu'on nous rend, toute l'abondance et tout l'éclat qui nous environnent, n'étant que des récompenses attachées par le Ciel même au soin qu'il nous confie des peuples et des états, ce soin n'était pas assez grand s'il ne passait au-delà de nous-mêmes, en nous faisant communiquer toutes nos lumières à celui qui doit régner après nous.

> (My son, many excellent reasons have prompted me to go to a considerable effort in the midst of my greatest occupations in order to leave you these *mémoires* of my reign and of my principal actions. I have never

believed that kings, feeling as they do all the paternal affections and attachments in themselves, were dispensed from the common and natural obligation of fathers to instruct their children by example and by counsel. On the contrary, it has seemed to me that in this high rank of ours a public duty combined with the private, and that all the respects that are paid to us, all the affluence and brilliance that surround us being nothing but rewards attached by Heaven Itself to the care entrusted in us for people and for states, this care would be insufficient if it were not extended beyond us by making us hand down all our insights [toutes nos lumières] to he who shall reign after us.) (49/21–22)

The first two words—the apostrophe to his son—clearly highlight that the text that follows has only one intended reader, the Dauphin. And by discreetly calling to mind the mortality of the king, the end of the paragraph evokes a scene of reading. There is indeed a "reign after us," and for the Dauphin a reign without his father: after him and without him. This is of course the principal reason for the king to go to such a "considerable effort in the midst of [his] greatest occupations." The *Mémoires* are first and foremost instructions, which, in the case of the king's premature death, would arrive to the Dauphin as a message from the other side of the grave, so to speak, in order to take the place of the living father's instruction "by example and by counsel." The main verb used in the first sentence of the text accentuates this effect: many good reasons have led the king to decide to *leave behind* the *Mémoires* for his son.

Within the scene of reading emerging here, the question of the *Mémoires'* authorship loses much of its importance. The text is written in the conditional mode. Every section seems to contain an unspoken *if*: If, my son, I should die before you, which is the only circumstance under which you will see this text, *then* I would want you to know that . . . This allows the king and his team of writers to carefully construct a place of enunciation separated from the sole intended reader of the text by a premature death. Through this gesture from the other side of the grave, *in potentia*, the text represents an extreme authority.[21] It arrives to its intended reader

21. Premature death was, of course, much less of an anomaly in the seventeenth century than today. The threat must have loomed large in Louis XIV's life both due to the fact that his two male predecessors died prematurely (Henri IV assassinated in 1610 and Louis XIII from illness when his oldest son was only four years old) and to the threats to his own life (in the civil war-like chaos of La Fronde, when Louis XIV was still a young boy, and above all through the severe illness that nearly killed him in the summer of 1658 before he turned twenty years old). It is worth noticing that James VI of Scotland (subsequently James I of England) makes a similar move allud-

as a claim on a future beyond the life of the author, although one that the Dauphin will still be free to disregard. In this sense, the (implicit) conditional mode accentuates the tenuous ambition of absolutism about controlling the future, as addressed in the introduction of this chapter. The king's "considerable effort," his travail if not his œuvre, will be received by the Dauphin as a political testament bequeathing to him "toutes nos lumières." The English rendition "all our insights" conveys only part of what the French *lumières* entails, since the original promises the transmission not only of what is seen (the insight), but also and above all the light that makes possible the very act of seeing. What is at stake from the opening of the text is thus the transmission of the extreme authority that is consubstantial with this light and that enables what Louis XIV will soon call the "eyes [one is tempted to say: the *gaze*] of a master" ("des yeux de maître") (53/24) in his emphasis on enlightened kingship conceived in terms of visual supremacy that runs throughout the whole text. Quite naturally the sections of the *Mémoires* covering the events of 1661 play an important role here, since they narrate how Louis XIV himself came to possess this necessary light when he started his personal reign at the tender age of twenty-two. Similarly, the way in which the text presents itself is crucial insofar as it presents the key to what follows, not only to us as modern readers but also to the fatherless son about to become Louis XV.

The backdrop for this royal intervention par excellence is a long description of the bleak state of the kingdom before Louis XIV's 1661 decision to govern on his own after the death of Mazarin, including references to the Franco-Spanish War (1635–59), intrigues at court, and most noteworthy to the civil war–like unrest known as La Fronde (1648–53), which in retrospect came to stand for the last serious challenge to the emerging absolutist monarchy. It is therefore significant that this description is framed by two passages on kingship and mastery, or the absence thereof:

Dès l'enfance même, le seul nom des *rois fainéants* et de maires du palais me faisait peine[22] quand on le prononçait en ma présence. Mais il

---

ing to premature deaths in the opening of the *Basilikon Doron* that he wrote for his son Prince Henry in 1598: "And because the hour of death is uncertain to me, as unto all flesh, I leave it as my Testament, and latter will unto you" (4). Otherwise, these two projects are, however, more different than one might think initially. The place of enunciation becomes more crucial in the *Mémoires* through the way they try to bring together precepts and examples; cf. the discussion in section 4 (67–68) of Pierre Ménard's *Académie des princes* (1646), where the *Basilikon Doron* was included.

22. Interestingly, an earlier version of the manuscript had "honte et dépit" (shame and spite); cf. Hoffmann, "Sun-Eye and Medusa-Head," 21.

faut se représenter l'état des choses: des agitations terribles par tout le royaume [...]

[...]

Je commençai à jeter les *yeux* sur toutes les diverses parties de l'État, et non pas des yeux indifférents, mais des *yeux de maître*, sensiblement touché de n'en voir pas une qui ne m'invitât et ne me pressât d'y porter la *main*; mais observant avec soin ce que le temps et la disposition des choses me pouvaient permettre. *Le désordre régnait partout.*

(Even from childhood, the very name of *do-nothing kings* and of mayors of the palace distressed me when it was uttered in my presence. But one must remember the circumstances: terrible disorder throughout the kingdom [...]

[...]

I began, therefore, to cast my eyes over all the various parts of the state, and not casual eyes, but *the eyes of a master*, deeply struck at not finding a single one that did not call on me and did not urge me to bring my *hand* to it; yet carefully observing what time and circumstances would allow me. *Disorder reigned everywhere.*) (51, 53/23, 24; my emphasis)

The medieval *rois fainéants* (do-nothing kings), manipulated by the mayors of their palace and therefore kings only in title but not in function, cast a long shadow, reaching up to Louis XIV's own father, whom the text never once names. Louis XIII's presence is collapsed alongside all of the king's other predecessors, if not into a less-favorable collective entity, like the *rois fainéants*. This almost becomes explicit a few pages later when the king expresses his wish that neither his son nor his further successors will ever take a first minister (as Louis XIII had in Richelieu), so that "le nom en sera pour jamais aboli en France, rien étant plus indigne que de voir d'un côté toutes les fonctions, et de l'autre le seul titre de Roi" ("the name will forever be abolished in France, there being nothing more shameful than to see on the one hand all the functions and on the other the mere title of king") (65/31).

If France had once turned into a shameful kingdom of disorder, as portrayed here, it was because of a disorder in the execution of kingship: a weak royal hand and an absent royal gaze. The last sentence in the passage above—quite possibly the most frequently quoted words of the whole text—expresses the dysfunctional governance of the state already through its grammatical form: the verb *régner* is used with an inanimate, abstract noun in an impersonal, metaphorical sense instead of with an actual reigning sovereign as its active subject. This accentuates the morass of the do-nothing kings. The negative form of the noun stresses the void in the preponderant and exclusive place from where an important influence has gone missing and a preponderant and exclusive role is no longer being played.[23] The disorder is at once politically, semantically, and syntactically the expression of an absence of royal agency.

However, a latent change is already present in the *passé simple* in the opening of the second passage quoted above: "Je *commençai* à jeter les yeux..." ("I *began* to cast my eyes..."). The time was not yet ripe, but soon the royal eyes and the royal hand would no longer be indifferent to the demands of a state in sore need of a true Master. Although disorder still reigned everywhere, the imperfect tense describing this regrettable state of affairs—the *imparfait* of "régnait"—was already pierced by a first *passé simple* preparing the change to come. Against this backdrop, the sections that follow in the *Mémoires* tell the story of the reign of an enlightened king who takes matters into his own hands, governs by himself—through an endless series of sovereign actions expressed by further uses of the *passé simple*—thereby introducing light and order where disorder and darkness once reigned.

Returning now to the first paragraph of the *Mémoires*, as quoted above, I draw attention to the presence of two overlapping discourses—a co-presence that runs throughout the whole text—namely that of a discourse of political theology and the language of exemplarity. In the opening of the text, Louis XIV makes a tacit distinction between public and private—on the one hand, "the greatest occupations [...] of [his] reign," and, on the other, "paternal affections and attachments," "the common and natural obligations of fathers"—which then becomes explicit in the opening of the third sentence: the "public duty" he has as a king, the "private [duty]" he has as a father. This distinction between the man and his function—private and public—runs through the long third sentence to

---

23. I allude here to the definition of this sense of the word from the *TLF*: "RÉGNER, verbe intrans. [...] B. [Le suj. désigne une chose] / 1. Occuper une place prépondérante, exclusive; exercer une influence importante; avoir un rôle prépondérant, exclusif." (REIGN, intransitive verb [...] B.—[The subject is a thing] / 1. To occupy a preponderant or exclusive place; exert a significant influence; have a preponderant or exclusive role.) The definition gives examples of a particular use when "Le suj. désigne un fléau, une maladie" (The subject denotes a curse or disease), among which the sentence commented upon here could have been cited. Dictionaries from the period have many examples of similar uses, but the definitions are less precise. The first edition of the *Dictionnaire* of the French Academy is closest: "Regner. [...] Il se dit aussi fig. et signifie, Dominer. [...] Il signifie fig. Être en crédit, en vogue, à la mode." (Reign. [...] It is also said figuratively and signifies, to dominate. [...] It signifies figuratively, to be held high, in vogue, fashionable.")

the end of the paragraph and reappears in its very last line: the royal *function* is beyond the king as a mortal man and will be carried on by "he who shall reign after us," or in other words, you after my death, your son after your death—the function always surviving the death of the individual king. For, as royalists know, *le roi ne meurt jamais*; the king never dies. The very first paragraph of the text thus exposes the absolute monarchy's grounding in political theology: it is indeed "Heaven Itself" that invests the *body politic* of the king with glory ("all the affluence and brilliance that surround us") and a duty ("the care entrusted in us for people and for states") well beyond the limits of his *body natural* ("beyond us" ["au-delà de nous-mêmes"]). In this way, private and public duties merge in the paternal care for royal instruction, a care that assures that the king never dies (since paternal instruction here ultimately serves the purpose of royal succession) and of which this text is a supreme expression.

From the beginning, the text builds from the analogy of three patriarchal figures: Father (in the biological sense), King, and God. This hierarchically ordered analogy finds its most explicit expression later in the 1661 *Mémoires*, when Louis discusses the importance of displaying religious humility in a sentence that links exemplarity and politics in a striking way that will probably sound suspect to most modern readers:

> Notre soumission pour lui [Dieu] est la règle et l'exemple de celle qui nous est due. Les armées, les conseils, toute l'industrie humaine seraient de faibles moyens pour nous maintenir sur le trône, si chacun y croyait avoir même droit que nous, et ne révérait pas une puissance supérieure, dont la nôtre est une partie. Les respects publics que nous rendons à cette puissance invisible, pourraient enfin être nommés justement la première et la plus importante partie de notre politique, s'ils ne devaient avoir un motif plus noble et plus désintéressé.

> (Our submission to Him [God] is the rule and the example for that which is due to us. Armies, councils, all human industry would be feeble means for maintaining us on the throne if everyone believed he had as much right to it as we and did not revere a superior power, of which ours is a part. The public respects that we pay to this invisible power could indeed justly be considered the first and most important part of our entire policy if they did not require a more noble and more disinterested motive.) (104–5/57)

Doesn't this passage evoke blatant manipulation and cynical propaganda in a way that points directly forward to totalitarian regimes of the twentieth century? Yes and no. In order to grasp the nuances of that comparison, I will tease out the different layers of meaning in the passage.

First of all, the wording points back to the first paragraph of the *Mémoires* in the way it anchors royal power in an exemplary display of public respects: "The public respects that we pay to this invisible [divine] power" (from the paragraph just quoted) is the example for "all the respects that are paid to us" (from the opening paragraph of the *Mémoires*). The reader is thus at the heart of the project and at the heart of absolutism. At the same time, it should be stressed that this is *not* a genealogy of royal power. The passage does not say anything about the historical or political origin of the royal claim to power; there is no reference to a foundational event, nor to a construction or justification of that claim itself. In the *Mémoires*, as in absolutism in general, the king's position is taken for granted since it is God-given; he is, so to speak, always already on the throne. This point of the *Mémoires* provides modern readers with a privileged glimpse of the inner workings of absolutism, since its enunciative position gives us little reason to suspect that it takes part in or reenacts a strategy of manipulative propaganda. And this is even more the case for the passage here, since it gives advice about the political use and efficacy of manipulation. Therefore, if the passage evokes the "means for maintaining us on the throne," it is in response to a factual, not a legal or normative challenge. It would certainly still be a problem "if everyone believed he had as much right to it [the throne] as we," but only because of the *might* of this collective "everyone" and not because they were actually *right*.

The passage enumerates three different "means for maintaining us on the throne," all of which Louis XIV deems feeble and ineffective, although throughout his reign he deployed them with unprecedented efficacy and ruthlessness: first, brute force ("[l]es armées"); second the rule of public and private law widely construed ("les conseils"); third, an even wider category of governmentality encompassing all man could possibly do in order to successfully maintain the king on the throne and which we today might call the whole biopolitical system ("toute l'industrie humaine"). Importantly, the fourth "means," which is the main topic of the paragraph under discussion and the answer to the challenge raised, evokes at once a top-down and a bottom-up process: royal participation in a divine mystery (with perceived agency from above) and the royal subjects' very real reverence for the hierarchy (agency from below). The conservation of the patriarchal hierarchy is dependent on the perfect confluence of these two processes, divine-right monarchy being the immanent, visual instantiation of this transcendent, invisible power. Indeed, the elevation of the royal throne itself requires an act of submission that points to the superiority of the invisible power that justifies it.

A passage at the end of the *Mémoires* for 1667 provides an even more condensed expression of the same idea, in a discussion of the importance that the sovereign not stray from the path assigned by Christianity. Again, the perspective here is pragmatic, not genealogical. What is at stake is the conservation of power (through royal example) not its constitution (through Christian maxim), which is taken for granted, given, or in the more technical language of the passage: "préposé" ("instituted"; literally, previously imposed).

> Il n'est point de maxime plus établie par le christianisme que cette humble soumission des sujets envers ceux qui leur sont préposés. Et, en effet, ceux qui jetteront la vue sur les temps passés reconnaîtront aisément combien ont été rares, depuis la venue de Jésus-Christ, ces funestes révolutions d'États qui arrivaient si souvent durant le paganisme.
>
> Mais il n'est pas juste que les souverains qui font profession de cette sainte doctrine se fondent sur l'innocence qu'elle inspire à leurs peuples pour vivre de leur part avec plus de dérèglement. Il faut qu'ils soutiennent par leurs propres exemples la religion dont ils veulent être appuyés, et qu'ils considèrent que leurs sujets, les voyant plongés dans le vice et le sang, ne peuvent presque rendre à leur personne le respect dû à leur dignité, ni les reconnaître pour les vivantes images de celui qui est tout saint aussi bien que tout puissant.

> (No maxim is more established by Christianity than this humble submission of subjects to those who are instituted over them; and indeed, those who would inquire into past times will easily see how rare, since the coming of Jesus Christ, have been those ghastly revolutions that occurred so often under paganism.
>
> But it is not fair for the sovereigns who profess this holy doctrine to rely on the innocence that it inspires in their people in order to live, for their part, in greater indiscipline. They must sustain by their own example the religion whose support they desire and consider that their subjects, seeing them immersed in vice and in blood, can hardly render to their person the respect due to their rank, nor recognize in them the living image of Him who is all-holy as well as all-powerful.) (307–8/245)

Paul Sonnino's translation of "il n'est pas *juste*" as "it is not *fair*" in the sentence just after the paragraph break may be surprising at first, but it reveals a deep understanding of the logic at work. The French adjective *juste* refers here to a pragmatic *justesse*, which is closer in meaning to a term like "appropriateness" or even "prudence," rather than to an absolute "justice." Hence the presence of the modifier "ne peuvent presque" ("can *hardly*"). The royal indiscipline does not in any way invalidate or cancel the sovereigns' claim to power (unsurprisingly, we are very far from any theory of resistance and the contemplation of limitations on royal power), but it is nonetheless an obstacle to its practical conservation. The sovereigns' moral conduct is necessary because confronted with their indiscipline, "their subjects [...] can hardly render to their *person* the respect due to their *rank*" ("leurs sujets [...] ne peuvent presque rendre à leur *personne* le respect dû à leur *dignité*"). In this case, respect is still due, since it is in no way canceled by the sovereigns' indiscipline, but it is rendered pragmatically difficult if not close to impossible. Basically, this passage merges a discourse of exemplarity with one of political theology in order to enable the king's subjects to react in the way dictated by religion. The example performed by the royal person (his physical, mortal body of flesh and blood) must work in tandem with the dignity with which it is invested (his divinely infused political body).

At this point it is important to recall the discussion in the introduction to the book regarding the structural similarity between the logic of absolutism explored here and the logic of exemplarity as such. As showed there, the workings of exemplarity are dependent on a vertical elevation or exception. That is why, in a certain sense, all exemplarity is royal, and the logic of exemplarity itself stands in a relation of solidarity with that of kingship.[24]

In light of this wider discussion, it would be tempting to see an even more sweeping claim in the passage from the *Mémoires* on the central role of the public display of religious devotion than what is rendered in Sonnino's English translation. That is to say, the example of "submission" and "public respects" offered by the king is not only "the first and most important part of our entire *policy*," but quite literally the grounding of absolutist *politics*, tout court. The first submission in respect to a God-given hierarchy becomes exemplary for the submission to figures of authority in general. Exemplarity is "la première et la plus importante partie de notre *politique*" insofar as it is the principle that grounds and conserves orderly, hierarchical life in the polis.

The enunciative situation of the text adds further complexity. In the passage in question, the king mobilizes the exemplarity of all three patriarchal levels. The Dauphin should learn to follow his father's example and

24. See section 3 of the introduction, especially 30–33.

publicly display his submission to the divine Father so that the people of France, when the Dauphin becomes king, can in turn follow his example in their submission to him, the new king and father of France. But, at the same time, this advice from father to son about exemplary conduct is rooted in more than mere self-interest. Indeed, if anything, it is a reflexive move probing the *limits* of political self-interest.

This notion brings me back to the conditional clause in the last sentence of the passage in question. It is not obvious how to render its meaning in English: the public display of royal religious devotion "pourraient [. . .] être nommés"—"could [. . .] be considered," or perhaps rather "could [. . .] have been considered"—the core element of royal politics, if it hadn't been for the fact that it ought to have "a more noble and more disinterested motive." The apparent cynicism of the preceding demystification of royal politics is thus tempered and even questioned from within. The gesture toward the allusively evoked "more noble and more disinterested motive" is pursued further in the subsequent sentence that opens the next paragraph of the text:

> Gardez-vous bien, mon fils, je vous en conjure, de n'avoir dans la religion que cette vue d'intérêt, très mauvaise quand elle est seule, mais qui d'ailleurs ne vous réussirait pas, parce que l'artifice se dément toujours, et ne produit pas longtemps les mêmes effets que la vérité.

> (Watch out, my son, I implore you, not to approach religion with only this idea of self-interest, very bad when it stands alone, but which, moreover, would not succeed for you because artifice always comes out and does not long produce the same effects as truth.) (105/57)

"*[J]e vous en conjure*" ("*I implore you*"): In accordance with the "more noble and more disinterested motive" announced in the preceding sentence, the political consideration here is only secondary, as highlighted by the adverbial locution "d'ailleurs" ("moreover," "by the way"), which introduces the practical efficacy of artifice as if it were an afterthought. Prior to that, the father's implicit emphasis on their relation hammers in a moral message, in and beyond the text, no less than three times: imperative warning ("Watch out"), apostrophe ("my son"), and imploration. It is as if he hopes that the etymological meaning of the verb *conjurer* would be activated by a semi-magical insistence on the bond uniting them, in a *con-jurer,* a communal invocation between father and son, the act of calling upon religion in order to call into existence a more primary—that is: a "more disinterested," less interested, less instrumental—relation to religion. For, as Furetière makes explicit in his definition of *conjurer* that aligns most closely with its use here, "*conjurer*, also signifies, to pray with insistence and forcefully in the name of what one respects the most, of what one holds dearest."[25] Indeed, what is at stake here is precisely the public respect the Dauphin will pay to religion (which should be what he respects the most) and his real motivation for doing so (which should be his profound respect, rather than his self-interest). Therefore, another more specific meaning of the verb is also at play, closer to the present-day meaning of the English cognate: "*conjurer*, also signifies, to chase away with certain words or charms Demons, a tempest, etc. When one does it in the name of God, this is called to exorcise."[26] It could even be tempting to read the passage above as a first attempt at exorcising from the mind of the Dauphin the dangerous—and dangerously alluring—spirit of Machiavellian instrumentalism.

But what message exactly does the passage convey? Rereading the sentence from the perspective of a young sovereign in need of instruments for governing his land efficiently, there is another lesson here, formulated in terms of self-interest. At a surface level, the lesson of exemplarity is quite simply that dissimulation does not work. Superficial exemplarity is not enough. In addition to being morally and theologically bad, artifice is also politically ineffective. Not only will it not fool God (as spelled out soon afterward in the text: "à son égard, l'extérieur sans l'intérieur n'est rien du tout, et sert plutôt à l'offenser qu'à lui plaire" ["in his view, the external without the internal is nothing at all and serves more to offend him than to please him"] [105/58]), but it will not even fool the sovereign's own subjects for long. It may certainly work for a while, producing the same exterior expressions of faith as authentic devotion, "the same effects as truth" (we could say the same "truth effect," in analogy with the "reality effect" of Roland Barthes), but not for long. A self-interested display of devotion only works if it does not "stand alone," but is the expression of true faith. Therefore, although the father recommends that his son should embrace—or rather, *needs* to embrace—truth and authenticity over political artifice for more noble reasons, it will at the end of the

---

25. "Conjurer, signifie aussi, Prier avec instance et fortement au nom de ce que l'on respecte le plus, de ce qu'on a de plus cher." Furetière, *Dictionnaire universel*, "Conjurer."

26. "Conjurer signifie aussi, Chasser avec certaines paroles ou charmes les Démons, la tempête, etc. Quand on le fait au nom de Dieu, cela s'appelle exorciser." Furetière, "Conjurer." It is also worth noticing the very first definition of the verb, whose resonance lends urgency to royal politics by spelling out the nefarious consequences of a failed exemplarity: "CONJURER. v. act. / Conspirer contre le Prince ou l'État." (CONJURER. active verb / To conspire against the King or the State.)

day also produce more politically beneficial effects. Exemplarity understood as exemplary submission is truly "the first and most important part of our entire politics," but it should not be named as such in public (this reflection is possible only in the *arcana imperii* of absolutism), or even be approached as such by the Dauphin. The Dauphin should display signs of religious submission in public, not because a religion that is true is in his interest, but because it is actually true. But this also means, somewhat perplexingly, that it is in his own political interest to follow an apolitical, disinterested motive rather than one of self-interest, in a second-order utilitarian orientation of sorts.

My analysis of these few key passages from the *Mémoires* serves to highlight both the crucial function and the precariousness of exemplarity within the absolutist hierarchical system. The father and son are certainly united in the first-person plural of the axiomatic starting point: "Notre soumission pour lui [Dieu] est la règle et l'exemple de celle qui nous est due." ("Our submission to Him [God] is the rule and the example for that which is due to us") (104–5/57). This first-person plural is the king who never dies from the opening paragraph of the *Mémoires*, voicing the confluence of political theology and exemplarity that sustains the whole system. But father and son are separated by the father's lingering doubts about the one weak link in this chain, the single point on which everything hinges and where the system may start to unravel: the wholeheartedness of the next sovereign's own faith. Indeed, it is tempting to go a step further by reading the affective energy and the convolutedness of the text at this point as the expression of an even more fundamental fissure: the father separated from himself, as if of two minds (and not only two royal bodies), by his lingering doubt about the wholeheartedness of his own faith. Hence the warning, the *con-juration* and the exorcism observed above, in a paradoxical appeal to a second-order self-interest. And hence the surprising continuation of this argument in the following paragraphs of the text, where the king turns away from his usual procedure of instructing his son "by example and by counsel" (21), putting the examples from his own life aside and, after first assuring his son that "[c]e n'est pas à moi à faire le théologien avec vous" ("[i]t is not for me to play the theologian with you") (106/58), doing exactly that, through a multipage accumulation of arguments and proof for the existence of God.

4. The Utility of "These Mémoires"

It should come as no surprise that the word "example" already appears for the first time in the second sentence of the *Mémoires*. What is more natural for a father than wanting to teach his son by example and by counsel, that is: not only by *telling* but also by *showing*, not only in *theory* but also in *practice*? It is important to note the order of the two terms: first "by example," then "by counsel," which is the way the king proceeds throughout the *Mémoires*, first retelling a prominent action or event from his reign, and then presenting concrete advice extracted from this episode. There is, however, a considerable difference between the instruction provided by the king's text and the common paternal method of instruction described in its first paragraph, although they both work "by example and by counsel." For while fathers normally instruct their children by example in the presence of the children, the king is here making his past actions present to his son through narration—that is, through representation. The opening of the text thus displays an immense faith in the power of the written word and in the force of the king's written example.

The text further develops this paternal exemplarity in the second paragraph. Louis directly states that he hopes that, through these *mémoires*, he "pourrai[t] vous être [au Dauphin] aussi utile [...] que le saurait être personne du monde" ("could be as useful to you [the Dauphin] [...] as [...] anyone else in the world would know how to be") (49/22). The negation of any utility to be found on this earth hints at another source of instruction, namely, "Heaven Itself" from the preceding paragraph. This divine instruction is exploited by the court's chief theologian and preceptor for the Dauphin, Bossuet, in his *Politique tirée de l'Écriture sainte* (Politics drawn from the very words of Holy Scripture), originally destined for his pupil and now considered the most important political treatise from the early reign of Louis XIV. The scholarship has worked out in great detail the radical pedagogical differences between Bossuet's political textbook and the king's *Mémoires*, starting with the striking observation that the latter does not contain a single reference to the Bible.[27] However, this observation should not obscure the extent to which the *Mémoires'* whole pedagogical enterprise relies on a patriarchal hierarchy that is profoundly Judeo-Christian, as demonstrated in detail in the preceding section.

How can it be that Louis's example can be so powerful, even more useful than all other examples (in the world)? As the king points out in the continuation of the paragraph, this is not exactly a question of talent or experience: "ceux qui auront plus de talents et plus d'expérience que moi, n'auront pas régné, et régné en France" ("those who might have greater talents or more experience than I would not have reigned, let alone in France") (49/22). Rather, it is a matter of perspective, of the

27. See, for example, Halévi, "Le sens caché des *Mémoires*," 455.

king's visual, spatial, and cognitive privilege: "plus la place est élevée, plus elle a d'objets qu'on ne peut ni voir ni connaître qu'en l'occupant" ("the higher the position, the more things it entails that can neither be envisaged nor understood without occupying it") (49–50/22). This is not only a striking departure from Machiavelli, who famously, in his dedicatory letter for the *Prince*, justifies his own less-elevated point of view by referring to the way in which cartographers adopt a lower perspective in order to better describe mountains and other high points,[28] but it also brings forth a new discursive strategy compared to earlier instructional texts written by kings for their offspring.

Pierre Ménard, Sieur d'Yzernay, provides a useful ground of comparison in this regard, in the instruction manual for the young Louis XIV that he dedicated to Mazarin in 1646, *L'académie des princes, où les rois apprennent l'art de régner de la bouche des rois. Ouvrage tiré de l'histoire tant ancienne que nouvelle* (The academy of princes, where kings learn the art of ruling from the mouth of kings, gathered from ancient as well as present-day history). The prince's perspective is absent from the sections justifying the project, not only from Ménard's own dedicatory letter but also from the introduction of each text constituting the volume, written by kings ranging from the biblical David to James I of England (the *Basilikon Doron* constitutes the third of four books in the volume). The reason for this absence becomes clear at the end of the dedicatory letter when Ménard announces a second instructional volume (never to be realized, it seems) to complement *L'académie des princes*, where he will let the kings "qui ont déjà donné les préceptes [. . .] donner aussi les exemples" (who have already given the precepts [. . .] also give the examples).[29] Louis XIV was only eight years old when this book was published, and it is not very likely that he was able to make use of its teachings, or even that he read it at all.

It seems, however, that Paul Pellisson had Ménard's project in mind in the following note that he wrote to the king during his work on the *Mémoires*: "Des princes qui ont écrit pour leurs enfants, les uns n'ont laissé que des préceptes sans histoire, ce qui est moins agréable; les autres que l'histoire sans préceptes, ce qui est moins utile: la perfection est peut-

---

28. In the "Dedicatory letter to Lorenzo de' Medici," Machiavelli justifies the pertinence of his reflections (that is, the reflections of "a man of very low and humble condition") by making an analogy to the situation of those who draw maps: "For those who draw maps place themselves on low ground, in order to understand the character of the mountains and other high points." Machiavelli, *The Prince*, 4.

29. Ménard, *L'Académie des princes*, unpaginated dedicatory letter to Mazarin.

être à joindre les deux."[30] (Among princes who wrote for their children, some only wrote precepts without history, which is less pleasant; the others only history without precepts, which is less useful: perfection would maybe consist in bringing the two together.) Whether the *Mémoires* actually succeeds in realizing the Horatian ideal of *dulce et utile* (pleasant and useful), the project seems very much driven by such an ambition, bringing together the two aspects of royal education in one volume in an effort to instruct "by example and by counsel," in a constant back-and-forth between the representation of and the reflection on the exercise of power.

Importantly, this shift in royal pedagogy is much more than a methodological improvement that reaches the same end. Rather, the new discursive strategy expresses a different vision of kingship, a vision *from above*, so to speak, which assumes the full political, epistemological, cognitive, and thus pedagogical consequences of the fact that sovereignty cannot be shared. Within such a paradigm, the insights of political theory lose much of their potency and pertinence. It should therefore not be a great surprise that the reign of Louis XIV saw a marked decline in the production of major political treatises as compared to the preceding decades, nor that Louis XIV increasingly relied on artists rather than jurists to affirm his sovereignty.[31]

It is tempting to read the contorted language in the passage just quoted from the *Mémoires* as an expression of this very shift in the conception of kingship: "ceux qui auront plus de talents et plus d'expérience que moi, n'auront pas régné, et régné en France" ("those who might have greater talents or more experience than I would not have reigned, let alone in France") (49/22). What exactly does the expression "n'auront pas régné" mean here? A direct translation of this use of the French *futur antérieur* would give "will not have reigned," but Paul Sonnino's translation with "would" is better, in that it renders the modal use of the tense, conveying a sense of doubt, while marking a distance, which is already present in the first "auront" (which is therefore well translated as "might have" instead of "will have"). Indeed, since the king's position is so elevated, the generalized "talents" and "experiences" evoked are not really relevant

---

30. *Œuvres de Louis XIV*, ed. Grouvelle, 1:144.

31. See Church, "The Decline of French Jurists as Political Theorists"; and, in a more polemical vein, see Halévi, "Louis XIV: La religion de la gloire." Halévi evokes a "découronnement de la théorie politique" (discrowning of political theory) (183–86), observing in passing that the two major political treatises of the age were not written by jurists but by a theologian, namely, Bossuet (*Politique tirée des propres paroles de l'Écriture sainte* [Politics drawn from the very words of Holy Scripture]) and by Louis XIV himself (the *Mémoires*), cf. 184.

for the case at hand. What is placed at a distance here thus seems to be the very meaning of the verb *régner* (and even more, "régner en France"). For within this conception of kingship, what can non-sovereign readers, from their lowly point of view, even pretend to know about ruling? If, therefore, this way of justifying the project of the *Mémoires* may seem paradoxical, it is because it brings our attention to paradoxes that are undergirding absolutism itself.

Interestingly, these insights are expressed in the first publicly available documents that mention the *Mémoires*, namely, in the submissions to the 1677 poetry competition awarded by the French Academy discussed in section 2.[32] In reflecting on "[le] soin que prend le Roi de dresser lui-même les Mémoires de son règne pour servir d'instruction à ce jeune prince" (the care taken by the king in writing himself the *Mémoires* of his reign, to serve as instruction for this young prince), several of the five poets who had the honor of seeing their submissions published quite naturally turn to the image of the royal hand to convey the privileged royal perspective. They dream the same dream as the king about a book that will have a political impact beyond the life of the author, thanks to the absolute master's sovereign hand that participates in the documentation of his own exploits, indeed that *needs* to participate, since, as one anonymously published poem expresses: "la main qui les fait [les exploits] peut seule les écrire" (only the hand that brings them [the exploits] about can write them).[33]

The two prize poems written by future members of the French Academy both show an acute awareness of the strain placed by the single sovereign hand of the king on the Dauphin's position, as next in line to the highest position, but not quite there yet. As Bernard le Bovier de Fontenelle makes clear, the task is daunting and there is only one possible way to succeed, namely by imitation:

A moins qu'on l'imite, en vain on lui succède.
Que le Sceptre est pénible après qu'il l'a porté![34]

32. See 49–50, including for the reference in the following sentence to the topic proposed (50n9).

33. Here and in what follows, the 1677 prize poems are quoted from the 1695 re-edition of *Recueil de plusieurs pièces d'éloquence*, 23–27 (the winning poem by La Monnoye) and 173–92 (four other poems, including the one by Fontenelle). The names of the two authors are only given alongside their publication in the *Mercure galant* (see 50n9). The passage quoted is from "III. Pièce sur le même sujet" (III. Piece on the same subject), which lacks any indication of the author (180).

34. *Recueil*, 173.

(Unless one imitates him, in vain one succeeds him. / How heavy the scepter is after he has carried it!)

The scepter is indeed a heavy burden for the one who will carry it after the greatest of kings. The son can only prepare by somehow absorbing his father's "grande âme" (great soul),[35] which is exactly why the hand that carries the scepter also needs to communicate the most secret lessons of kingship.[36] The final two lines of Fontenelle's poem envision, from the father's perspective, a point in the future when his mission will have succeeded:

Il attend qu'il le suive un jour d'un pas égal,
Et dans son propre Fils se promet un rival.[37]

(He expects that he one day will follow him on equal footing, / And in his own son envisions a rival.)

Bernard de La Monnoye, whose poem won the prize from the French Academy, pushes the oedipal drama one step further. The middle of the poem envisions, again from the perspective of the king, his son reading the history of his reign, filled with jealousy before all his heroic exploits:

Un feu pareil au tien s'allume dans ses veines,
Et ce Lion naissant épris d'un beau courroux
Te voudrait à son tour pouvoir rendre jaloux.[38]

---

35. *Recueil*, 177.

36. The verses that explicitly refer to the royal hand run as follow: "Peuples le croirez-vous? de cette même main / Dont le Foudre vengeur ne part jamais en vain, / Sous qui l'audace tremble et l'orgueil s'humilie; / Il trace pour ce Fils l'Histoire de sa vie." (Peoples, will you believe it? With this same hand / From which the avenging lightening never parts in vain / Under which audacity trembles and pride is confounded / He draws for this son the history of his life.) *Recueil*, 174.

37. *Recueil*, 177.

38. *Recueil*, 25. Interestingly, the verses that explicitly refer to the double function of the royal hand do so by invoking the necessity of reaching the heart of the royal subjects: "Toi-même, pour l'instruire aux sublimes projets, / Pour lui mieux assurer le cœur de tes sujets, / Tu veux, de cette main qui sait dompter le Tage, / Lui tracer de ton Règne une fidèle image." (Yourself, in order to instruct him about your sublime projects / To better ensure him the hearts of your subjects / You wish, with this same hand that knows how to tame the Tagus / To draw for him a faithful image of your Reign") (27). The sublime projects of the father can only be faithfully—sublimely—captured in writing by his own hand, which will necessarily ensure the best instruc-

(A fire equal to yours is kindled in his veins, / And this Lion being born, filled with a beautiful wrath, / Would wish in turn to be able to make you jealous.)

More than his actions and his exploits, the poems above all thus portray the father as seeing how his son mirrors his fire ("un feu pareil"), the motivation that caused them. It is this fire, this wrath, that potentially could produce a rivalry of absolutist wills, although it only exists at this stage as an uncertain possibility for the future. The perspective of the Dauphin himself is nearly entirely absent, except in the somewhat timid accumulation of modal verbs: "Te voudrait [. . .] pouvoir rendre jaloux" (Would wish [. . .] to be able to make you jealous). The dream remains that of the father, as does the sovereign hand.

Returning to the opening pages of the *Mémoires* proper, I find the strongest formulations of the promise from father to son about the utility of the book he is reading. The Dauphin will learn how to adopt the perspective of the absolute monarch, which he can only do through the example of the person who presently enjoys the supreme vision, comprehension, and power intrinsic to this perspective. The final consequence of this ascent from low to high ground appears in the continuation of the text. The third paragraph considers the difficulty in obtaining sincere advice free from flattery from the crowd of people surrounding the king, as compared to the advice from a father whose only passion is his son's greatness. The fourth paragraph identifies books and histories as a possible source of such disinterested advice in the dense sentence quoted in the opening of this chapter:

> Je me suis aussi quelquefois flatté de cette pensée, que, si les occupations, les plaisirs et le commerce du monde, comme il n'arrive que trop souvent, vous dérobaient quelque jour à celui des livres et des histoires, le seul toutefois où les jeunes princes trouvent mille vérités sans nul mélange de flatterie, la lecture de ces Mémoires pourrait suppléer en quelque sorte à toutes les autres lectures, conservant toujours son goût et sa distinction pour vous, par l'amitié et par le respect que vous conserveriez pour moi.

> (I have also sometimes been flattered by the thought that if the occupations, the pleasures, and the affairs of this world should, as all too often

---

tion, and consequently better ensure that the son will be as admired as his father. However, a doubt is still audible in "mieux assurer" (better ensure); the guarantee can never be complete.

happens, take you away from books and from histories, where alone, however, princes find a thousand truths unmixed with flattery, the reading of
these *mémoires* might somehow compensate [suppléer] for all the other
readings, always preserving its taste and its quality for you through the
friendship and the respect that you would preserve for me.) (50/22)

This paragraph interestingly echoes certain aspects of the opening sentences of the text (analyzed in detail, 55–60). First of all, I note the same
discreet evocation of a life without and after the father at the end of the
sentence; by now, the book even more clearly exists as if to take his place,
prolonging, as it were, their friendship (in the sense of affection, amity,
fellowship). But the sentence also presents a *business* transaction in both
the etymological and casual meaning of the word: in the opening paragraph, the king was writing the *Mémoires* "avec assez de travail pour moi,
parmi mes occupations les plus grandes" ("[with] a considerable effort in
the midst of my greatest occupations") (49/21); now the busy life of the
Dauphin balances this statement: "les occupations, les plaisirs et le commerce du monde" ("the occupations, the pleasures, and the affairs of this
world"). In the midst of all his business, the father is so concerned about
the resources available to his son that he takes it upon himself to give him
the means to succeed.

It is against this backdrop that the passage raises the following implicit
question: What if the Dauphin is too busy to consult the examples from
literature and history? The answer is as straightforward as it is surprising.
In that case, says the king, "the reading of these *mémoires* might somehow
compensate for all the other readings." What shall readers think of this
strange concurrence of modesty and forcefulness in the same statement,
where the words "might somehow" ("pourrait [. . .] en quelque sorte")
seem to undermine the statement's message, while the hyperbolic "*all*
the other readings" ("toutes les autres lectures") radicalizes the message
even further? And what about the opening of the sentence: "I have also
sometimes been flattered by the thought that [. . .]"? Why only *sometimes*? And why use the term "flattered" when the sentence is part of an
argument warning precisely against flattery? In French the construction
is reflexive: "Je me suis [. . .] quelquefois flatté de cette pensée, que . . . ,"
but the pride inherent in the literal meaning of the reflexive verb *se flatter*
does not seem to stem only from the king's own achievement as a writer,
but also from the future actions of his son. The sentence shows the king
dreaming of his son's future success and of his own role as its enabler. It is
a fantasy of mastery, of continued mastery, channeled from father to son,
through the sweet taste of kingship.

This leaves the reader with the trickiest element of the sentence in question, namely, the main verb. The English verb "compensate" here is not a satisfying rendition of the French *suppléer*. In what way can the reading of the king's *Mémoires* be a supplement to—*suppléer à*—all the other readings? There is a profound ambiguity in the French verb *suppléer* that the early texts of Jacques Derrida made us acutely aware of, an ambiguity between the supplement as *completion* and *replacement*—which, I claim, also occurs in this sentence by Louis XIV.[39] It is the same ambiguity that resonates in the rest of the sentence through the strange concurrence of modest and forceful elements.

Let me reconsider the situation from the perspective of the text's intended reader. The Dauphin has access to a set of books and histories that he can trust, but the set is also incomplete; they do not directly address him (hence their freedom from flattery). The king's text, on the other hand, fills this lack by providing a source outside this set of examples, thereby also replacing that which was incomplete. In short, the king's *Mémoires* take the place not only of the example of the living father, but also of the formerly incomplete set of books and histories. The replacement of "books and [. . .] histories" by the royal *Mémoires* in the fourth paragraph of the text is thus the most direct and forceful expression of a displacement within the logic of exemplarity—from ancient examples to the sole example of the king himself—a displacement already announced in the first two paragraphs of the text, through their insistence on his own perspective and, above all, on his own *lumières*, in the dual meaning of

39. Is this ambiguity attested in the period the *Mémoires* were written? While contemporary dictionaries provide definitions of the verb *suppléer* evoking the idea of *completion* (Furetière, 1690: "Rendre une chose complète, parfaite et suffisante" [Render a thing complete, perfect and sufficient]) and *compensation* (l'Académie française, 1694, what it calls a "neutral" meaning: "Suffire pour réparer le manquement, le défaut de quelque chose" [Suffice in order to repair the lack, the defect of something]), the idea of supplement as *replacement* is present in one of the examples given by Furetière for the noun *abréviation*: "Écriture en abrégé, qui se fait avec plusieurs titres et caractères qui *suppléent* les lettres qu'on omet, et qu'il faut deviner, quand on veut écrire plusieurs choses en peu d'espace, ou avec diligence" (my emphasis). Furthermore, the database ARTFL-Frantext proves helpful in identifying the following two sentences by contemporary authors where the indirect construction *suppléer à* is used in a way that evokes its function in the sentence from the *Mémoires*: (1) "et pour suppléer en quelque façon à ce qu'il [Aristote] ne nous a pas dit." Corneille, *Trois discours sur le poème dramatique*, 65; (2) "en ce cas leur supérieur leur tiendrait lieu de livres, suivant l'expression de S Augustin [. . .]; et qu'il suppléerait à toutes les connaissances, qu'ils pourraient acquérir par l'étude." Mabillon, *Traité des études monastiques*, 3–4.

insight as well as the light that enables the supreme royal gaze. The Dauphin is thus asked to adopt the perspective of the king; that is to say, to perform the paradoxical task of following his father's example by becoming his own example. And the paradox only becomes more striking by taking into account that the *Mémoires'* royal ambition was formulated at the same historical moment that a team of leading scholars was brought together in order to create a vast library of readable editions of classical Greek and Roman texts for the education of the Dauphin, "ad usum delphini."[40]

Where does all this leave the reader? In what follows, I consider where it leaves the Dauphin: how the ambiguous approach to exemplarity identified above runs through the whole project of the *Mémoires* in a vacillating attitude about how the all-important royal *lumières* can be transmitted.

5. The Paradoxes of Absolutist Exemplarity

The structure of the *Mémoires* faithfully respects the paternal model of instruction "by example and by counsel" laid out in its first paragraph. The work is organized as a continuous back-and-forth between the narration of events from the king's reign and the exposition of the lessons the Dauphin should draw from them. Instruction takes place through the transformation of recent French history into examples. The result is a rhetoric of exemplarity through which the king recasts his actions as exemplary, his reign as a "permanent lesson,"[41] and his person as the Example par excellence, the Exemplar, the only example needed.

But how exactly does this rhetoric of exemplarity work? How are the *Mémoires* supposed to instruct the Dauphin? How can a written text come anywhere close to "communiquer toutes nos lumières à celui qui doit régner après nous" ("hand down all our insights [toutes nos lumières] to he who shall reign after us") (49/22)? I suggest that the opening of the text presents discreetly hidden reading instructions to the Dauphin. One of the very last introductory paragraphs, before the beginning of the actual narration of the events from the year 1661, describes how the king, when

40. The collection "ad usum delphini," directed by Pierre-Daniel Huet, distinguished savant and the Dauphin's assistant tutor, includes sixty-five volumes published from 1674 to 1691. For a discussion of exemplarity in relation to the actual education of the Dauphin, see Mormiche, "Éduquer le Dauphin." For a wider discussion of the Dauphin's education, see Mormiche, *Devenir prince*; Preyat, *Le Petit Concile de Bossuet*; and the most recent biography, Lahaye, *Le fils de Louis XIV*.

41. Goubert, introduction to *Mémoires*, 13.

he was younger and Mazarin was still first minister, had prepared himself for the moment when he would reign on his own:

> Je ne laissais pas cependant de m'éprouver en secret et sans confident, rai-sonnant seul et en moi-même sur tous les événements qui se présentaient, plein d'espérance et de joie quand je découvrais quelquefois que mes premières pensées étaient celles où s'arrêtaient à la fin les gens habiles et consommés, et persuadé au fond que je n'avais point été mis et conservé sur le trône avec une aussi grande passion de bien faire, sans en devoir trouver les moyens.

> (I did not fail, however, to test myself in secret and without a confidant, reasoning alone and to myself about all the events that arose, full of hope and joy whenever I would discover that my first thoughts were the same with which able and experienced people finally concluded, and deeply convinced that I had not been placed and preserved upon the throne with such a strong passion to succeed without being able to find the means.) (53/24)

Just as the father had prepared himself for taking the helm of the state by trying to foresee the right decision in every situation, he invites his son to predict, while reading about the king's exemplary exploits, the lessons that the king would subsequently draw from them. The Dauphin should "test [him]self in secret, reasoning alone and to [him]self about all the events" presented to him in the text.

What the text describes here is a game of decision-making. Like his father, the son has to analyze the situation correctly and then settle for the appropriate course of action, although he is for now safely exempt from its execution. It could be tempting to compare this scene to a student practicing chess by observing the game of a master, trying to predict at each stage what the strongest move will be. The analogy is fruitful in the way it maintains the tension between decisions based on intuition ("my first thoughts") and on analysis (that "with which able and experienced people finally concluded").[42] But in doing so, the analogy also highlights

---

42. Two further complications that I will not develop here: First, for the anal-ogy to operate, we would need to consider chess an art and not a science (the same way decision-making is an art, as is "the art of governing"). Moreover, there is an important difference not accounted for here, since a game of chess, unlike a scene of decision-making from the real world, can be communicated without added com-plexity, that is: without an added level of interpretation. The Dauphin is obviously thrown into a situation where the king's own (necessarily subjective, and normally

a major tension underlying this pedagogical model. The success produced by this process, as described by the king, is not exactly the result
of the training per se—it does not consist in the transmission of specific
knowledge, nor even in an analytical skill—but seems rather to reside in
a process of self-discovery.

The nature of this experience is well worth further reflection. First of
all, the king's insistence on its strictly private nature is striking. The young
king is present for important decisions, but only as an observer, not a par-
ticipant. He stresses the secrecy of his self-education "about all the events
that arose" four times in one single sentence: "in secret," "without confidant," "reasoning alone," "to myself."[43] There is of course an important
political message for the Dauphin here, as so often elsewhere, regarding
the necessity of royal dissimulation. However, I propose that the obses-
sive focus on secrecy and privacy points to the fact that this experience is
necessarily private. The young and still uncertain king's experience interpreting external events is reflexive in nature: the testing of his skills is obviously a self-testing ("to test myself," "m'éprouver"), but in a much more
literal way than one might first believe. Indeed, his success in this test
proves to him that he already has what it takes. Not only has he been chosen by a transcendent authority for the task ("placed and preserved upon
the throne"), but he has been endowed with the ability to succeed. It is
as if, through this decisive experience, his "passion to succeed" itself becomes a promise of his imminent success in the decisions that lay ahead.
Therefore, the outcome of the process is "hope and joy." His autodidactic
project ultimately provides him with a stronger sense of a vigorous royal
I, which will very soon be ready to assume the agency of the master reserved for the political center stage.

But for now the king is still only observing. The position of passivity
described by the king in this passage remains similar to that of the Dauphin in front of the *Mémoires*. It points out a path of initiation and self-
discovery that can lead the still-timid royal reader to embrace royal mastery, if only the son will give the text the attention it deserves, following
the paternal example by excelling at the *game* of royal decision-making,
playing the sovereign in order to become sovereign.

---

quite complacent) representation of the events creates an additional screen between
the Dauphin and the situation.

43. It is symptomatic in this regard that Sonnino's English translation does not
translate the apparently redundant words "et sans confident." His translation still has
a triple insistence on the privacy of the act, while the fourth one ("and without a
confidant") is reintroduced by me.

The nature of the curious initiation to the execution of kingship described by the king can be further explored by reflecting on a structural analogy between this experience and the self-realization of the Cartesian cogito. Like the cogito, the royal sovereign self finds itself through introspection in private, before turning to the external world with the confidence of somebody who is its rightful "maître et possesseur." In both cases, the ultimate result of self-observation is a strong sense of entitlement: the confirmation that the subject (royal or Cartesian), at some deep level, can trust his own judgments of the world. Quite naturally, this sense of entitlement implies a shift from external to internal authority, which puts pressure on the logic of exemplarity. Not surprisingly, there is in René Descartes's *Discours de la méthode* a similar reversal to the one just observed in Louis XIV's *Mémoires*: the narrator rejects ancient examples and offers his own experience instead for the reader to imitate (in the case of the *Mémoires*, this is obviously limited to the text's only intended reader), as a new kind of example replacing all others. Both the *Mémoires* and the *Discours de la méthode* contain a dream of self-birth, an absolute beginning founded only on itself. At the same time, neither the cogito nor the royal self is the ultimate source of its authority. In Descartes's philosophy, the existence of God and whether this existence is necessary in order to reject the hypothesis of the evil demon—a necessity that would bring a menacing circularity into the argument—is of course a major point of contention, which will not be addressed here.[44] It is interesting, however, to observe a similar circularity lurking in the *Mémoires*. Although the obvious source of royal authority is God, the passage above works more as a proof of God than of anything else. The king's self-testing and self-discovery convince him that he is part of a greater plan that "has placed and preserved [him] upon the throne" and will guarantee that he will continue "to find the means" "to succeed" in the future. His sense of entitlement functions, in other words, both as proof and as an effect of the invisible, divine plan.

It is important to stress that the juxtaposition above does not necessarily show a Cartesian influence, or a Cartesian foundation for absolutist kingship, as has often been claimed. It could in fact easily be the other way around, the vigor of the Cartesian cogito growing out of the sovereignty of an increasingly autonomous royal self under French absolutism

---

44. Without going into detail, one observation is necessary to bring out the full pertinence of the juxtaposition that follows: even if the Cartesian system is deemed valid without recourse to the existence of God, the cogito is not the ultimate source of authority, since its authority relies on a faith in the evidence of self-evidence.

as it unfolds in the century following the Wars of Religion and of which Louis XIV's representation in the *Mémoires* is only one (although a particularly forceful, not to say extreme) instantiation.

It is now time to return to the reading instructions offered to the Dauphin in the passage quoted above and its immediate message about kingship. The increased weight put on self-discovery through the parallel with the cogito recalls the tension between intuition and analysis discussed above in relation to the chess analogy. The king finds the means to succeed in himself; he realizes that he has what it takes, and in the process it becomes clear that the royal art of decision-making depends more on intuition than on transferable analytical skills.

This tension inherent in the logic of royal exemplarity is also, I assert, constitutive of French absolutism in general. This claim brings me back to the discussion of the contradictions of the concept of absolutism itself in the introduction to this book: the uneasy coexistence of, on the one hand, a more modern and analytical form of governing ("centralized," "rationalist," "disenchanted," "bureaucratized," "procedural," and "scripted" would be other terms for the same impulse, observable at all levels of the governing body) and, on the other, the model's premodern foundation in the glorious exceptional decision of an absolute will. The following passage from the 1662 *Mémoires* is an example of royal advice where the rationalizing impulse is so strong that readers can wonder how much leeway is left for the absolutist will. This is thus Louis XIV adopting the voice of analytical reason:

> Ne vous étonnez pas si je vous exhorte si souvent à travailler, à tout voir, à tout écouter, à tout connaître. Je vous l'ai déjà dit, il y a grande différence entre les lumières générales qui ne servent ordinairement qu'à discours, et les particulières qu'il faut presque toujours suivre dans l'action. Les maximes trompent la plupart du temps les esprits vulgaires; les choses sont rarement comme elles devraient être. La paresse s'arrête aux notions communes, pour n'avoir rien à examiner et rien à faire. L'industrie est à relever les circonstances particulières, pour en profiter; et on ne fait jamais rien d'extraordinaire, de grand et de beau, qu'en y pensant plus souvent et mieux que les autres.

> (Don't be astonished if I so often exhort you to work, to see everything, to listen to everything, to know everything. I have already told you: there is a vast difference between general insights [lumières] that are usually useful only for discussions and particular ones that must almost always be followed in practice. Maxims are most often misleading to vulgar minds.

Things are rarely as they should be. Laziness stops at common notions in order to avoid thinking and acting. The effort lies in evoking particular circumstances in order to profit from them, and one never accomplishes anything extraordinary, great and wonderful without thinking about it more often and better than others.) (160/95)

The problem raised by this passage appears more explicitly if the double negative in the last sentence is unpacked: What are the conditions for doing something "d'extraordinaire, de grand et de beau" ("extraordinary, great and wonderful")? Such an inquiry is, of course, in no way surprising within the framework of the education of a future absolute monarch. Greatness, exception, and beauty all merge in the exemplary heroic exploits that will help display the glory of the sovereign. The rest of the passage is remarkable, however, in the way it avoids resorting to a traditional language of royal exemplarity, which refers to insights that come from the high position only the sovereign can access. The only virtue alluded to is the less-than-heroic diligence necessary to avoid the "laziness" of "vulgar minds." Otherwise, the message is one long reminder that kingship consists, above all, in hard work. The Dauphin needs to see all, hear all, know all; he needs to think more and better than others, as his father puts it. The passage certainly evokes the *lumières* that the situation calls for, but unlike the opening paragraph of the *Mémoires* discussed above, these are insights that do not obviously require a royal perspective or a divinely infused intuition to be comprehended. On the contrary, it would not be far-fetched to see the whole passage as motivated by early signs of a certain royal laziness in the intended reader of the text.[45] For while "[l]aziness stops at common notions in order to avoid thinking and acting," what the Dauphin needs is insight into the particular circumstances of the situation.

This passage reminds the reader that it was Louis XIV who famously spoke of "le *métier* de roi" ("the *craft* of the king").[46] At the same time, it is less clear how an approach oriented toward an analytical mastery of particular circumstances can be combined with a logic of exemplarity. The combination risks rendering both the royal example and the *Mémoires*

45. The main source for the Dauphin's reputed laziness is Saint-Simon. For references and a further discussion of the character of the Dauphin, see da Vinha, "Monseigneur le Dauphin, fils de Louis XIV."

46. See Louis XIV, "Réflexions sur le métier de roi" (1679), included in Louis XIV, *Mémoires, suivis de Manière de montrer les jardins* (ed. Cornette), 333–35.

useless. The king himself voices a similar concern in the following reflection, before rejecting it by mobilizing the power of habit:

> Je ne puis même m'empêcher, mon fils, de faire là-dessus une réflexion avec vous: car en considérant combien il est vrai que tout l'art de la politique est de se servir des conjonctures, je viens à douter quelquefois si les discours qu'on en fait et ces propres Mémoires ne doivent pas être mis au rang des choses inutiles, puisque l'abrégé de tous les préceptes consiste au bon sens et en l'application que nous ne recevons pas d'autrui, et que nous trouvons plutôt chacun en nous-même. Mais ce dégoût qui nous prend de nos propres raisonnements n'est pas raisonnable; car l'application nous vient principalement de la coutume, et le bon sens ne se forme que par une longue expérience, ou par une méditation réitérée et continuelle des choses de même nature, de sorte que nous devons aux règles mêmes et aux exemples l'avantage de nous pouvoir passer des exemples et des règles.

> (I cannot even refrain, my son, from reflecting on this with you, for considering how true it is that the entire art of politics consists of playing on circumstances [les conjonctures], I sometimes begin to wonder if its discussion and these very *mémoires* must not be classed as useless things, since the summary of all its precepts lies in good sense and in dedication, which we do not receive from others, and which we find rather in ourselves. But this disgust [dégout] with our own reasoning is not reasonable, for dedication comes to us primarily through habit, and good sense is developed only through long experience or through repeated and continual meditation on things of a similar nature, so that we owe to rules and to examples themselves the advantage of being able to dispense with examples and with rules.) (165/99)

Exemplarity here seems to be a ladder that the Dauphin can throw away once he has ascended to the high position from which he will reign, once he has come to fully espouse the perspective of a prince. This only accentuates, however, the question of how the final step is to be taken, how the final transition is to be achieved. The question is very much the same as in the discussion in the opening of this section, regarding the royal art of sovereign decision-making:

> Mais quand dans les occasions importantes, ils [nos ministres] nous ont rapporté tous les partis et toutes les raisons contraires, tout ce qu'on fait ailleurs en pareil cas, tout ce qu'on a fait autrefois et tout ce qu'on peut

faire aujourd'hui, c'est à nous, mon fils, à choisir ce qu'il faut faire en effet; et ce choix-là, j'oserai vous dire que si nous ne manquons ni de sens ni de courage, nul autre ne le fait mieux que nous; car la décision a besoin d'un esprit de maître et il est sans comparaison plus facile de faire ce que l'on est, que d'imiter ce que l'on n'est pas. Que si l'on remarque presque toujours quelque différence entre les lettres particulières, que nous nous donnons la peine d'écrire nous-mêmes, et celles que nos secrétaires les plus habiles écrivent pour nous, découvrant en ces dernières je ne sais quoi de moins naturel, et l'inquiétude d'une plume qui craint éternellement d'en faire trop ou trop peu, ne doutez pas qu'aux affaires de plus grande conséquence, la différence ne soit encore plus grande entre nos propres résolutions, et celles que nous laisserons prendre à nos ministres sans nous, où plus ils seront habiles, plus ils hésiteront par la crainte des événements, et, d'en être chargés s'embarrassent quelquefois fort longtemps de difficultés qui ne nous arrêteraient pas un moment.

(But when, on important occasions, they [our ministers] have reported to us on all the sides and on all the conflicting arguments, on all that is done elsewhere in such and such a case, it is for us, my son, to decide what must actually be done. And as to this decision, I shall venture to tell you that if we lack neither sense nor courage, another never makes it as well as we. For decision requires the spirit of a master, and it is infinitely easier to act according to what one is than to imitate what one is not. For if one almost always notes a difference between the letters that we go to the trouble of writing personally and those that our most able secretaries write for us, detecting in the latter a certain lack of naturalness and the concern of a pen in perpetual fear of including too much or too little, have no doubt that in affairs of greater importance there is an even wider distance between the decision that we make ourselves and those that we allow our ministers to make without us, where the more able they are, the more afraid they are to take events upon themselves, and hesitate sometimes over difficulties that would not stop us for a moment.) (75/38)

The middle of this paragraph contains a passage first quoted in section 2 (52–53), addressing the difference in style between letters written by the king himself and those written by his secretaries. There will always be a perceivable disparity due to the fearful and timid—if not shaky—hand of the secretary. For Sainte-Beuve and Halévi, who both quote this passage, this point is decisive for the text's authorship: the royal provenance of both this passage and the *Mémoires* in general can be felt through the absence of such fear and hesitation.[47] The point made by the king is of course paradoxical (as Sainte-Beuve and Halévi are well aware of), since the passage itself was most likely written by the king's team of writers, possibly even the very same secretaries that it denounces. The importance of the paradox only increases when readers consider the wider context inside which it occurs. The paragraph above zooms in on the moment when some of the most important decisions are made. The difference between the royal hand and that of his secretaries is seemingly analogous to a similar difference between the king's own decisions and the equally fearful and timid approach of the highest ministers allowed to decide in the king's place. Just as the hand of the master is needed in order to properly write the letters, the spirit of the master is also needed in order to effortlessly make the right decision.

The paragraph thus forcefully conveys an ideal about the perfection residing in the touch of the sovereign hand of the master, as much in the making of political decisions as in their expression. If there is any meaning at all in the notion of an essence at the core of absolutism, it would reside in this dream about the single hand of the sovereign master drawing its own portrait through deeds and words. An absolutism whose surface shows us a version of M. C. Escher's remarkable lithograph of a hand in the process of drawing itself, hiding another reality a little less paradoxical but just as complex: a collectivity of hands drawing this hand in the process of drawing itself. Absolutism is, then, the many hands collaborating in the cultural production of sovereign single-handedness, but also the necessary, indeed the constitutive, effacement of this collaboration. If, thus, the provenance of the *Mémoires* is paradoxical, it is a paradox of absolutism itself. I return to this paradoxical provenance in the next chapter's reading of Charles Le Brun's paintings at the Hall of Mirrors at Versailles: as I will argue there, the central painting of the gallery that now carries the title *Le Roi gouverne par lui-même, 1661* (The King governs on his own, 1661) was, in fact, originally conceived as a depiction of the originless self-creation of Louis XIV as an absolute monarch.

For now, however, the perspective remains that of his son: the scenario of the Dauphin at the cusp, at the threshold of power—so close but not yet able to channel the sovereign decision. The opposition at the end of the paragraph is seemingly straightforward: the king is doing what he is meant to do, insofar as he incarnates the "spirit of the master," while

47. See 53n18 above for the references.

the king's highest ministers can only imitate what they are not. But what about the Dauphin? Does he already embody the "spirit of a master"? Will he become one? Could he really adopt the spirit of the master by following the example of the king, although this would seemingly imply that he is "imitating something he is not"? The king's answer to the last question is remarkable. Yes, he seems to reply, his son could become a master through *hard work*. The following excerpts read like a self-help manual for kings in distress, based on the exemplary testimony of somebody who pulled himself out of prior difficulties:

> Quant au travail, [. . .] [j]e ne vous avertirai pas seulement là-dessus que c'est toutefois par là qu'on règne, pour cela qu'on règne, et que ces conditions de la royauté qui pourront quelquefois vous sembler rudes et fâcheuses en une aussi grande place, vous paraîtraient douces et aisées s'il était question d'y parvenir. [. . .] Je m'imposai pour loi de travailler régulièrement deux fois par jour, et deux ou trois heures chaque fois avec diverses personnes, sans compter les heures que je passerais seul en particulier, ni le temps que je pourrais donner extraordinairement aux affaires extraordinaires s'il en survenait. [. . .] Je ne puis vous dire quel fruit je recueillis aussitôt après de cette résolution. Je me sentis comme élever l'esprit et le courage, je me trouvai tout autre, je découvris en moi ce que je n'y connaissais pas, et je me reprochai avec joie de l'avoir trop longtemps ignoré. [. . .] Il me sembla seulement alors [par le travail] que j'étais roi, et né pour l'être. J'éprouvai enfin une douceur difficile à exprimer, et que vous ne connaîtrez point vous-même qu'en la goûtant comme moi. [. . .] La fonction du roi consiste principalement à laisser agir le bon sens, qui agit toujours naturellement et sans peine.

(As to work, [. . .] I shall not merely tell you that this is nonetheless how one reigns, why one reigns, and that these demands of royalty which may sometimes seem harsh and painstaking to you from such a lofty post would appear delightful and pleasant to you if it were a question of attaining them. [. . .] I made it a rule to work regularly twice a day for two to three hours at a time with various persons, aside from the hours that I worked alone or that I might devote extraordinarily to extraordinary affairs if any arose. [. . .] I cannot tell you what fruits I immediately gathered from this decision. I could almost feel my spirits and my courage rising. I was a different person. I discovered something new about myself and joyfully wondered how I could have ignored it for so long. [. . .] It was only then [by the hard work] that I knew that I was king, and born to be it. I experienced, finally, a sweetness that is difficult to express, and that you

will not know yourself unless you taste it like I did. [. . .] The function of
the king consists primarily in letting good sense do its work, as it always
does naturally and effortlessly.) (61–62/29–30)

The king is thus an instrument through which a rational, if not Cartesian, good sense naturally expresses itself.[48] But to make it to this point of
natural mastery, the master-to-be needs to realize that sovereignty starts
at home, with the sovereign imposition of a harsh self-rule: "Je m'imposai
pour loi de travailler régulièrement" (literally: "I imposed on myself as
law to work regularly"). In other words, the Dauphin has to make a wager: he has to work, although in the beginning it does not make sense to
him at all, although it is "harsh and painstaking," in order to finally be able
to taste the sweetness of kingship, and finally believe that he is indeed
king, finally know that he was born to be king.

This approach worked for the king himself, he tells his son. In fact, the
passage above is perhaps best read as a conversion narrative: immediately
after his decision, the king found himself to be entirely different ("tout
autre"; "a different person," in Sonnino's freer translation). But if this is indeed a conversion narrative, it importantly does not depend on external
divine intervention. It didn't happen on the way to Damascus, but in the
comfort of his own study. The seeds of his radical transformation were
there inside him all along: "je découvris *en moi* ce que je n'y connaissais
pas" (my emphasis; literally: "I discovered *in me* what I didn't know was
there"). What the king found in himself through a process of literal self-
discovery was a royal sovereign self. Again, surprisingly, this transformative self-discovery did not emerge from his most glorious acts of kingship
(ceremony or war; while handling the scepter or the sword), but rather
from his least glorious ones: through the discipline of his daily routine.
And yet, what he found was exactly royal glory, in the deeper theologico-
political sense of a perceived absolute sovereignty, as discussed in the introduction to this book (see esp. 22–27).

Significantly, the king links this transformation and its persistence to
the *taste* of kingship, a taste that only kings can know: "I experienced,
finally, a sweetness that is difficult to express, and that you will not know
yourself unless you taste it like I did." It is important to insist that this notion of taste is pre-Kantian and has nothing to do with judgment. Rather,
it is the premodern sweetness (*douceur*) magisterially analyzed by Mary

---

48. Cf. the well-known opening sentence of *Discours de la méthode*: "Le bon sens
est la chose du monde la mieux partagée" ("Good sense is the best distributed thing
in the world"). Descartes, *Discours de la méthode*, 14 (French)/15 (English).

Carruthers as it pertains not only to knowledge and persuasion, but also to ethics and medicine. "Sweetness is medicinal; it heals and restores."[49]

Beyond Carruthers and medieval studies, la douceur has recently been a vibrant research topic in early modern French studies in France, with at least three important collective volumes published since 2003.[50] However, their approach is often predominantly rhetorical and aesthetical, focusing on the *use* of sweetness in persuasion, in reflections on and the practice of art, and especially writing. Even reflections on "la douceur du politique" (the sweetness of politics)[51] have a very different focus than what readers encounter here, accentuating rather the function of meekness and clemency in politics, the possible mobilization of sweetness within a manipulative framework, and so on. As opposed to this field of inquiry, which interrogates sweetness as a political tool (its *effect*), in Louis XIV's use of the term here, sweetness refers to an affective reaction, the pleasurable taste that the king enjoys when he finally coincides with his role (and hence closer to conversion, salvation; as a metaphysical category[52]). It is only the sweet taste born from the execution of kingship that can definitively liberate the sovereign from "this disgust [dégout] with our own reasoning." This was how it worked for Louis XIV, according to the account he gives his son, and the king could only hope that his son would reach the same conclusion through a similar wager.

This surprising version of Pascal's Wager ("kneel and you will believe"[53]) offers a solution to the pedagogical challenge of exemplarity that I engaged earlier. The point is not only for the Dauphin to use his father's example to learn the art of reigning (which itself, as this chapter has shown, implies the deployment of exemplarity as "the first and most important part of our entire politics"), but also to persuade him that he is

49. Carruthers, "Sweetness," 1010.

50. Prat and Servet, *Le doux aux XVIe et XVIIe siècles*; Baby and Rieu, *La Douceur en littérature de l'Antiquité au XVIIe siècle*; Boulègue et al., *La Douceur dans la pensée moderne*.

51. This is the title of Méchoulan's contribution to *Le doux aux XVIe et XVIIe siècles*, ed. Prat and Servet, 221–38.

52. There is also an important parallel between the sweetness mobilized by Louis XIV and his team of writers here and the role assigned by François de Sale to "la douceur" in his *Introduction à la vie dévote* (1609), along the lines of Parish's observations in "'Une vie douce, heureuse et amiable.'"

53. This expression, which sums up admirably concisely the perplexing key argument of Pascal's Wager (fragment 680 of the *Pensées*), is not formulated by Pascal, but based on Althusser's reading: "Pascal says more or less: 'Kneel down, move your lips in prayer, and you will believe.'" Althusser, "Ideology and Ideological State Apparatuses," 168. See also in this regard Pepper, "Kneel and You Will Believe."

himself the new Exemplar, that he has indeed "been placed and preserved upon the throne," and that this was done "by Heaven Itself," as his father made sure to remind him in the first paragraph of the text.

As in Pascal's Wager, there is a peculiar exemplarity at work here, one that helps the interlocutor to bypass his own reason and rationality by letting bodily habits and repetition take over instead: he follows the example of the one who has already wagered and who is now tasting the sweetness of that choice. It is important to notice, however, that in Pascal this is a desperate solution, proposed as the last resort to an interlocutor who has realized that he is *not* the master, inviting him to embrace, as it were, his non-mastery in a final attempt at reaching faith through what is known in Pascal scholarship as "l'abêtissement" (from the perplexing use of the verb *abêtir* [to render stupid, like a beast] at a crucial moment of the Wager argument).[54] Here, it seems like the only way—or the last hope—for the Dauphin to embrace sovereignty is through a similar "abêtissement": not through sovereign reason, but through its "beastly" abdication.

At the very least, the argument in the *Mémoires* expresses a clear sense of desperation. The reflection quoted above lingers on this point, moves on, then returns to it, and uncomfortably so, in a way that suggests that the whole enterprise of the *Mémoires* is on shaky ground, or even that this train of thoughts could cause the whole edifice to crumble. The fatherly unease becomes evident when the king returns to the same point at the end of his reflection, adding yet another argument, playing his last, des-

54. The critical passage from Pascal's Wager runs as follows: "Travaillez donc, non pas à vous convaincre par l'augmentation des preuves de Dieu, mais par la diminution de vos passions. Vous voulez aller à la foi, et vous n'en savez pas le chemin; vous voulez vous guérir de l'infidélité, et vous en demandez le remède: apprenez de ceux qui ont été liés comme vous, et qui parient maintenant tout leur bien [. . .] Suivez la manière par où ils ont commencé: c'est en faisant tout comme s'ils croyaient, en prenant de l'eau bénite, en faisant dire des messes, etc. Naturellement même cela vous fera croire et vous abêtira." ("Work then, on convincing yourself, not by adding more proofs of God's existence, but by diminishing your passions. You would like to find faith and do not know the way? You would like to be cured of unbelief and ask for the remedies? Learn from those who were bound like you, and who now wager all they have. [. . .] Follow the way by which they began: they acted as if they believed, took holy water, had masses said, etc. This will make you believe naturally and mechanically.") Pascal, *Pensées*, fragment 680. The last words, "et vous abêtira," are untranslatable, but do convey an idea of persuasion utilizing a "mechanical" aspect of the human constitution, as conveyed by Roger Ariew's translation given here. But that translation entirely loses the resonances of "la bête" (the beast) at the root of the verb *abêtir*. For a further discussion of the need to reassess the Pascalian "abêtissement," see Bjørnstad, *Créature sans créateur*, 184–85.

perate fatherly card, as it were: the guilt trip, the blame game, the son's immense debt to his father. The passage brings together many of the elements discussed earlier in this chapter, starting with the hint at the premature death of the king himself and his imploration from the other side of the grave:

> [S]'il arrive que Dieu vous appelle à gouverner avant que vous ayez pris encore cet esprit d'application et d'affaires dont je vous parle, la moindre déférence que vous puissiez rendre aux avis d'un père à qui j'ose dire que vous devez beaucoup en toutes sortes, est de faire d'abord et durant quelque temps, même avec contrainte, même avec dégoût, pour l'amour de moi qui vous en conjure, ce que vous ferez toute votre vie pour l'amour de vous-même, si vous avez une fois commencé.

> ([I]f God should call upon you to rule before you will have acquired that spirit of dedication and of affairs that I am describing to you, the least deference that you could pay to the advice of a father, to whom I venture to say that you owe a great deal, is to do initially and for some time, even with compulsion, even with disgust, for the sake of me who implores you, what you will do your entire life for your own sake once you have begun.) (63/30)

The *Mémoires* are thus the dream that the father will live on beyond his (premature) death in the examples and advice gathered in this book and integrated into the life and reign of his now-sovereign son. But at the same time, it is the nightmare that his effort will have been in vain, the realization that the future is beyond the reach of absolutism.

6. Conclusion: "So many ghastly examples"

Although the king had promised his son at the outset of the text that he would include the errors and mistakes that he made during his reign,[55] speaking about his own shortcomings is seemingly not something that comes easy to him. This chapter ends with a brief look at the one place

---

55. The king is "persuadé qu'il est d'un petit esprit, et qui se trompe ordinairement, de vouloir ne s'être jamais trompé, et que ceux qui ont assez de mérite pour réussir le plus souvent, trouvent quelque magnanimité à reconnaître leurs fautes" ("convinced that it befits a small mind, which is usually mistaken, never to admit a mistake, and that those who have enough merit to succeed most often find a certain greatness in recognizing their errors") (51/22–23).

where he comes closest to actually doing so while recounting what was indeed a major moral flaw and a clear deviation from the path of exemplary virtue, namely, when he tasted in his love life a very different kind of sweetness than the one that was the fruit of his hard and disciplined work as a king.

This reflection arises after the end of his affair with Louise de La Vallière in 1667. At this point he had acknowledged their only surviving child (out of four in total, with one more to come) and given her, he tells his son, "un établissement convenable à l'affection que j'avais pour elle depuis six ans" ("an establishment suitable to the affection that I had borne for her for six years") by making her a duchess. The king concedes his unexemplary conduct: "cet attachement dont l'exemple n'est pas bon à suivre" ("this attachment whose example should not be followed") (310/246). However, rather than acting as an occasion for the son to learn from his father's failure, the account quickly turns into yet another story about relative success: a crisis contained, a catastrophe averted. First of all, the king minimizes his failure: after all, even princes are not absolutely immune to the common failings of the rest of humankind, the father explains to his son. Second, the text foregrounds how, thanks to the precautions he had taken, the king never let down his guard, never let his sovereignty slip away from him; despite his heart being conquered, he always made sure to remain in control of his time and his judgment. The king seems to imply that this challenge is thus an occasion to display heroic greatness, not unlike on the battlefield. After a detailed description of the precautions that served him so well, the king ends his thoughts with the following lofty peroration:

> Je vous avouerai bien qu'un prince dont le cœur est fortement touché par l'amour, étant aussi toujours prévenu d'une forte estime pour ce qu'il aime, a peine de goûter toutes ces précautions. Mais c'est dans les choses difficiles que nous faisons paraître notre vertu. Et d'ailleurs, il est certain qu'elles sont d'une nécessité absolue et c'est faute de les avoir observées [ces précautions], que nous voyons dans l'histoire tant de funestes exemples des maisons éteintes, des trônes renversés, des provinces ruinées, des empires détruits.

> (I will confess to you that a prince who is deeply in love is so taken by his affection for his beloved that he would have difficulty in taking in [goûter] all these precautions. But it is in difficult things that we display our virtue. And moreover, it is certain that they [the precautions] are an absolute necessity, and it is from not having observed them that we see in history

so many ghastly examples of houses extinct, of thrones overthrown, of provinces devastated, of empires destroyed.) (312/248)

"[S]o many ghastly examples": History is thus a storehouse of tragic examples of what will happen when precautions are not taken and virtue not displayed. The tragic resonance is even stronger in the original French: the adjective *funeste* (ghastly) in "tant de funestes exemples" was, together with *sanglant* (bloody), the primary synonym for the adjective *tragique* in the seventeenth century. Therefore, the royal precautions serve as virtue-induced damage control in order to prevent a bad example from history from being replayed as tragedy on the contemporary political stage. They are "an absolute necessity" in order to enable the protagonist and sole agent of history to rewrite the tragic script in a way that inscribes him and his passions into an exemplary and edifying account. In other words, these prescriptions are "an absolute necessity" for the survival of absolutism, which is why the king works so hard to transmit them to his successor, especially in the case of his premature death, as envisioned here.

Although these precautions emerge from a specific reflection on love and amorous passions, it is tempting to consider them as an exemplary synecdoche of the lessons the Dauphin should glean throughout his reading of the *Mémoires*. While the overall purpose of the *Mémoires* is certainly to prepare the Dauphin for greatness through glorious exploits on the center stage—quite possibly the battlefield—of history, a major part of the actual lessons proposed to him is the less glorious but all-important avoidance of tragedy through a very different war with himself.

The use of the verb *goûter* suggests that this reflection is closely related to the passages discussed above that aim to communicate the eventual sweetness of kingship to the Dauphin. It is certainly difficult for a prince in love to "*goûter* toutes ces précautions": difficult to "take [them] in" in Paul Sonnino's freer translation, more literally to "taste" them in the sense of appreciating. The execution of these precautions will certainly seem "rudes et fâcheuses" ("harsh and painstaking"), as stated in one of the other passages on the work needed to succeed (61/29). Only later will the Dauphin taste their sweetness, while for the moment he may be so overwhelmed by the more obvious sensual pleasure that he risks falling into its trap.

Interestingly, as readers, we risk stumbling for a moment, alongside the father and the son, as we make our way through the last sentence of the quotation. "And moreover, it is certain that they [the precautions] are an absolute necessity, and it is from not having observed them that *we* [. . .]"—what is the logical subject of this sentence? By interrupting the reading here, it sounds like it is *we* who have not observed the precautions, like it is *we* who are about to fall, if not already falling. But then we realize with a sigh of relief that we were not the actors but only the observers in the sentence: ". . . it is from not having observed them that *we see* in history so many ghastly examples. [. . .]" When it comes to the matter at hand, we as readers are only observing at a safe distance, experiencing, but only vicariously, as when watching the staging of a tragedy or reading history. It is as if the progression of the sentence performs the effect that it hopes to have on its only intended reader: By taking him to the edge of the precipice of tragedy, by making him observe those who did not respect the precautions, by making him lose his footing for a brief moment—maybe it can bring him to wager now on a royal sweetness to come, in time to avoid falling.

But does the king, does the text's royal voice, really believe in its own exemplary power to effectuate such a change? Hardly. Rather, I claim, in conclusion, that the complacency of this passage is only equaled by its desperation, a desperation that is also observable in its grammar.

The passage displays the absolute prince for us to study from several angles, as expressed through the use of four different personal pronouns: "je" (I), "vous" (you), "il" (he), and "nous" (we)—observing, acting, falling, and resisting to fall. Importantly, the father's "we" is *not* a majestic plural, not an official royal "we" into which his son is included. Instead, this "we" that brings together the "I" of the writing father and the "you" of the reading son and thereby gives this passage—and also the text as a whole—its coherence is broken with temporal disjuncture. Its enunciative *now* is a present when only the father can act, while the *now* of its reception belongs to the fatherless son. As an educator, the king speaks monologically into the void; as a royal protagonist at an uncertain point in the future, the Dauphin will be radically alone. Bridging this abyss, the fragile "we" marks separation more than conjunction. Aside from the proper royal "we" whose grammatical plural always hides a logical singular (since sovereignty cannot be shared), there is no first-person plural in the grammar of absolutism, and this fact risks undermining the whole enterprise of the *Mémoires*. The "we" that permeates the *Mémoires* is an ineffectual discursive construction which might work within a legal fiction that serves to enable dynastic continuity across generations (a theoretical "we" constituted by a series of discrete sovereigns), but hardly as the site of an actual royal communion that transforms the king's son into an enlightened and disciplined sovereign at an indeterminate point in the future.

Instead, the king can certainly dream: dream the dream of an absolutism where the realm of his omnipotence includes not only his son's disposition and the ability to write a book that could replace all others, but also control over the future itself. Dream the dream of a glorious greatness without example but that might still somehow be emulated. This phantasmatic daydream that the whole absolutist culture tried to turn into reality has left its traces on every page of the *Mémoires*, and I shall soon show it inscribed in the ceiling of the Hall of Mirrors in Versailles. However, this daydream is at the same time the nightmare inside which the son was doomed to live: a pale moon on the firmament of the bright sun, forever getting ready to wield a scepter too heavy for him to handle. It is tempting to see the occasional desperation expressed in the text as a sign of awareness of this contradiction: the father erecting himself— not only with his own scepter but also with his pen—into his son's most ghastly example.

CHAPTER 2

Mirrors of Absolutism

1. Introduction: Our Body in This Space

In a remarkable series of videos first published on their YouTube channel in 2012, the French luxury brand Dior uses the décor of political absolutism as the backdrop for staging a dream of dazzling beauty. In "Secret Garden—Versailles I–IV," beauty in the shape of elite female models moves through the empty château and garden, in a dreamlike, carefree, enchanted atmosphere, far removed from any of the niceties of ordinary life. Although the short films flaunt the garden's alluring peace and secrecy as a retreat from the château, it is the sparkling splendor of the shots within the château that imbues this universe with its otherworldly energy. These short films are studies of movement, slowed-down or frozen movement, but also of awe, through close-ups of mouths half-open, heads tilted backward, as if the models marvel at the world, this world, in which they magically yet naturally find themselves. Although the videos seem whimsical and disorganized, there is a central point structuring both movement and marvel, from which the women are always about to depart but to which they also constantly return: the central gallery of the château, named after the mirrors decorating its walls. Beauty and glamour are born in front of these mirrors in the Hall of Mirrors. And not only born but also conceived, as it were, in a haunting primal scene, displayed repeatedly starting from the very beginning of the first video.[1]

In this chapter, I argue that the enchanted dream of marvel and awe emerging from this space outside time is not only what Dior promises viewers in these clips, but also what the gallery itself promised the king

---

1. The first of these videos, to which I will return at the end of the chapter, can be seen here: https://vimeo.com/41499247. A shorter version is available here: https://www.youtube.com/watch?v=3Vpw3nQLv7g.

and his court from the outset. But whose dream would that be? For Louis XIV and his court, it was a dream of absolutism collectively dreamt by the king, his image-makers, and the court, if not the nation; a glorious mirror of *gloire*, inviting those present to take part—and revel—in the splendor, his splendor, their splendor. For us today, it is a similar invitation to bask in an idealizing mirror, expertly channeled by Dior, troublingly close to the dream of absolutism from yesteryear, as will be explored further when I return to the Dior videos at the end of the chapter.

In many ways, the proximity, familiarity, and availability of the material studied here may seem to be diametrically opposed to those of Louis XIV's *Mémoires* in the preceding chapter. While there I explored the workings of absolutism according to a document that was radically unavailable at the time of its production, written for a royal audience of one, in this chapter I turn to what was the most conspicuous self-expression of French absolutism under Louis XIV, at the architectural and political center that was Versailles. Today, even those who haven't made the pilgrimage to Versailles know of the Hall of Mirrors, and both real-life and virtual visitors can easily imagine themselves in the position of a seventeenth-century beholder. We are in their position, although as part of a different crowd, not only observing but experiencing the lavish gallery in front of these vast mirrors, underneath Charles Le Brun's enormous paintings of Louis XIV's major exploits. Our body in this space. And while the king's *Mémoires* remain somewhat of a secret today, that is hardly the case for Versailles, with more than five million guests annually, firmly establishing it as one of the foremost tourist destinations worldwide, as it actually had been throughout most of the ancien régime after the permanent relocation of the court and the government there in the early 1680s.[2]

It is a central claim of this chapter that, surprisingly, the importance of royal mirrors and mirroring has been taken for granted and not ana-

2. Going by the less-than-scientific rankings in *Travel and Leisure* travel magazine, Versailles is number four among the world's most visited palaces (number two in Europe, only after the Louvre) and number forty-three among the world's most visited tourist attractions (number twelve in Europe). These rankings are based on visits to the palace proper, not including visitors who come only for the Versailles gardens. For seventeenth- and eighteenth-century tourism to Versailles, see the impressive volume produced for the 2017–18 Versailles / New York Met exhibit "Visitors to Versailles (1682–1789)." After the French Revolution forced Louis XVI to leave Versailles for Paris in 1789, the palace would never again be a royal residence. It fell into disrepair, and despite becoming the Museum of the History of France in 1837 and being the site of important political ceremonies through the following century, it wasn't until the second half of the twentieth century that the palace again became a cosmopolitan destination.

lyzed in a systematic way in the immense scholarship on Versailles and the Hall of Mirrors. More precisely, I will single out two privileged yet understudied instances of the king seeing himself and try to tease out their significance for our understanding of the gallery and for the symbolic construction of French absolutism in general. In the first instance, Louis XIV encounters Le Brun's painting for the first time, as described by Le Brun's biographer, Claude Nivelon. The second instance is a discreet mirror scene depicted in the middle of the gallery's central painting; while the painting portrays the king at the moment absolutism was born, the mirror presents a puzzling reflection of the royal face at that moment, visible only for the king within the painting. These mirror scenes of the king are generally ignored by the scholarship, and in the few instances when they have been given any attention, it has been in passing, as if the scenes were transparent and their meaning self-evident. As I argue, this is not at all the case, and the full meaning of these royal mirrors depends on the wider context of the mirrors adorning the east wall of the gallery that now give it its name. What did the court and the courtiers see in these mirrors? What was their social function? What did it mean to be seen seeing oneself? What did the king see? And not least, what do we, twenty-first-century visitors and scholars, see?

Approaching the Hall of Mirrors through this set of questions takes my discussion well beyond the scope of what any modern reader can know with absolute certainty. It means engaging in a project of open-ended interpretation, rather than one of positivist documentation and decoding, as most of the scholarship on Versailles does. It means *not* taking our knowledge of artistic projects and contemporary descriptions and testimonies as the last word of the inquiry but rather as a starting point for deeper engagement with the material. It means acknowledging that even from our twenty-first-century vantage point, what we can see and what our predecessors saw in these mirrors of absolutism are not at all obvious. In other words, it means approaching the Hall of Mirrors *not* as absolutism reduced to a carefully curated and controlled expression of *mere* propaganda, whose message and modalities we know ahead of time, but as the expression of the dream that absolutism itself was—and, as suggested by the Dior videos, still is.[3]

---

3. Over the last few decades, our knowledge of every stage of the artistic process behind the décor of the Hall of Mirrors has increased dramatically, from the project's origin with the commission and conception of the gallery, via the décor's actual material production in its various stages, to the attempts at controlling the way in which it was received. In particular, there was a surge in research around the time of

2. An Age of Mirrors

In the twenty-first century, we live our lives surrounded by our reflection. Our mirror image is available to us, perhaps even imposed upon us, in the bathroom, at the gym, in stores, in elevators and restaurants, to the extent that it is difficult to imagine what it was like to live without the ubiquity of mirrors. As Narcissus knew from seeing his reflection in still water, there have always been mirror effects. The mirror is not exactly a human-made invention but rather a technological enhancement of what nature already provided. Many premodern cultures produced smaller-sized, lower-quality mirrors made of polished metal. And during the Renaissance there was a mirror craze, spurred on by technological advances and a renewed interest in self-expression, going hand in hand with the birth of the self-portrait in the arts. However, until the construction of the Hall of Mirrors at Versailles, mirrors had never been used so profusely and lavishly for any purpose. Indeed, when the not yet fully finished gallery opened to the public on December 1, 1682, it may very well have been the

---

an unprecedented €12 million restoration in the mid-2000s, further spurred by the dynamic presence of the Centre de recherche du château de Versailles (CRCV; the Palace of Versailles Research Center) founded in 2004 and located within the confines of the palace grounds. The first stages of the output from this process focused on the detailed material history of the décor, based on new discoveries made during the restoration, both regarding its genesis (1677–84) and the ways in which it had been reshaped through successive restorations. Grounded in scientific analyses of the layers and constitution of the extant décor, this work was quite naturally positivistic rather than hermeneutic in orientation. It aimed at providing factual, often technical, knowledge about artistic artifacts and their provenance rather than exploring their meaning or impact from the perspective of the beholder. See the lavish official account for a general audience that brings together a dream team of scholars and conservators in *La galerie des Glaces* (English edition: *The Hall of Mirrors*) and the more pointedly scholarly accounts in Volle and Milovanovic, *La galerie des Glaces après sa restauration*. There was a wider set of inquiries in the following years, but the positivistic orientation toward documentation and decoding remained predominant. The single most important monograph of the last decade is symptomatic in this regard. In *Versailles ou la disgrâce d'Apollon*, former director of the research board of the CRCV Gérard Sabatier synthesizes decades of research and seminal publications, while already announcing on the book jacket that this is a project of "décryptage" (decoding). The central chapter on the meaning of the Le Brun paintings carries the subtitle "Explication des tableaux de la Galerie de Versailles et de ses deux salons," as if there were only one correct interpretation, which the chapter then proceeds to deliver, relying closely on the official descriptions and guidebooks from the period. My objection here is methodological: this scholarship does an enormously erudite job in terms of documentation and decoding, but leaves much to be said and done when it comes to actual interpretation and analysis. See in this regard 122n46.

first time many of those present were able to see their own upright, full-length reflection.[4]

This is an interesting kind of "first" in the annals of innovation: the promise of it had been present from times immemorial, in the full-length reflection so alluringly close to being available to anybody standing at the edge of a still lake. But precisely for that reason, the yearning would have been stronger: the dream to control finally the reflection, to master what had always been there but only fleetingly and at an awkward angle. Nobody would have been more attuned to the promise of mastering the art of reflection than the court at Versailles, where that dream was pursued not only through innovations in mirror technology for the château but also in the unprecedented deployment of natural mirrors in the gardens, especially the Grand Canal, in what have evocatively been called "mirrors of infinity."[5] The Hall of Mirrors opens up a different form of infinity to humankind, since now even the full-length mirror image is emancipated, freely available to the human gaze indoors.

What did they see? Themselves, certainly, and they did so in a fuller, more integral way than ever before, possibly also with a clearer reflection, thanks to the quality of the mirrors. However, the most radical novelty lay in seeing themselves in context, situated, embedded: seeing themselves seeing, among so many others who also saw themselves for the first time. These were certainly mirrors of beauty, but a beauty belonging to the place, to the space, to the court. Quite objectively, the mirrors created a marvelous effect of increased space and splendor in the gallery by multiplying the splendor already there. While the king's *Mémoires*, as analyzed in the preceding chapter, fostered a royal self focused on interiority—the being rather than the seeming of piety and self-discipline—the mirrors of Versailles established a new intersubjective space, a space that for the first time made looking into a mirror image eminently social and public and not only a matter of private self-contemplation. Earlier mirrors did not do that, could not do that.

Mirrors had of course always been an indispensable tool for individuals to prepare and control their public appearance during private grooming practices. There are noteworthy instances already in ancient art: for

4. The general discussion in this and the following paragraphs relies on Melchior-Bonnet, *The Mirror*; and Pendergrast, *Mirror Mirror*. For more on the Versailles mirrors specifically, the discussion in Melchior-Bonnet, *The Mirror* (35–69, esp. 46–48) remains the most extensive, but see also Berger, "Galerie des Glaces"; DeJean, "Power Mirrors"; and the brief synthesis in Maral, "The Marbles and the Mirrors."

5. Weiss, *Mirrors of Infinity*, 21–41.

example, in recovered frescos in Pompeii, showing women intently gazing into handheld mirrors. These are intimate scenes. The beholder remains alone with her mirror, and the mirror itself remains private (as was most likely the case for the fresco itself). The mirror here functions as a private prosthesis of sorts, an extension of faculties limited by humans' natural constitution. It is worth pausing a moment to consider the nature of this limitation: without mirrors, people's faces and appearances would forever remain invisible to them, while publicly available to everybody else. With technological advances that allowed for larger mirrors with clearer images, their utility for grooming purposes expanded; compared to the dark and possibly blurry facial reflection from earlier times, Renaissance men and women who could afford a Venetian crystal mirror could catch a fuller glimpse of their appearance, including gestures and movements. Not only actors would have rehearsed in front of mirrors, but also courtiers, in search of the seemingly artless, unrehearsed grace of sprezzatura. And yet here, too, the mirror remains a private tool or prosthesis, which, at the very most, anticipates an appearance in public. "This is how I present myself to the public eye." Compared to such a pre-public, intimate role, the Versailles mirrors represent something radically new. Now, the individual's public appearance is reflected, unfiltered and immediate. These mirrors made it possible for individuals to see themselves as public beings; each person thus becomes, literally, a res publica, a public thing, possibly for the very first time. It was the public eye itself that was looking back from the other side of the mirror.

What the mirrors reflected, then, was the beholder in front of the mirror, embedded in a social structure made up of fellow beholders. This was also the exact moment when the court permanently settled at Versailles, the final step in a historical development through which the crown transformed French nobility from heroic warriors to refined courtiers. Importantly, Louis XIV's domestication of the nobility did not only entail their physical separation from both Paris and their original estates at what until recently had been nothing but a hunting lodge in the countryside. As first analyzed by the German sociologist Norbert Elias, in the new social sphere at Versailles, members of the nobility domesticated their own affective reactions in order to conform to a court society where ideals of self-control and self-discipline adhered to rigid and hierarchically structured expectations of conduct, which took the place of more openly aggressive modes of behavior.

It is worth stressing that it was not only the courtiers who were caught in this hierarchically structured web of expectations, but also the king.

The court was certainly a structure of domination, but as such it was constituted by a network of interdependences to which even the king was beholden and within whose boundaries he therefore needed to negotiate. Jacques Revel beautifully captures this complex dynamic in the following dense passage, which suggests the extent to which the dynamic relies on the trope of mirroring: "From the top down, the curial order shapes behavior according to the place and the rank of each person within a rigorous hierarchy, and the etiquette's function is to regulate in detail this discipline that is unequal but equally imposed on everyone. From the bottom up, it's all of society that contemplates the spectacle of the court, a model offered for all to admire and imitate."[6] Essentially, social conformity operates through the aspirational mirror presented by court society as such and for each person in it by the level above them in the hierarchy. Whether called *politesse*, *étiquette*, or *civilité*, the spectacle of the court situates everybody in a hall of mirrors of social expectations.

At once a symbol and a tool, the vast public mirrors at Versailles both inaugurate and enable this brave new world, where the perfect mastery of the self's exterior was of paramount importance. Therefore, the tale these mirrors tell is not only an uplifting one about individuals' emancipation and empowerment through access to their public images. Rather, the same process through which Versailles became an object of admiration and imitation for the rest of France and the whole of Europe submitted the aristocrat courtiers to a tightly disciplined life lived on display. At a collective level, then, the mirrors showed the nobility an image of their new reality, situated, *framed*, contained, in a space dominated by the necessity of observing others and themselves. Indeed, just as courtiers saw an affective outburst as a sign of weakness, so they construed the need to consult the mirror, as if the beholder was not already in control of their appearance, of the physicality of their body moving around in this new,

---

6. "Du haut vers le bas, l'ordre curial conforme les comportements à la place et au rang de chacun au sein d'une rigoureuse hiérarchie, et l'étiquette a pour fonction de régler dans le détail cette discipline inégalitaire mais également imposée à tous. Du bas vers le haut, c'est la société tout entière qui contemple le spectacle de la cour, modèle offert à l'admiration et à l'imitation." Jacques Revel, quoted from Croix and Quéniart, *Histoire culturelle de la France*, 143, where no source for the quotation is given. The conceptual analysis leading to the quoted sentence can be found in Revel, "La cour," but without this at once beautiful and beautifully dense synthesis, which I retain here. For Norbert Elias's analysis, see *The Court Society* and *The Civilizing Process*, as well as Roger Chartier's introduction to the French edition of the former in *La société de cour* and the discussion by Revel in "La cour."

glamorous social space. As everybody knew all too well, the public eye looking back from the other side of the mirror was importantly always the gaze of the sovereign, Louis XIV.

The issue of the mirrors' social function and impact can be addressed in a more technical way, by examining their specific function within the wider décor of the gallery. Some scholars have drawn attention to the fact that the mirrors occupy a prominent part of the décor that had traditionally featured history paintings, the highest genre within the hierarchy of painting, as prescribed by the Royal Academy of Painting and Sculpture. Should, as Felipe Chaimovich has proposed, the "[v]irtual, contemporary, and interactive [mirror] images [that] took possession of salons and galleries throughout France," starting in the Hall of Mirrors, be considered "*pictures* of the history of the reign of Louis XIV"?[7] If so, should the lack of a fixed perspective in mirror images as compared to the tightly controlled composition and message of traditional history paintings be interpreted as a social leveling or rather as a further reinforcement of difference? Chaimovich argues forcefully for the latter, stressing how the mirrors reproduced rather than interrupted social and generic expectations about hierarchy, but his argument needs to be revisited in the context of my discussion here, since it ignores the function (and even the presence) of the history painting in the vault just above the mirrors.[8]

I argue that the history of the architectural use of mirrors prior to the Versailles gallery yields a similar point.[9] There is, in fact, a tradition for such an architectural use of mirrors, albeit at a more modest scale, going back at least as far as mid-sixteenth-century Renaissance Germany. And in the decades before the construction of the Versailles gallery, there was a conspicuous presence of mirrors in the decoration of domestic spaces for the French monarchy and in the mansions of the financial elite (in Paris, Vaux-le-Vicomte, Saint-Germain-en-Laye, and even at Versailles). Moreover, recent scholarship has highlighted the important role played by Charles Le Brun in their construction.[10]

7. Chaimovich, "Mirrors of Society," 364, 360; emphasis in original. See also Legge, "The Mirror and Manners."

8. I refer to Chaimovich's article for the pertinence of its central intuition, which serves to pinpoint an overlooked structural relation between mirrors and history paintings, although the article has shortcomings in terms of contextual precision and conceptual depth.

9. This paragraph relies on the discussion in Bazin-Henry, "Charles Le Brun et les décors de miroirs"; Berger, "Galerie des Glaces," 56–58; and Sabatier, *Versailles ou la disgrâce d'Apollon*, 114. See also Bazin-Henry, "Tromper les yeux."

10. See especially Bazin-Henry, "Charles Le Brun et les décors de miroirs."

While these mirrors were all located in private domestic rooms, there is at least one important prior example of a mirrored room of state: the Salón de los Espejos (Hall of Mirrors), which was the ceremonial center of the Royal Alcázar palace in Madrid.[11] It is difficult to assess or even imagine this space today, since it was destroyed with the rest of the building in a fire in 1734. We know of its appearance mainly through royal portrait paintings and a partial reconstruction, based on inventories from 1636 and 1686, of the arrangement of its decoration. At 10.5 by 19.5 meters, the room was significantly smaller than the Versailles gallery (10.5 by 73 meters); from the mid-1640s, it featured eight eagle-frame mirrors in total, located symmetrically in pairs of two on each side of the doors placed at the center of the short ends of the room. With each mirror measuring approximately 65 by 85 centimeters, they would not necessarily have struck us as particularly noteworthy, surrounded as they were by paintings that were not only much larger but also major masterpieces from the royal collection, at the time the most important collection in Europe. And yet, they were prominent enough that what was at first known quite simply as "el salón nuevo" (the new room) came to be named for its mirrors, which also tended to feature conspicuously in royal portraits with the room as their backdrop, as is the case in Juan Carreño de Miranda's circa 1675 portrait of Charles II (fig. 4).

From a French perspective, the Salón de los Espejos is most noteworthy as the solemn setting where Philip IV in October 1659 received a delegation of French dignitaries sent by Louis XIV to officially ask him for the hand of his daughter Maria Theresa. This was a decisive event in the lead-up to the signing of the Peace of the Pyrenees a few weeks later, thus marking the beginning of the end of decades of war between the two countries (thereby preparing the ground for the events of 1661 discussed elsewhere in this book). No wonder that it was in preparation of this visit that the room's decorative program was given its definitive form, under the direction of official court decorator Diego Velázquez and in close collaboration with the king himself. In addition to the eight mirrors, the décor featured thirty-one masterpieces from the royal collection (including paintings by Titian, Rubens, Tintoretto, and Velázquez himself) and a massive fresco in the vault of the hall representing the myth of Pandora

11. The most important source on all matters related to the Salón de los Espejos remains Orso, *Philip IV and the Decoration of the Alcázar of Madrid*, chapter 2: "The Decoration of the Hall of Mirrors." See also Barbeito, *El Alcázar de Madrid*; Berger, "Galerie des Glaces," 57–58; Brown, *Velázquez*, esp. 11, 189–94, 244–51; and Sancho, "L'espace du roi."

FIGURE 4. Juan Carreño de Miranda, *Charles II of Spain* (ca. 1675). Oil on canvas. Prado, Madrid, Spain. Photograph: Wikimedia Commons.

(by a team of Italian painters, commissioned by Velázquez). Unlike the Hall of Mirrors at Versailles, this room did not display a preplanned cycle or program. Scholars have nevertheless pondered the "message" of the room's decorative program, highlighting the inclusion not only of mythical themes but also of history paintings of recent historical events that position the Spanish monarchy as defenders of Christendom; however, they have not come to any firm conclusions.[12] It is noteworthy in the context of my discussion here that none of these interpretations contain any mention of the mirrors' symbolic function, even when the room is presented as an important instantiation of the "gallery of princely virtue" tradition.[13] It is unclear to what extent the Hall of Mirrors at Versailles should be considered as an attempt to rival the Salón de los Espejos, but if so, it would certainly not have been through the display of mirrors alone, but also through the wider decorative program, where both the material signifiers (the space, mirrors, painted surfaces, and further decorative elements) and the signified (the "message" conveyed) contributed to more or less tacit claims about military, political, technological, and also cultural hegemony. These claims were naturally more subdued in the Hall of Mirrors at Alcázar, given the context of peace and dynastic intermarriage. As developed in section 5, the case of the Hall of Mirrors at Versailles is very different, starting with its portrayal of the political situation in the early 1660s.

There are two other noteworthy instances where mirrors feature conspicuously in architecture in a context intimately linked to the public celebration of dynastic power prior to the Hall of Mirrors. First, obliquely related to the preceding case, there is the concluding act of the French-Spanish truce: the meeting between Louis XIV and Philip IV on the border between the two countries at Pheasant Island in the Bidassoa River in the Pyrenees region just off the Atlantic coast, in early June 1660. A well-known tapestry designed by Le Brun in 1663 as part of the History of the King series and first produced around 1670 focuses in on the solemn moment when the two kings greet each other just after having signed the treaty and before Princess Maria Theresa is handed over by her father to her husband (fig. 5). Many scholars have spilled much ink in seeking to identify which dignitaries from the two courts the tapestry includes and also regarding its representation of fashion and style.[14] However, very few scholars have commented upon one of the visually most striking features

12. See especially Orso, *Philip IV and the Decoration of the Alcázar of Madrid*, 87–117; but also Brown, *Velázquez*, 244–49; and Berger, "Galerie des Glaces," 57–58.

13. For the notion of "gallery of princely virtue," see the discussion below, 132.

14. For the most comprehensive discussion of the conception, production, and diffusion of the History of the King tapestries, see Meyer, *L'histoire du Roy*. For the most complete record of the contemporary French and Spanish sources of the June 1660 event and also the most thorough discussion of the various preparatory paintings and studies for that specific tapestry, see Colomer, "Paz política, rivalidad suntuaria." None of the modern sources I have consulted contain any information about

FIGURE 5. *Entrevue de Louis XIV et de Philippe IV d'Espagne dans l'île des Faisans, le 6 juin 1660* (Meeting of Louis XIV and Philip IV of Spain on Pheasant Island, June 6, 1660) (ca. 1665–80). Tapestry, manufactured at Gobelins, from the series "History of the King," by the workshop of Jean-Baptiste Mozin, after a design by Charles Le Brun. Embassy of France, Madrid, Spain. Photograph © RMN-Grand Palais / Art Resource, New York.

of the scene, which is also what makes it relevant to my argument: the enormous mirror in the center of the tapestry right behind the two kings, in which the kings' facial expressions are clearly reflected.[15] The reason for this silence may very well be that there is quite simply not much that can be said about it—or about the rest of the décor—with any level of certainty. The mirror does not seem to be mentioned in the many written sources describing the event, nor does the rest of the décor portrayed in the tapestry (a décor itself consisting of tapestries) match our detailed knowledge of the actual décor.[16] For my purposes, however, the presence

whether Le Brun or his collaborator, Adam Frans van der Meulen, were present at the events in 1660, or about what the sources of the design would have been if not.

15. Given the large size of the tapestry (348 by 597 cm), there is no doubt as to the visibility of the reflection. The reflection is also present in all the various preparatory paintings, as well as in the later etchings of the tapestry.

16. Jonathan Brown provides the following terse summary of what we know from written sources about the décor of the central room of the pavilion where the meet-

of the mirror in this iconic representation of the event emphasizes the connection between mirrors and the ceremonial celebration of dynastic authority and seems to suggest that size does indeed matter. In any case, at least one copy of the tapestry would have been present at Versailles in the decade leading up to the construction of the Hall of Mirrors, although scholars know very little about its actual decorative use.[17]

The second conspicuous architectural use of mirrors to celebrate dynastic power prior to Versailles is of a different order and magnitude. There is an important Mughal seventeenth-century tradition of *shish mahals* (Crystal Palaces, or Palaces/Halls of Mirrors) inspired by the construction of two such pavilions by Emperor Shah Jahan around 1631–32 as part of the Lahore Fort (in modern Pakistan) and Agra Fort (in modern India). The decoration of these spaces relies massively on complex mirror work, but rather than large pane mirrors, they include mirror mosaics, which create an astonishing gleaming effect through thousands of small mirrors along with other stones and crystals.[18] In her 2018 reassessment of the important ways in which contact with India changed both the material world and the imaginary of seventeenth-century France, Faith Beasley ends with an intriguing investigation into whether this contact is also reflected in the Versailles mirrors.[19] She makes a compelling case that French travelers like François Bernier and Jean-Baptiste Tavernier, "frequent visitors to the courts at Agra and Dehli [where they] would have witnessed such spectacular displays [of mirror mosaics]," would have described these mosaics to the French court upon their return.[20] Without necessarily following Beasley's bold thesis about a decisive influence or even a direct imitation, it seems plausible to include the Mughal mirrors within a wider set of examples handed down from the imperial or dynastic predecessors that Louis seeks to outshine. For Beasley, the Versailles mirrors are symptomatic of the wider tendency to suppress and erase

---

ing took place: "To adorn their side of the room, the French chose four tapestry panels representing Scipio and Hannibal; the Spaniards, intending to represent their ruler as defender of the faith, chose four scenes from the Apocalypse." Brown, *Velázquez*, 250. Brown discusses the tapestry in some detail (250), but without commenting on the seeming discrepancy with the written record, nor with any mention of the mirror. The only explicit mention I have found of the mirror represented in the tapestry is by J. A. Emmens in "Les Menines de Velazquez," 64–65, but there, too, it lacks any further discussion.

17. See Meyer, *L'histoire du Roy*, 132–36, 138–40.

18. See Koch, *Mughal Architecture*, esp. 132, but also 94, 115.

19. Beasley, *Versailles Meets the Taj Mahal*. See especially the last section of the book, entitled "Reflecting Grandeur: Mirroring India," 265–68.

20. Beasley, 265.

the origins of the seemingly unique royal beauty of Louis XIV, as ana-lyzed by Claire Goldstein.[21] As I shall argue in what follows, the mirrors do in fact themselves become a figure for such a suppression, a figure of pastlessness.

Returning now to France, popular accounts of the history of the mirror often describe the Hall of Mirrors at Versailles as the result of a decisive technological breakthrough. Until the 1660s, glass blowers in Venice had a monopoly in mirror-making technology. The production of the Versailles mirrors was the result of a sustained and systematic case of industrial espionage, masterminded by Louis XIV's leading minister, Jean-Baptiste Colbert. The story is quite spectacular and would make for a promising Hollywood blockbuster, including as it does sex and sui-cide, power and poisoning, bribery and blackmailing, kidnapping and shoot-outs. And the last mirror was mounted in the nick of time, the night before the formal inauguration of the gallery in November 1684. The one element this story is missing, however, is the technological breakthrough. The Versailles mirrors are certainly an important part of a wider technological development headed toward such a breakthrough, and the display of the 357 mirrors in the Hall of Mirrors (21 individual mirrors constituting each of the 17 arches facing the 17 arcaded windows overlooking the gardens) is situated toward the end of this development. They are a testimony as much to a new French mastery of an extremely sophisticated artisanal production process as to an unprecedented pro-duction capacity. But technologically, there is nothing related to the Ver-sailles mirrors, either in size or quality, that could not already have been done by glassblowers in Venice decades earlier, except the mere scale of the enterprise.

The 1680s were certainly crucial years of innovation in the history of mirror making, in what a leading specialist has called "a context of techni-cal effervescence." However, it wasn't until the second half of the decade that, for the first time, mirrors were successfully made by casting, the pouring of molten glass onto a metal table, rather than by blowing. Ber-nard Perrot, a Jewish glassmaker from Orléans, famously demonstrated this emerging technology to the Royal Academy of Sciences in 1687. The Paris-based Thévart company, under the decisive influence of another glassmaker, Louis Lucas de Nehou, seems to have spearheaded the use of casting in the production of large mirrors. Despite the immense profit at stake in this technological revolution and the royal letters patent granted to the Thévart company in 1688, it wasn't until 1691 that the first two-

21. See Goldstein, *Vaux and Versailles.*

meter mirrors were produced, at which point four were presented to the king.[22]

Somewhat perplexingly, perhaps, the definitive breakthrough in mirror-making technology happened soon *after* the initial opening of the gallery, which turns out to have been the monumental celebration *prior* to the final technical breakthrough that it is commonly assumed to be the result of. The new plate-glass technology not only liberated the size of mirrors from dependence on the lung capacity of the glass blower, but also opened up the prospect of a more industrialized production process. The actual realization of the innovation's promise was, however, slow in coming. Despite the monopoly granted by the French state to successive instantiations of the Manufacture royale des glaces since the mid-1660s, persistent technical and administrative challenges meant that Venetian glass was still half as expensive as French glass in the 1680s. It wasn't until the turn of the century that not only the technological but also the commercial hegemony shifted north. And it was only then that the somewhat reliable production of a genuine full-length mirror in one piece, not a composite as at Versailles, became possible, with panes up to five times larger than the largest panes in the Hall of Mirrors, which measure a modest 72 by 90 centimeters.

3. A Gallery Celebrating Greatness

What was new about the Versailles mirrors, then? As just outlined, it wasn't so much the technology itself as the political will and ambition

---

22. The specific elements and chronology of the decisive technological innovation growing out of the 1680s effervescence remain notoriously obscure; cf. Hamon, "Les commandes de glaces," especially the section "Un contexte d'effervescence technique" to which I allude at the beginning of the paragraph; and Belhoste, "La glace dans la galerie," esp. 149–54. According to Hamon, "What can be said, in short, about the invention of casting, as little known as it is disputed, is that it was an idea circulating in glassmaking circles at the time, which the best of the protagonists surely attempted." ("Ce que l'on peut dire, en bref, de l'invention du coulage, aussi mal connue que disputée, c'est qu'il s'agissait d'une idée qui circulait dans le milieu verrier du temps, à laquelle s'essayaient sans doute les meilleurs d'entre les protagonistes.") Hamon, "Les commandes de glaces." Within such a discussion, it certainly makes sense to surmise, as Hamon does, that "the Great Gallery was a pilot project between two [production] processes: blowing and casting" ("que la Grande Galerie a été un chantier pilote entre deux procédés: soufflage et coulage"). However, the presence of innovative elements pointing forward to the emerging shift (most importantly the increased thickness of some of the glass used) only becomes significant in retrospect and does not in any way question the place of the Versailles mirrors themselves *prior* to the shift.

at work in their production and assembly. The mirrors certainly helped express the magnitude of the outsized ambition of the wider decorative program inside which they appeared. They were a loud and flashy royal statement, saying above all else: "Because I can." But at a different level, they also added something qualitatively new, which made them the source of an energy we can still perceive in the Dior videos and which situates them at once very far from and quite close to us. Rather than the origin of something objectively new in the annals of technological innovation, it is my contention that the Hall of Mirrors was a tipping point in the display and symbolism of mirrors. To better grasp the significance of the Versailles mirrors, then, I examine more closely the wider decorative program inside which they are situated. More precisely, I shift temporarily away from the mirrors and up toward the ceiling. Considering these two elements of the gallery together, the ceiling paintings along with the mirrors, is very seldom done.[23] And yet, I argue, it is there, at the center of the hall's iconography, that the mirror's symbolism is most powerful, even though the ceiling includes no actual glass mirrors.

Interestingly, most of the early testimonies from the Hall of Mirrors do *not* actually focus on the mirrors.[24] One exception is the description of the not yet fully finished gallery from December 1682 in the French gazette *Le Mercure galant*, which evokes the way the mirrors "multiplient un million de fois cette Galerie, qui paraît n'avoir point de fin" (multiply the gallery a million times so that it appears to have no end).[25] But even this seemingly exuberant qualification, where the number "a million" explicitly points to a seeming endlessness, only appears within a detailed enumeration of the various elements of the décor. The mirrors are first presented as blind windows facing the real ones in a context where other, less inventive, features, such as trophies, in bas-relief and painted, and the

23. For two notable exceptions, see Rossholm Lagerlöf, "La Galerie des glaces at Versailles (1678–1684)"; and Bazin-Henry, "Charles Le Brun et les décors de miroirs." Rossholm Lagerlöf discusses "the use of huge mirrors" as "a peak of visual effect," which is, however, also "an aesthetic threat in relation to the paintings" (187, cf. 187–91), but without considering the mirroring taking place through—and in—the paintings themselves. Bazin-Henry does exactly that in an important section entitled "Dialogue entre glaces et peintures" (Dialogue between mirrors and paintings) (paras. 28–30), to which I will return below, 142–43. Otherwise, the article is mainly focused on artistic choices in terms of influence and sources, and less interested in questions of meaning and effect.

24. See in this regard the two syntheses by Saule, "The Hall of Mirrors during Louis XIV's Reign," and by Ziegler, "'His house at Versailles.'"

25. "Description de la Grande Galerie de Versailles," *Mercure galant*, December 1682; quoted here from *Les fastes de la Galerie des Glaces*, 34.

materials of pilasters and capitals—which to modern observers seem less glitzy—receive more attention. Other descriptions mention the mirrors in passing, matter-of-factly, if at all.

This lack of attention to the gallery's mirrors becomes less surprising once we realize that it did not yet possess its modern name of La galerie des Glaces (The Hall of Mirrors), highlighting mirrors as the room's primary feature. Instead, the hall was known as La Grande Galerie (The Great Gallery). This name refers to its size, of course, but more importantly to the fact that it was intended for the celebration of the reign of the king, who at this point, in the early 1680s, was known less by his number in the chain of the many French kings called Louis than by the simple title Louis le Grand (Louis the Great). It was in 1671 that the city of Paris first conferred upon the king this epithet that many other great rulers had only received posthumously, but it wasn't until the 1680s that absolutist culture caught up with the full implications of it, in what Olivier Chaline has called "a significant turning point" "in the evolution of Louis' glory."[26] It is in this process that the mirror as object and symbol comes to assume a new meaning for the figuration of greatness.[27] In order to understand how, it is important to consider not only how and why the mirrors were produced, but also, and above all, the decorative program inside which they are located.

From the outset, the plan for the vault had been to portray the king's major exploits, on the battlefield and beyond, through the traditional analogic use of ancient models: originally Louis would appear under the guise of Apollo, then through the labors of Hercules. The royal painter Charles Le Brun and his studio's drawings reveal his vision for both projects; the former project survives only in a few early drawings (fig. 6), while the latter is fleshed out in great detail in numerous drawings, including a scaled-down representation of the whole gallery measuring nearly two meters wide (fig. 7). In both cases, Louis would have been

26. "Dans l'évolution de la gloire de Louis, la décennie 1680 représente un tournant significatif." Chaline, *Le règne de Louis XIV*, I:168.

27. Louis XIV would have to wait until the nineteenth century to get his famous epithet of "the Sun King," although the sun symbolism was there from the beginning. It is important to observe, however, that Versailles is *not* a celebration of Louis XIV as the Sun King, and even less so as the project nears its completion in the 1680s. See in this regard Sabatier, *Versailles ou la disgrâce d'Apollon*, starting with the book's title and the very first sentence on the back cover: "*Versailles ou la disgrâce d'Apollon* entend briser l'image convenue mais fausse de palais du Soleil que Versailles n'a jamais été" (*Versailles or the disgrace of Apollo* intends to break the received but false image of the palace of the Sun that Versailles never was).

FIGURE 6. Charles Le Brun, Project for the vault of the Hall of Mirrors of Versailles, with scenes from the original Apollo design (ca. 1679). Ink, ink wash, black chalk. Musée du Louvre, Paris, France. Photograph © RMN-Grand Palais / Art Resource, New York. Photograph: Thierry Le Mage.

glorified through an implicit analogy between the exploits of the ancient deity and those of the present king, not unlike Le Brun's earlier series of monumental easel paintings exhibited at the Louvre, which celebrate the grandeur of Louis through association with the figure of Alexander the Great (fig. 8). By the late 1670s, the once-omnipresent trend of portraying Louis XIV through references to Alexander the Great had already long been out of fashion,[28] but now what seemed to be at stake was the traditional use of ancient models as such. The rejection of the Hercules project was a dramatic last-minute decision, described by Le Brun's disciple and biographer, Claude Nivelon, in the following terms:

> Toutes les études nécessaires étaient faites pour l'exécution de ce beau sujet, qui était agréé, mais le Conseil secret de Sa Majesté trouva à propos et résolut que son histoire sur les conquêtes devait y être représentée. Ce changement subit, qui aurait embarrassé les plus habiles génies, ayant à changer si promptement d'idées, a servi au contraire à faire juger quelle était l'étendue du génie de notre auteur, représentant des actions qui étonneront la postérité, et donneront de l'occupation aux plus délicates plumes du Temps.[29]

28. See Grell and Michel, *L'École des princes.*
29. Nivelon, *Vie de Charles le Brun,* 486–87.

FIGURE 7. Charles Le Brun, Project for the vault of the Hall of Mirrors of Versailles, with scenes from the life of Hercules (ca. 1679). Watercolor and ink. Chateaux de Versailles, France. Photograph © RMN-Grand Palais / Art Resource, New York.

FIGURE 8. Charles Le Brun, *L'Entrée d'Alexandre le Grand dans Babylone* (Entry of Alexander the Great into Babylon) (1665). Oil on canvas. Musée du Louvre, Paris, France. Photograph: Wikimedia Commons.

(All the necessary studies were done for the execution of this beautiful subject [the Hercules project], which was agreed upon, but the secret Council of His Majesty found fitting and resolved that the history of his conquests had to be represented there. This sudden change, which would have perturbed even the most skilled geniuses, having to change ideas so quickly, allowed us on the contrary to judge the extent of our author's genius, having represented actions that will astonish posterity and occupy the most delicate quills of our Time.)

Importantly, the decision was not Le Brun's but was imposed on him from above and very much against his will by the "secret Council of His Majesty." This administrative entity, also known as the Conseil d'en haut (Council of State), was the highest decision-making authority of the monarchy and included leading ministers like Colbert and François-Michel Le Tellier, Marquis of Louvois, although it is safe to assume that the king himself must have been instrumental in the decision in question.

The passage from Nivelon is noteworthy for the way in which it accentuates the heroic achievement of Le Brun. The narrative device he deploys is one I return to in chapter 3 in the structure of a fairy tale celebrating the king himself: the completed preparation for the former project and the sudden change of plans merely serve to highlight the immensity of the challenge, which the hero nonetheless overcomes with tremendous success. Furthermore, the allusion to "the most delicate quills" refers to none other than Racine and Boileau, named official royal historiographers as recently as 1677, and with whom Le Brun would now rival in the direct representation of recent royal actions and conquests. The continuation of Nivelon's text tells how Le Brun withdrew for two days and reemerged with a sketch for the central painting of the gallery, which the Conseil approved with an order to continue along the same lines. The material outcome of this process is well-known, since viewers can still observe it in the vault of the gallery today, which contains close to 1,000 square meters painted by Le Brun and his assistants. More specifically, it shows us the king's heroic deeds—from the moment he decided to govern without a chief minister after the death of Cardinal Mazarin in 1661 (as portrayed in the central painting, analyzed in detail in section 5), via administrative reforms at home in the 1660s and heroic highlights from the Franco-Dutch War in the 1670s, until the victorious end of the war in 1678—within an allegorical framework where the king, dressed in Roman garb, is the only mortal surrounded by a cohort of mythical and allegorical figures.

It is important to stress that although scholars know the source of the decision to radically shift the representational regime and also the ultimate outcome of this decision, there are many elements of the process that remain unknown, despite the considerable progress made by scholarship on the gallery over the last two decades. First of all, scholars do not know how exactly the decision come about at such a late stage and why the Conseil d'en haut deemed this shift of representational paradigm "à propos" now and not earlier. It may be tempting to identify a trigger in the contemporary events just mentioned, like the recent victorious end of the war and the subsequent foregrounding of "le Grand" as a royal epithet, but the change is so radical that it needs to be considered within a much wider context, at once artistically, politically, and technologically. Second, Le Brun's exact role is at times less obvious than one might think, not only at the level of execution (distinguishing the work of the master from that of his large team of assistants) but also at the level of conception (distinguishing the contributions of Le Brun from those of Jules Hardouin-Mansart, the architect of the gallery, as well as from those of Paul Tallemant, the academician who served as Le Brun's learned consultant in matters of iconography and whose role has recently been characterized as that of a co-designer alongside Le Brun).[30] Finally, and most

---

30. Some early accounts, including that of Nivelon, tend to exaggerate Le Brun's role to the detriment of that of Mansart and Tallemant, most blatantly the follow-

importantly for my discussion here, scholars know very little about how, when, and why the immense display of mirrors entered into the mix and whether it even makes sense to speak of a "mix" at all. Alexandre Maral authoritatively observes that "[t]he mirrors are absent from all the recorded projects and seem to have appeared at a fairly late date."[31] Robert Berger, on the other hand, is able to suggest "that mirrors were already being considered in conjunction with the Apollo cycle—that is to say, from the initial stages of the planning of the Galerie" by drawing attention to a mirrored door figuring as one option for the north end of the gallery in an early drawing.[32] And while it is customary to assume that the reason the mirrors are present in the gallery is above all due to the influence of Colbert and Hardouin-Mansart, Sandra Bazin-Henry has recently made a strong case for the role of Le Brun.[33] And yet, despite all that scholars don't know and probably cannot know about the intent and purpose behind the inclusion of the mirrors in the décor, and perhaps even about the agency behind the decision, it is obvious that the mirrors contribute to the overall celebration of the greatness of the king in an important way. Indeed, although it is far from certain that these were coordinated efforts,

---

ing one in the *Mercure galant*: "Monsieur Le Brun en a fait tout le dessein. C'est-à-dire que les ornements, la sculpture et enfin toutes les choses qui contribuent à l'enrichissement de la Galerie, partent du génie de ce premier peintre de Sa Majesté." (Mr. Le Brun did the whole design. That is to say that the ornaments, the sculpture and finally all the things that contribute to the enrichment of the Galerie stem from the genius of this first painter of His Majesty.) *Mercure galant*, August 1681; quoted here from *Les fastes de la Galerie des Glaces*, 31–32. For Mansart and Le Brun, see Maral, "La galerie: une affaire d'architecte?" and Maral, "Architectural Work on the 'Grande Galerie,'" especially the final section, "Mansart or Le Brun?" (50–51). The reference to Tallemant as the co-designer of the gallery is from Milovanovic: "la collaboration des deux concepteurs du programme iconographique: Charles Le Brun et Paul Tallemant" (the collaboration of the two designers of the iconographic program: Charles Le Brun and Paul Tallemant). Milovanovic, "Les inscriptions dans le décor de la galerie des Glaces," 298.

31. Maral, "The Marbles and the Mirrors," 53. Maral adds that a similar lateness can be observed in the construction of the mirrors: while the construction of the décor is thought to have started in the spring of 1679 and an important sum was set aside for "glasswork" in 1680, the first payment to the mirror-maker Briot didn't occur until May 1682, only shortly before the first account of the gallery in the *Mercure galant* in August of that year. Maral, 53; cf. Maral, "Architectural Work on the 'Grande Galerie,'" 46–47.

32. Berger, "Galerie des Glaces," 56, cf. figure 89 for the sketch in question, which also occurs in Maral (but without comment of the apparent mirror), "Architectural Work on the 'Grande Galerie,'" 44.

33. Bazin-Henry, "Charles Le Brun et les décors de miroirs," para. 2.

it is tempting to see a parallel development in the unprecedented use of mirrors, on the one hand, and the reorientation of the representation of the king, on the other.

There is thus an intriguing overlap between the emphasis on bigger, better mirrors on the lower walls of the gallery and the push toward a more direct rendition of the king himself on the ceiling. By sidestepping the ancient models, the décor of the gallery conveys the dream of absolutism in its purest form: the collective dream about the king as an absolute agent, whose agency has no human source beyond himself and his divinely inspired will. Sovereignty is envisioned as a closed, self-sufficient system where self-reflection and mirroring take on a new meaning and importance. Instead of the traditional "mirror for princes"—a genre of political writing dating back at least to the early medieval period and in which the king can learn from a portrayal of the ideal prince that subtly mixes descriptive and prescriptive features—the decorative program at Versailles seems to encourage the king to contemplate only himself.

I turn now to the question of what the king saw in this gallery celebrating his greatness. What does the renewed emphasis on seeing and optics signify in the first place? How should we as modern viewers understand the accentuation of specularity within the framework of the mirrors, and what about the seemingly sustained and systematic effort to make the mirror image bigger, better, and more direct? To engage more thoroughly with the way in which the gallery reflects the king while considering these questions, in what follows I home in on two privileged yet understudied scenes where mirrors and royal self-contemplation are central: first, in the actual gallery during the king's first visit, as reported in a contemporary testimony (section 4); second, in an often-overlooked mirror scene in what is incontestably the most central painting of the gallery, portraying the enabling decision from 1661 alluded to above (section 5).

4. Making the King See What He Felt

To begin to understand what it is that the king saw in the Grande Galerie, let me evoke a scene. The moment is at the beginning of the 1680s. The main characters are the king, Louis XIV, and his painter, Charles Le Brun. Their eyes and heads are turned upward toward Le Brun's paintings adorning the ceiling of the Grande Galerie that celebrate the greatest actions from the reign of the greatest of kings. They are dwarfed by the verticality of the space in this scene.

The architectural space imposes on the beholder a posture that incites not only a certain visual impression but also a specific bodily experience.

The act of *looking up* situates us in a position of inferiority, of respect or submission, possibly of awe, as highlighted by the way we naturally open our mouth when looking upward. Before we read or interpret anything, before we even look, our bodies are prepared to be overwhelmed. Philosophers of religion like Mircea Eliade, for whom "height" is a transcendental pre-rational category, confirm these spatial intuitions. According to Eliade, "Simple contemplation of the celestial vault already provokes a religious experience."[34]

However, this correlation between height and religious experience may make it more delicate for secular powers to exploit unabashedly the vertical dimension, even when invested with the divine, as in the case of the French monarchy. This observation may, at the very least, help explain why Louis XIV had "only sporadically" been represented in ceiling paintings before Le Brun's project in the Grande Galerie.[35] The gallery accomplishes another significant "first" related to the decorative program: the depiction of the king surrounded by the gods and deities of antiquity, rather than humans, elevates him in a symbolic sense, in addition to his architectural elevation. In the words of Nicolas Milovanovic, "We can thus say that henceforth the heavens belong to him as much as [au même titre que] the divinities of Olympus."[36]

With the symbolic importance of this verticality in mind, I return to the scene of the king's first guided tour on the floor of the Grande Galerie. Looking up at the paintings in the vault, Louis XIV and Le Brun arrive at the one that today carries the inscription "Résolution prise de faire la guerre aux Hollandais, 1671" (Decision made to wage war against the Dutch, 1671). As the title already suggests, it portrays the key moment in the gallery's representation of the Franco-Dutch War of the 1670s, the origin of all the glorious achievements depicted elsewhere, and it does so through an excellent example of the allegorical novelty alluded to above, by placing the king between Mars and Minerva (plate 2). More precisely, to the right of the king, the god of war, Mars, invites him to ascend toward Victory and Fame, who await him on clouds higher up in the heavens. To the left, Minerva, the goddess of wisdom and prudence, shows him a representation of the horrors of war that she has woven in a tapestry. There is no reliable record of how Le Brun described the painting on the occa-

34. Eliade, *The Sacred and the Profane*, 118.

35. "La représentation du roi dans les peintures de plafond est sporadique jusqu'aux décors versaillais." Milovanovic, *Du Louvre à Versailles*, 213.

36. "On peut donc dire que le ciel lui appartient désormais au même titre que les divinités de l'Olympe." Milovanovic, 213.

sion, but it is likely that his description was quite close to a contemporary description in the *Mercure galant* that has been attributed to Le Brun:

[L]e Roi, animé par sa valeur [= Mars] à une conquête juste, délibérant en lui-même s'il la commencera, écoute la Sagesse [= Minerve] pour sur-monter par ses conseils les obstacles qu'elle lui fait remarquer dans son entreprise.[37]

(The King, spurred on by his valor [= Mars] to a just conquest, delib-erating within himself whether he will undertake it, listens to Wisdom [= Minerva] in order to overcome through her advice the obstacles that she makes him observe in his enterprise.)

The king's words, however, do exist in testimony from Claude Nivelon, disciple of Le Brun, in his book on the life of his master:

Ce conseil royal et secret, caractérisé de cette manière, fit témoigner à Sa Majesté, lorsque M. Le Brun lui en expliqua le dessein, ces paroles, en l'honorant de lui toucher sur le bras: "M. Le Brun, vous m'avez fait voir des choses que j'ai ressenties."[38]

(This royal and secret council, characterized in this way, made the king declare [témoigner], when Le Brun explained its composition to him, the following words, while honoring him by touching his arm: "Mr. Le Brun, you have made me see things that I felt.")

This passage merits a careful close reading, not only of the words directly attributed to Louis XIV—the way he sees the gallery as a portrait of his emotions ("Mr Le Brun, you have made me see things that I felt")—but also of Nivelon's framing of these words. Importantly, the reason that there is a story to tell at all is that it bears witness to an unusual public

37. "Explication de la Galerie de Versailles," *Mercure galant*, December 1684; quoted here from *Les fastes de la Galerie des Glaces*, 53. The *Mercure galant* article is introduced as having been written by "Mr. Lorne Peintre" (*Mercure galant*, Decem-ber 1684, 2), that is, François Lorne, who was to be received into the Royal Academy of Painting and Sculpture in 1686. For these details and the attribution of the article to Le Brun, see Sabatier, *Versailles ou la disgrâce d'Apollon*, 135.

38. Nivelon, *Vie de Charles le Brun*, 501. This anecdote is well-known in the schol-arship, but it has never been submitted to a serious analysis, as if the meaning and implication of these words were self-evident, cf. e.g., Sabatier, *Versailles ou la disgrâce d'Apollon*, 154; and Milovanovic, "The Portrait of the King," 146.

display of royal emotion. The king is moved by the painting, and this un-expected interior movement then provokes two different public expressions from the king—one audible and another visible: the king *declares* (*témoigne*), and he *touches*. These two verbs of affection—*témoigner* and *toucher*—announce what the third verb denoting the action of the king, *honorer*, says explicitly: the painting glorifies not only its motif but also, through the king's reaction, its maker. Thereby, the painter's disciple foregrounds a chiasmus that seems to have been a commonplace at the time: Le Brun is not only "the painter of the King" but also "the King of painters."[39]

From a historical distance, we may wonder whether the king's affective reaction, as described by Nivelon, could be read directly on his body or his face. We don't know, obviously, but it seems reasonable to assume that it couldn't. The king's impenetrable countenance was well known. According to court chronicler Duke of Saint-Simon, the king was "parfaitement maître de son visage, de son maintien, de son extérieur" (perfectly in control of his face, his appearance, his exterior), and foreign diplomats remarked that he was "capable de dissimulation totale" (capable of total dissimulation).[40] It is against this background that the king's affective reaction in Nivelon's story stands out, since it is precisely a question of a "royal and secret council," or as Le Brun emphasizes in his description of the same painting: the king "deliberating within himself." If the king makes a public expression of his well-mastered emotion, it is because the painting makes him see the least public aspect of his own exercise of power: royal deliberation in secrecy, the process of making a solitary decision, the workings of the "mystery of State."

It might be reasonable to object that Louis XIV's lack of expression is nothing more than the impenetrability constitutive of the majesty of any king. After all, the failure to govern his public display of emotions would, for any king, inevitably signal weakness or imperfection. His courtiers would interpret it as a deformation of his sovereignty. However, although impenetrability is related to absolutism in general, Louis XIV seems to

39. For one prominent example, see the *Mercure galant*'s coverage of the visit to the Hall of Mirrors by the ambassadors from Siam in November 1686: "Ce que cet Ambassadeur voyait alors, et tout ce qu'il avait déjà vu de Monsieur Le Brun, fut cause qu'il lui dit *qu'il était le Roi des peintres*. Ce qu'il a souvent dit depuis." (What the Ambassador saw then, and all that he had already seen by Mr. Le Brun, was the reason he told him *that he was the King of painters*. As he has often said since then.) *Mercure galant*, November 1686; quoted here from *Les fastes de la Galerie des Glaces*, 83; emphasis in original.

40. For these sources, see Halévi, "Le sens caché des *Mémoires*," 463.

have closely associated it with his own exercise of power, clearly distinguishing his approach from that of his immediate predecessors. That is at least what he teaches to his own successor. In his *Mémoires for the Instruction of the Dauphin*, the king evokes a time in the past

[...] quand tous ceux qui approchaient du roi ou du ministre avaient part aux secrets et presque aux résolutions, ou pouvaient du moins *les pénétrer par cent marques extérieures*. Je pense y avoir pourvu autrement; et de quelque sorte qu'on ait les yeux ouverts sur mes *desseins*, si je ne me trompe, ceux qui ne bougent du Louvre n'en savent guère davantage que ceux qui n'en approchent jamais.

([...] when all those who were around the king or the minister participated in their secrets and virtually in their decisions, or could at least *penetrate them through a hundred outward signs*. I think I have provided against this, and unless I am mistaken, however carefully one keeps an eye on my *plans*, those who never budge from the Louvre know hardly any more about them than those who never go near it.)[41]

Nothing surprising, then, in this lesson about the need for a radical disconnect between "outward signs" and the sovereign's intentions or "plans" (*desseins*). But it serves to highlight an intriguing opposition between the dissimulation of the king's plans, on the one hand, and the visibility of those of his painter, on the other. This opposition is even more conspicuous in French, since it is formulated through the same central concept of *dessein*: first, as used by the king about his plans that are kept secret; second, by Nivelon in his description of the scene with the king and his painter looking up at the painting above them: "Le Brun explained its composition to him [lui en expliqua le dessein]." In each case, the English translation of the term (as "plan" and "composition," respectively) is not entirely satisfactory; the meaning of the French term seems to be wider, as if pointing to something grander. The *dessein* of an action, be it political or artistic, refers to the signifying motivation that stands behind and before that act (causally and temporally) and which only finds its expression through the act; it is at the level of conceptualization rather than execution.[42] Politically speaking, the king needs to keep the *dessein* secret,

---

41. Louis XIV, *Mémoires, suivis de Manière de montrer les jardins*, 167–68; Louis XIV, *Mémoires for the Instruction of the Dauphin*, 100–101; my emphasis.

42. The *dessein* brings together the *thrust* with which and the *goal* toward which a grand action unfolds. This untranslatable dimension of the term is nicely captured in

as dictated by the nature of sovereignty itself; for, as successful rulers had always known and Bodin had made explicit in the preceding century, sovereignty cannot be shared. But what should viewers think about the legibility of his painter's *desseins*, and specifically in a history painting, which was the most dignified genre at the time and was so exactly because it was entrusted with the task of capturing royal actions that expressed the sovereign's own grand *desseins*?

I focus first on what happens after the painter has helped the king interpret the painting above them. Once Le Brun has explained and decoded the allegories, the meaning of the painting seems clear. The painter's words have helped the king move from incomprehension to understanding, indeed to the understanding that the *dessein* of the painting somehow corresponds to his own secret *dessein* at the moment portrayed: his own sovereign *dessein* at the exact moment it took shape. The king's reaction to the painting upon understanding it—in other words, upon *seeing* what it is really about—is itself a confirmation of the medium's transparency and therefore already a sign of the success of the enterprise.

That same transparency is at the heart of the Petite Académie's effort to guide the visitors of the gallery through detailed inscriptions at the bottom of the paintings and numerous printed *explications* of the gallery. The scene analyzed here of Le Brun showing the king the gallery most likely took place before the inscriptions were added, but soon enough the painting that today carries as its inscription the pithy title "Résolution prise de faire la guerre aux Hollandais, 1671" (Decision made to wage

---

the main (twentieth-century) definition from the *TLF*: "Conception par l'esprit d'un but à atteindre, d'une fin à réaliser." (The mind conceiving of a goal to reach, an end to realize.) Furetière's general definition is very brief: "Projet, entreprise, intention" (Project, enterprise, intention), but two of the first four examples he gives bring us close to our context here: "Ce Prince a de grands *desseins*, il ne veut pas qu'on penetre dans ses *desseins*." (This prince has great plans, he doesn't want people to penetrate his plans.) As for the artistic use of the term, we learn that "DESSEIN, est aussi la pensée qu'on a dans l'imagination de l'ordre, de la distribution et de la construction d'un tableau, d'un Poème, d'un Livre, d'un bâtiment" (*dessein* is also the thought that one has in the imagination about the order, the distribution and the construction of a painting, a poem, a book, a building). As for my distinction between conceptualization and execution, see the following remark from the *TLF*: "Alors que *dessein* implique la détermination d'un but, d'une fin, *plan* ou *projet* impliquent l'intention et la combinaison réfléchie des moyens propres à l'exécution du dessein." (While *dessein* implies the determination of a goal, *plan* or *project* implies the intention and the reasoned combination of the means suitable for the *dessein's* execution.) *TLF*, "dessein," Rem. 1.

war against the Dutch, 1671) came with an elaborate tripartite inscription in Latin, following the tripartite movement of the painting (and of the king's decision) from left to right: "MINERVA BELLI LABORES FORTIS-SIMO PRINCIPI RETEGIT" (Minerva makes the king see all the miseries of war); "DE BELLO INEUNDO CONCILIUM" (Deliberation to go to war); "MARS TRIUMPHOS PARAT" (Mars promises victory).[43]

The scholarship on the Hall of Mirrors commonly implies that there is no distance or gap between the *dessein* of the painter and the expression of this plan in the vault of the gallery, nor is there any opacity within the artistic *dessein*. In his effort to clarify the signification of his work, the painter draws on the iconographic alphabet of the tradition, as firmly documented by Cesare Ripa in his *Iconologia* (1593) and adapted for the French context in Jean Baudoin's richly illustrated translation from 1636. Therefore, scholarship implies, all that the inscriptions and descriptions of the gallery do is translate back into words the iconographic elements on the wall, while spelling out their composite meaning. As Nivelon's description of the scene made explicit: the words are there in order to "faire voir," make the beholder see. For viewers today, it is even easier, for the former curator of the gallery, Nicolas Milovanovic, has beautifully gathered all the signifying elements from the tradition in an online icono-graphic catalogue on the château's website: one click on an image brings up a description of it, while another click lists all of the other occurrences of the same figure in the gallery.[44] Hence the title of Gérard Sabatier's chapter on the meaning of the gallery in his important 2016 synthesis of decades of work on Versailles: "'Une éloquence de montre': Explication des tableaux de la galerie de Versailles et de ses deux salons" ("An elo-quence of display": Explication of the paintings of the gallery at Versailles and of its two salons).[45] His chapter is an *explication* in the same sense as

43. Bjørnstad, "'Plus d'éclaircissement touchant la grande galerie de Versailles,'" 339. The Latin inscriptions were written by Paul Tallemant, the academician who as-sisted Le Brun in the conception of the gallery's iconographic agenda. My English translations are based on Tallemant's own translations to the French. ("Minerve fait voir au Roi tous les malheurs de la guerre. / Délibération de faire la guerre / Mars promet la victoire.") For the early history of the inscriptions and descriptions of the gallery, including the rediscovery of the long-lost original Latin inscriptions and Tallemant's French translations, see Bjørnstad, "'Plus d'éclaircissement touchant la grande galerie de Versailles'"; and Vuilleumier Laurens and Laurens, *L'âge de l'in-scription*, chapter 12: "Le chantier de Versailles et la péripétie des inscriptions latines, puis françaises à la lumière des récentes découvertes."

44. Milovanovic, *Versailles, la galerie des Glaces.*

45. Sabatier, *Versailles ou la disgrâce d'Apollon*, chap. 5.

the painter's decoding of the painting for the king and the *explications* of the period for a wider audience, without any room for ambiguity.[46]

This need for absolute transparency with regard to Le Brun's *dessein* for his paintings in the vault of the gallery is closely linked to the primacy of drawing (*dessin*) over color (*coloris*) in academic painting at the time. As highlighted by Jacqueline Lichtenstein in her seminal discussion of "The Clash between Color and Drawing" in *The Eloquence of Color* (1989), "Only drawing exercises a control over painting that is both aesthetic and pedagogical. It represents in painting the principle of centrality that defines the royal politics that the academicians are expected to uphold in the world of fine arts."[47] Significantly, the two terms *dessein* (plan, composition, as discussed above) and *dessin* (drawing, outline, design) weren't yet distinct at the time.[48] Such a blurriness might be surprising to a modern observer, but less so once we realize that drawing itself was "always defined as an abstract representation, a form of a spiritual nature, whose origin resides solely in thought,"[49] as opposed to the sensorial materiality of the *coloris*. This lack of distinction nevertheless points to the importance of a certain approach to the arts within the absolutist agenda: "If drawing must rule in painting so that discourse may rule over paint-

46. Do I thereby contest the transparency of the signification, against both the scholars from the Petite Académie and present-day specialists? At the very least, it is tempting to see the presence of rivaling inscriptions and *explications* and at times a sharp polemics between different ways of labeling and explicating the project as an indication of the energy that went into holding the signification together in order to assure its transparency. It is also worth noting a tension in Sabatier's approach at the few occasions where he suggests that there are layers of meaning *not* accounted for by the official *explications*, most importantly in his reading of *Résolution prise de faire la guerre aux Hollandais, 1671*. The period descriptions of this painting don't mention at all what Sabatier considers to be the fundamental focal point between Minerva and Mars—namely, the allegory of Justice. Though it seems logical that this omission suggests that more care is needed in following the decoding proposed by the period *explications* elsewhere, this is not what Sabatier concludes. Instead, he ends his "explication" of the painting by quoting the words from Nivelon describing the scene with the king and Le Brun analyzed here, without any further comment, as if its meaning were also obvious (154).

47. Lichtenstein, *The Eloquence of Color*, 152. This and the following quotations are all from the chapter "The Clash between Color and Drawing; or, The Tactile Destiny of the Idea" (138–68).

48. As attested by Richelet in 1680: "Quelques modernes écrivent le mot de dessein étant terme de peinture sans e après les deux s; mais on ne les doit pas imiter en cela." (Some moderns write the word *dessein* being a term of painting without e after the two s; but one should not imitate them in this.) Richelet, *Dictionnaire français*, "dessein."

49. Lichtenstein, *The Eloquence of Color*, 149.

ing, this truth is even more imperative when the discourse and painting in question concern representation of the king. This truth explains the high risk of historical painting, whose privileged position at once reflects the interests of the king, of discourse, and of drawing."[50] It is this truth that is policed by the Petite Académie and confirmed, first by the king's reaction, then by that of modern scholars, at the point of intersection between political opacity and artistic transparency brought into focus by the place of *dessein* in history painting.

In retrospect—the very specific retrospect provided by the contemporary history paintings in the Hall of Mirrors—the royal *desseins* are visible. It is the course of history itself that flows from these decisive moments. But on the canvas, the king's emotions remain invisible in his facial and corporal expressions, in contrast to the narrative of emotions felt but not seen by the king at the time of deliberation. This contrast takes on its full meaning in the context of the very real cult of royal impassiveness of the 1680s. The topic of composition proposed by the French Academy in 1681 for its annual award competition is symptomatic in this respect: "On voit le Roi toujours tranquille, quoique dans un mouvement continuel." (One always sees the king calm, although in continuous movement.) The speech pronounced by academician Jean Doujat during the award ceremony aptly zeroes in on what he calls the king's "constant evenness of mind" ("constante égalité d'esprit"):

> Cette vertu si rare, plutôt vantée que possédée par les anciens philosophes, mais inconnue à notre siècle hors l'âme du Grand Louis, est sans doute ce qui fait le véritable héros, et qui le rend maître de tout ce qui est hors de lui en le rendant maître de soi-même. [. . .] Il est toujours le même parce que quoi qu'il puisse arriver, il n'arrive rien qui lui soit nouveau.[51]

> (This virtue, so rare [his constancy of mind], more often paraded than possessed by the ancient philosophers, but unknown in our century outside the soul of the Great Louis, is without doubt what makes a real hero, and what makes him master of everything that is beyond him by making him master of himself. [. . .] He is always the same because whatever may happen, nothing happens which is new to him.)

Louis is, therefore, not only the most royal of kings, but also more stoic than the Stoics. Real heroism starts at home, in the affirmation of an

---

50. Lichtenstein, 149.
51. *Les Panégyriques du roi*, ed. Zoberman, 187.

absolute and serene self. In other words, the king becomes master of his body politic by first being the master of his body natural, by tightly controlling passions and emotions that seek to express themselves in his body natural.

Far from being apolitical, emotions are thus at the heart of politics. Pascal provides a surprising indication of this when he mobilizes explicitly political terminology in order to denounce the human deformation implied in the pursuit of sexual pleasure: "[D]ans le plaisir, c'est l'homme qui succombe au plaisir. Or il n'y a que la maîtrise et l'empire qui fasse la gloire, et que la servitude qui fasse honte." ("In pleasure, it is man who yields to pleasure. Now mastery and empire alone bring glory, and subjection alone brings shame.")[52] The sovereignty of the self in relation to emotional perturbations is expressed through an analogy with political sovereignty. Racine's *Phèdre* provides another striking example of this analogy, this time moving from political control to control of the body, in the often-quoted lament of the deeply troubled eponymous heroine in the opening of act 3: "Moi, régner! Moi ranger un État sous ma loi, / Quand ma faible raison ne règne plus sur moi." ("I, reign! You'd trust the State to my control / When reason rules no longer in my soul.")[53] In fact, the various ways in which the French noun *émotion* functions in the seventeenth century already calls for such an analogy. In his *Dictionnaire universel* from 1690, Furetière records the use of *émotion* not only to denote what today we would call a psychological perturbation or psychological state, but also a political meaning of the term as "the beginning of sedition" (commencement de sédition).[54] In both cases, emotion is a movement that threatens the equilibrium of the body in question. And in the case of the king, who inhabits two bodies (body natural and body politic), the link is obviously even stronger. In order to remain the sovereign of his kingdom and to avoid provoking *public emotions* (in the sense of sedition), public emotions that could risk disturbing the body politic, he must first and foremost control the emotions of his body natural, emotions that are always already political, since they mark the body of the king.

This is the background against which the scene of the king contemplating his own portraits on the ceiling of the Hall of Mirrors—the images of the "things [he] felt" at crucial moments of his reign—is not only an intriguing anecdote but becomes an occasion to ponder what the pub-

52. Pascal, *Pensées*, fragment 648.
53. Racine, *Œuvres complètes*, 1:847; Racine, *Phaedra*, 54.
54. Cf. Furetière, *Dictionnaire universel*, "esmotion."

PLATE 1. Charles Le Brun, *Le Roi gouverne par lui-même, 1661* (The King governs on his own, 1661) (1679–84). Oil on canvas, marouflage. Hall of Mirrors, Château de Versailles, France. The exact direction of the gestures by Minerva and Mars in the painting is not obvious in this reproduction, since the angles are distorted in the projection from the curved surface of the ceiling of the gallery to the flat surface of the two-dimensional reproduction. Photograph: Wikimedia Commons.

PLATE 2. Charles Le Brun, *Résolution prise de faire la guerre aux Hollandais, 1671* (Decision made to wage war against the Dutch, 1671) (1679–84). Oil on canvas, marouflage. Hall of Mirrors, Chateaux de Versailles, France. Photograph © RMN-Grand Palais / Art Resource, New York. Photography: René-Gabriel Ojéda / Franck Raux / montage Dominique Couto.

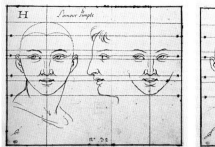
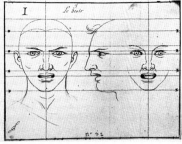

PLATE 3. Charles Le Brun, *L'amour simple* (Simple love) and *Le désir* (Desire) (late seventeenth century). Pen and brown ink and black chalk on white paper. Musée du Louvre, Paris, France. From Jennifer Montagu, *The Expression of the Passions: The Origin and Influence of Charles Le Brun's "Conférence sur l'expression générale et particulière"* (New Haven, CT: Yale University Press, 1994), 135.

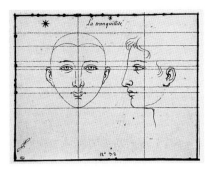

PLATE 5. Charles Le Brun, *La tranquillité* (Tranquility) (late seventeenth century). Pen and brown ink on white paper. Musée du Louvre, Paris, France. From Jennifer Montagu, *The Expression of the Passions: The Origin and Influence of Charles Le Brun's "Conférence sur l'expression générale et particulière"* (New Haven, CT: Yale University Press, 1994), 18.

PLATE 6. Charles Le Brun, *Le Roi gouverne par lui-même, 1661* (The King governs on his own, 1661) (extreme detail) (1679–84). Oil on canvas, marouflage. Hall of Mirrors, Château de Versailles, France. Photograph: Wikimedia Commons.

PLATE 4. *Facing page:* Charles Le Brun, *Le Roi gouverne par lui-même, 1661* (The King governs on his own, 1661) (detail) (1679–84). Oil on canvas, marouflage. Hall of Mirrors, Château de Versailles, France. Photograph: Wikimedia Commons.

PLATE 7. Charles Le Brun, *Le Roi gouverne par lui-même*, 1661 (The King governs on his own, 1661) and *Faste des puissances voisines de la France* (Splendor of the neighboring powers of France) (1679–84). Oil on canvas, marouflage. Hall of Mirrors, Château de Versailles, France. Full view of the central section of the vault of the Hall of Mirrors. Photograph: Wikimedia Commons.

lic display of royal emotions says about absolutism, the self-image of the sovereign, and the role of the arts.

Before addressing these issues directly, I would like to foreground an important parallel between the problematic status of royal emotions and the general problem of the expression of emotions in painting at the time of Le Brun. What is at stake is the expression of the soul, or in René Démoris's concise formulation: how "to bring out [and] make appear an object [. . .] which is irredeemably elsewhere," an object "which is not visible and generally not accessible through the senses, which only can be grasped thanks to the mediation of the body."[55] Le Brun himself proposes the most radical response to this dilemma in his famous 1668 lecture entitled "Sur l'expression générale et particulière." Le Brun aims at establishing a perfect monosemy, an absolute key for reading the passions based on the expressions of the human face, hence the well-known drawings representing the exterior movements of the passions—love, hatred, desire, rage, or rapture (*ravissement*)—which complemented the lecture (fig. 9).[56] Le Brun's taxonomic ambitions notwithstanding, his contemporaries Nicolas Poussin and André Félibien perceived the problem in a very similar way. This proximity is clear in the following quotation where Félibien is describing Poussin's aesthetics:

En parlant de la peinture, [Poussin] dit que de même que les vingt-quatre lettres de l'alphabet servent à former nos paroles et exprimer nos pensées, de même les linéaments du corps humain servent à exprimer les diverses passions de l'âme pour faire paraître au-dehors ce qu'on a dans l'esprit.[57]

(Speaking of painting, [Poussin] says that in the same way that the twenty-four letters of the alphabet serve to form our speech and express our thoughts, so do the alignments of the human body serve to express the various passions of the soul, to make appear outside what one has in the mind.)

The human body is here considered an interface "pour faire paraître" (to make appear) that which is in the soul or the mind. However, several ele-

---

55. "[Comment] faire sortir, [. . .] faire apparaître un objet [. . .] irrémédiablement ailleurs," "[un objet] non visible et en général non accessible aux sens, saisissable seulement grâce à la médiation du corps." Démoris, "Le langage du corps," 43. This and the following paragraph are indebted to Démoris's article.

56. See the critical edition by Montagu in *The Expression of the Passions*.

57. Félibien, *Mémoires*; quoted here from Démoris, "Le langage du corps," 39.

FIGURE 9. Charles Le Brun, *Le Ravissement* (Rapture) (late seventeenth century). Black chalk on white paper. Musée du Louvre, Paris, France. From Jennifer Montagu, *The Expression of the Passions: The Origin and Influence of Charles Le Brun's "Conférence sur l'expression générale et particulière"* (New Haven, CT: Yale University Press, 1994), 147.

ments of the preceding discussion suggest a clear awareness at the time that such a mechanistic model based on a one-to-one correspondence between the expressions of the body and the content of the soul is too simplistic. First of all, there are good reasons to doubt the efficacy and relevance of a straightforward legibility of the human face or body in the public space, in light of the discussion above regarding the increased pressure to modulate one's exterior in the "age of the mirror" and what Norbert Elias called the "civilizing process." These discussions could be framed in terms of strategy and self-interest; it is wise to be guarded in showing one's emotions. However, at the time, such a discussion would rather have been articulated in terms of dignity and decorum. In other words, it is not about which strategy the individual adopts to attain a particular end, but rather which ethos to embody. This is very much the case for comportment manuals, which present a positive version of this message, formulated as an ideal to which readers should adhere. And even more so for the negative, critical version of the message, when laughter and ridicule sanction the break of decorum, as in comedy.[58] Obviously,

58. This is the sense in which comedy is a "public mirror"; cf. Norman, *The Public Mirror*.

these considerations will have a bearing on the actual human bodies depicted in painting, once those portrayed are no longer men in the abstract but men and women in socially situated scenes. Indeed, this will *always* be the case, since the demands of behaving in accordance with one's dignity is always there. Hence the appearance of passages like the following, again from Félibien:

Car il est certain que la colère paraît autrement exprimée sur le visage d'un honnête homme, que sur celui d'un paysan; qu'une Reine s'afflige d'une autre manière qu'une villageoise; [...] la douleur des personnes de condition et d'esprit, n'est jamais accompagnée de messéance et de trop d'emportement.[59]

(For it is certain that anger appears differently expressed on the face of a gentleman than on the face of a farmer; that the distress of a Queen is expressed differently than that of a woman from a village; [...] the pain of persons of condition and of spirit is never accompanied by impropriety and too violent outbursts.)

Therefore, the problem of how to represent the highest dignity (the distress of a queen, or even higher: the emotions of an absolute king) accentuates the need for another procedure beyond the mere soul-body correspondence outlined by Le Brun in his 1668 lecture. Put bluntly, Le Brun's typological vocabulary is radically unable to express the impassive king's lack of expression. Hence the tendency to resort to Ripa and Baudoin's allegorical vocabulary, as alluded to above. This was, in other words, a pictorial language that preexisted Le Brun, who gave it his own inflection.[60] Although the paintings in the vault of the Grande Galerie at Versailles are the fullest expression of this allegorical language under absolutism, it was deployed by Le Brun from early on in the personal reign of Louis XIV. The following passage from Félibien's book *Le portrait du Roi* from 1663 describes a now-lost painting

59. Félibien, *Entretiens*, 2:345–46.

60. See Virginie Bar's description in the conclusion of her important *La peinture allégorique au Grand siècle*, 378: "L'usage du vocabulaire allégorique est original chez cet artiste [Le Brun] et oscille entre les allégories dont la compréhension nécessite simplement de consulter les livres de Ripa et Baudoin, et les figures bien plus complexes qu'il faut analyser beaucoup plus longuement." (In this artist [Le Brun], the use of allegorical vocabulary is original and oscillates between allegories whose comprehension simply requires the consultation of Ripa's and Baudoin's books, and much more complex figures that must be analyzed at much more length.)

of a young Louis XIV by Le Brun, singling out the presence of three allegorical figures:

> L'on juge assez que ces trois figures représentent l'Abondance, la Renom-
> mée, et la Victoire. Et parce que les plus grands peintres, aussi bien que les
> philosophes les plus savants, cachent souvent leur science, et la hauteur
> de leurs pensées sous des formes et des figures mystérieuses, lors qu'ils
> traitent des sujets extraordinaires et relevez: c'est aussi sous le voile de
> ces figures que le peintre a caché les grandes choses qu'il a eu dessein de
> représenter.[61]

> (One judges well enough that these three figures represent Abundance,
> Fame, and Victory. And because the greatest painters, as well as the wisest
> philosophers, often hide their science and the loftiness of their thoughts
> under mysterious forms and figures when they treat extraordinary and el-
> evated matters: it is also under the veil of these figures that the painter has
> hidden the great things that he had planned [a eu dessein] to represent.)

Elsewhere in the same text, Félibien states that "la beauté du corps [est] comme une marque de celle de l'âme," "une lumière qui provient de la beauté de l'âme" (the beauty of the body is like a mark of the beauty of the soul, a light which originates in the beauty of the soul),[62] but it is as if the royal body were overdetermined, having too many great and beauti-ful qualities to express, hence the need to portray it on a wider canvas. The mysterious figures of allegory seem necessary to convey the greatest things, which in this case is the point of intersection between the *dessein* of the painter and those of the king. Here, I claim, lies the political foundation for what Virginie Bar has called "the supremacy of the allegorical genre."[63]

The same reference to the "mysterious figures" of allegory reappears from Félibien's pen twenty years later, contemporary with the decora-tion of the Hall of Mirrors. As we saw in the introduction, *The Dream of Philomathe* stages a *paragone* between painting and poetry about the pre-ponderance of the two disciplines. Early in this exchange, the allegorical personification of painting asks her rival:

> Ne pouviez-vous pas employer vos talents d'une autre manière, sans vou-
> loir m'ôter la gloire que j'acquiers par l'excellence de mes Tableaux, et

61. Félibien, *Le portrait du Roi*, 76–77.
62. Félibien, 86, 87.
63. Bar, *La peinture allégorique au Grand siècle*, 15–16.

particulièrement dans ceux, où sous des figures mystérieuses je tâche à donner quelque idée de l'âme de ce grand Monarque?[64]

(Could you not put your talents to work in another manner, without wishing to deprive me of the glory that I acquire through the excellence of my Paintings, and particularly in those where, under the guise of mysterious figures, I endeavor to give some idea of the soul of this great Monarch?)

This passage echoes the circulation of glory evoked by Louis XIV himself in his statement to the Petite Académie, discussed in the introduction (22–23). The artist acquires his glory—as if by reflection—through the successful rendition of that of the king. However, the challenge here is of a different magnitude. For whereas the writers addressed by the king were to represent his glory through his glorious exploits (backed by the king's confidence that they would do marvels by giving form to the subject matter he provided), here the task is nothing less than the portrayal of his radically unavailable, glorious soul. The reason painting still prevails is its recourse to allegory: the monarch is so great that his soul can only be represented under the veil of mysterious, allegorical figures. Interestingly, a very similar justification of the allegorical mode appears in the opening lines of the *explication* of Le Brun's decorative program in the Hall of Mirrors quoted from above and which was possibly penned by Le Brun himself:

L'allégorie est la manière la plus ancienne d'exprimer les pensées par des caractères. Les lettres n'ont été en usage que longtemps après que les Égyptiens eurent, par des figures, laissé à la postérité les mystères de leur religion et les lois de leur État. [...] [C]ette science a été en usage de tout temps, principalement parmi les peintres et les sculpteurs, qui n'ont d'autres langages pour se faire entendre dans leurs ouvrages. [...] [Dans la Galerie de Versailles, pour] exprimer les différents mouvements qui ont fait agir ce Prince [Louis XIV] et les ennemis qui se sont opposés à ses desseins, il [Le Brun] ne s'est servi que des divinités qui nous sont les plus connues et qu'il a accompagnées de toutes les marques propres à les distinguer.[65]

(Allegory is the oldest way to express thoughts through characters. Letters were only in use long after the Egyptians had left, through figures, the

64. Félibien, *Le songe de Philomathe*, 469.
65. "Explication de la Galerie de Versailles," in *Mercure galant*, December 1684; quoted here from *Les fastes de la Galerie des Glaces*, 36–38.

mysteries of their religion and the laws of their State for posterity.[. . .]
[T]his science has been in use since the dawn of time, primarily among
painters and sculptors who do not have other languages with which they
can make themselves understood in their works. [. . .] [In the Gallery of
Versailles, in order to] express the different movements that made this
Prince [Louis XIV] and the enemies who were opposed to his plans act,
he [Le Brun] only made use of the divinities that are the most well-known
to us and that he accompanied with all of the signs suitable for distinguishing them.)

It is very difficult today to gauge the efficacy of such an attempt at portraying the movements of the king's soul without the mediation of the
body. Importantly, the emphasis on antiquity, primordiality, and mystery
in the last quotation is not at all gratuitous. The mystery of the allegorical
figures was a cipher meant to confer an aura of elevation, if not sacred-
ness, to the symbolic expression: a possible opening toward another level
of reality and thus tributary to the same verticality that the architecture
of the gallery imposes on its visitors.

However, this signifying force was under pressure in the seventeenth
century, and increasingly so at the moment of the construction of the
Grande Galerie at Versailles. From 1687 onward, it would be at the heart
of the *Querelle* between the Ancients and the Moderns. In retrospect,
many of the discussions regarding the decoration of the gallery at Versailles were already pointing forward to the *Querelle*, where the question
about how to best praise the king took on an urgency (still understudied)
for the two sides, as I shall argue in chapter 3. Against this backdrop, it is
not surprising that the accessibility of the gallery's message would wane
surprisingly fast in the following decades and, more importantly still, that
interest in its decorative program would fade. And yet, for the discussion
here, the powerful testimony given to Le Brun's painting by the one beholder who mattered, the king himself, is sufficient: "Mr. Le Brun, you
have made me see things that I felt."

But this makes it necessary to dwell one last time on the exact meaning of the verbal expression "make me see." Whereas the scene portrayed
in the painting displays "Minerva mak[ing] the king see all the miseries
of war," according to the original Latin inscription quoted above (121),
the communication was a bit less immediate in the scene *underneath* the
painting. At first glance, the mysterious figures veil the meaning of the
painting, for those not familiar with their allegorical signification. Nivelon's brief description is very explicit on this point, as mentioned earlier:
"This royal and secret council [that is, the scene represented in the paint-

ing], characterized in this way [that is, through Le Brun's verbal descrip-
tion], made the king declare . . ." It is thus a bit of an oversimplification to
state, as I did earlier, that the king is moved by the painting. Without the
painter's interpretative contribution, the allegorical meaning of the painting may even have remained hidden from the king. The emotional effect
is produced by the image and the words together.

But which effect exactly?

Nivelon's anecdote hints at a three-step process. First, at the historical
moment when the scene represented in the painting took place, during
the king's solitary deliberations before his decision to go to war with the
Dutch, the king felt a secret, isolated, confused, shapeless emotion (to use
the same words as the *Mercure galant* article quoted above). He may even
have reflected upon it, but his reflections and feelings remained secret;
his experience at that moment was unexpressed, and therefore situated at
the level of interiority. His will was certainly informed (namely, by God),
but it remained without any external form beyond the decision itself.
Then, twelve years later, looking up at the painting while listening to Le
Brun's words, the king sees himself deliberating, sees himself feeling, and
it is through the representation of this royal secret, finally seeing himself
from the outside—*now* seeing "things that [he] felt," "the different movements which made [him] act"[66] back *then*—that he comes to perceive his
body politic, and it is in this way that the experience becomes the experience of Louis le Grand, who coincides with his action, in a moment that
retrospectively establishes once and for all the sublime origin of absolutism, not only for the king's subjects but even for the king himself.

Finally, immediately afterward, the anecdote articulates this dual
consciousness when the king voices it to Le Brun, thereby leaving the
sole trace of this royal public emotion, an emotion captured in this story
about the king who was touched, the king who, in turn, quite literally
touches the painter. The anecdote thus both highlights the agency of the
king and also that of his painter: he who holds the *mirror* enabling the
king's sublime recognition—the recognition of himself as king.

If indeed the use of the word "mirror" is warranted here, I must further consider the status and function of this mirror. First of all, the royal
mirror in the vault of the Grande Galerie has a very different function
from the mirroring explored by Elias, with his focus on the social dynamics in court society (see 98–100). Whether that mirroring is actually

---

66. Expressed first with the words from Nivelon's anecdote ("[les] choses qu'[il a]
ressenties"), and then with the words from the quotation from the *Mercure galant*
above ("les différents mouvements qui [l']ont fait agir").

reflective (through the surface of the actual mirrors on the wall) or rather reciprocal (passing through the gaze of another person), it is always inter-subjective, serving to confirm the viewer's place in a sociopolitical space as well as in a preestablished hierarchy. Social mirroring is, however, not horizontal, given the extent to which it is driven by aspirational energies while ultimately serving to enforce a hierarchy, but its signifying struc-ture is certainly not vertical in the way discussed above in relation to the architecture of the gallery (see 115–16).

Furthermore, this royal mirror is different from that of the "mirror for princes" tradition in that the prescriptive or aspirational element seems entirely absent. This does not mean, of course, that the project is purely descriptive or realistic in any modern sense. Nor does it mean that Le Brun's royal mirror does away with the celebration of princely virtue that comes with the genre or with "halls of princely virtue" in general.[67] How-ever, Le Brun's direct rendition of the king's actions, accentuated by the almost exclusive focus on him and his emotions, radically displaces the function of the gallery, both for the king himself and for a larger public. Just like an actual mirror, itself a prosthesis that allows individuals to see beyond the limits of their natural constitution (e.g., their own appear-ance or what is behind them), the royal mirror in the vault of the gallery is a prosthesis that brings forth a visual record not only of past exploits but also of the hitherto radically unavailable origin of these royal acts, an enormous archive of what the king achieved and what he felt at different crucial moments of his early personal reign. In the process, a subtle shift is taking place, from the traditional focus on heroic outcome and victory (which is still emphasized but no longer as the epitome of kingship) to inception, decision, and deliberation, as in the painting under consid-eration here. The vault is a mirror of absolutism precisely in the sense that the king sees a reflection—*not* of a record of his dynastic legitimacy (which is entirely absent) but of the most sublime expressions of his soul during the most crucial decisions of his reign.

However, the success of this enterprise urgently hinges on the efficacy of the allegorical language. The gallery is designed not only to please and to instruct, but also to move. The anecdote therefore bears witness to an exemplary success: the *sublimity* of the moment portrayed is reflected in the mirror held up to the king and then confirmed by the king's reaction

---

67. For the latter notion, see Brown and Elliott, "The Hall of Princely Virtue"; and Berger's extension of it to the case of the Versailles gallery in "Galerie des Glaces," 91n18.

below the painting, in awe, with his mouth half-open, contemplating the origin of absolutism.

So, what is the status of the mirror and mirroring in this process? The question brings me back to the dynamics that Félibien highlighted in *Le portrait du Roi*, where the author characterizes Le Brun's portrait of the young Louis XIV as "une glace très pure" (a very pure mirror), a mirror where the painter, according to the words Félibien addresses to the king himself, "représente [. . .] toutes ces hautes qualités qui vous font aimer de vos sujets, craindre de vos ennemis et admirer de tout le monde" (represents [. . .] all these high qualities which make you loved by your subjects, feared by your enemies and admired by everybody).[68] As Louis Marin suggests in his influential reading of Félibien's book in a book with the same name, *Portrait of the King*, the function of this mirror (on the one hand, Le Brun's painting and, on the other, Félibien's description) in regard to the king is "[to] produce him or reproduce him—once more—as absolute monarch."[69]

However, the "very pure mirror" evoked by Félibien is first and foremost a private mirror reserved for the king. The situation is obviously not exactly identical to that of the Grande Galerie, which is, after all, much more than the king's exclusive mirror of absolutism. And yet, in the middle of this grand public mirror, there is, within the painting, a mirror that could qualify as "private," since it is only visible to the king. This private mirror is in fact situated at the exact symbolic center of the gallery, which is also the symbolic center of Versailles, and from our modern perspective, the symbolic center of classical France. I now turn to this scene.

5. A Mirror for One

The exuberant iconographic project in the Grande Galerie tells a story about self-origin. Importantly, this story does not incorporate the actual mirrors adorning the east wall of the gallery in any obvious way. The many guides to the gallery written in the first few years after its opening all stress the importance of the central painting (plate 1) instead of dwelling on the wonder of the mirrors. According to the modern French historian Joël Cornette, this painting constitutes a "unique document" in

68. Félibien, *Le portrait du Roi*, 87.
69. Marin, *Portrait of the King*, 212; translation modified. The original runs as follows: "le produire ou le reproduire—une fois de plus—comme monarque absolu." Félibien, *Le portrait du roi*, 259.

that it gives access to "the image the king had of himself, the nature of his power and of his action."[70] But such an assessment, relying on an implicit mirroring scene (the king seeing an image of himself), is not a modern invention, but, as I argue here, discreetly inscribed in the painting itself, in a way that connects specularity and self-origin.

Pierre Rainssant, who as a member of the Petite Académie wrote an official description of the gallery in 1687, most clearly emphasizes the painting's position among all the paintings in the gallery as the origin of the king's story. This is a painting "qu'on doit regarder comme le premier, puisqu'il renferme ce qui a été, pour ainsi dire, l'origine de toutes les belles actions, qui sont représentées dans les autres" (that should be considered as the first, since it contains what was, as it were, the origin of all the beautiful actions that are represented in the others).[71] As stated above, Le Brun conceived this painting first, after the Conseil d'en haut rejected the earlier plan narrating the king's exploits under the guise of Hercules, and it was its approval by the king and the royal Council that earned him the green light to pursue the project for the whole gallery.[72] Therefore, it not only represents the first originary *dessein* of the king, but also, on a very different level, that of the king's first painter. The architectural use of space further highlights its centrality: facing the king's private apartment, it was here the king would enter the gallery after his regular morning work session with his ministers, each time a new beginning, not from one of the two ends of the gallery, but from its exact center under this representation of the origin of absolutism.[73]

Today the central painting famously carries the inscription "Le Roi gouverne par lui-même, 1661" (The King governs on his own, 1661). It invites us to identify a state of affairs in the painting: absolutism as it was inaugurated in 1661. But this inscription is an eighteenth-century revision. The earlier inscriptions contemporary with the construction of the gallery, including the long-lost original Latin inscription, have a radically

70. "[Un] document unique, l'image que se faisait le roi de lui-même, de la nature de son pouvoir et de son action." Cornette, *Le roi de guerre*, 243.

71. Rainssant, *Explication des tableaux de la galerie de Versailles*, 2.

72. According to Nivelon, "M. Le Brun [. . .] produisit le premier dessin de ce grand ouvrage, qui est le tableau du milieu, qui fait le nœud principal de tout. Sur lequel lui fut ordonné d'en continuer la suite sur ces mêmes principes." (Mr. Le Brun [. . .] produced the first drawing of this great work, which is the middle painting, which constitutes the nodal point of it all. Based on which he was ordered to continue following these same principles). Nivelon, *Vie de Charles le Brun*, 487.

73. See Sabatier, *Versailles ou la disgrâce d'Apollon*, 135–36.

different emphasis, inviting us rather to see the foundational moment stressed by Rainssant.

So what exactly do visitors to the Versailles gallery see?

Looking up, one will see a large painting, which at first glance may seem quite crowded. The online iconographic catalogue identifies no less than twenty-one figures or groups of figures in the composition of this painting, while the painting discussed in the previous section only has eight.[74] The king can still be recognized easily; symmetry and light draw the gaze toward his central position. A more informed person (benefiting perhaps from one of the many guidebooks, if not from the assistance of Le Brun himself) will notice that among all these figures, the king is the only mortal. He is seated in front of the Three Graces (evoking the graces of his personality), and by his feet an allegory of tranquility (evoking the peace of the land) and a group of putti (representing the various diversions of court life) are seated. However, the king's own gesture and gaze suggest that the essential components lie elsewhere. To the immediate right of the king sits Minerva in her helmet and, following the direction of her gesture, are first an ironclad Mars on the clouds and, further up still, an allegory of glory holding up a crown of stars and the royal scepter for the king to reach toward.

This orientation seems to be contradicted by the present inscription under the painting, which draws our attention back to the right hand of the king: "Le Roi gouverne par lui-même, 1661" here symbolized by the hand firmly holding the helm of the state. However, Tallemant's original Latin inscription gives a richer account of what the painting is about—and perhaps also of what absolutism is all about. The inscription is tripartite, describing a movement at once upward and from left to right in the painting (a movement that is temporal as well as conceptual): "INTER PACIS ET FORTUNÆ FLORENTIS ILLECEBRAS / LUDOVICUS MAGNUS AD GUBERNACULA IMPERII ACCEDENS / GLORIÆ AMORE INCENDITUR" (Amidst the charms that peace and favorable fortune offer him / The king taking the government of his state / He is burning with love for glory).[75]

---

74. See http://www.galeriedesglaces-versailles.fr/html/11/collection/c17.html and http://www.galeriedesglaces-versailles.fr/html/11/collection/c21.html, respectively.

75. Bjørnstad, "'Plus d'éclaircissement touchant la grande galerie de Versailles,'" 336–38. My English translation is made with an eye to Tallemant's own translation into French ("Parmi les charmes que lui offrent la paix et la fortune favorable. / Le Roi prenant le gouvernement de son État / Il est épris de l'amour de la gloire"). See 121n43 for further details and references regarding the early history of the inscriptions.

It is important to realize the way in which the core of the painting is conceived in Latin: what we see is a king who takes power (government, *gubernaculum*), represented by the helm (also *gubernaculum*), two layers of meaning elegantly captured by one Latin noun. Where the sentence "Le Roi gouverne par lui-même" describes a state that lasts, Tallemant's inscription evokes a transition, a beginning, a point of origin; an actual *prise de pouvoir*, as in the title of Roberto Rossellini's 1966 film describing the same event (*La prise de pouvoir de Louis XIV*; English title: *The Taking of Power by Louis XIV*).

It is worth pausing for a moment here to stress that this idea of Louis XIV's dramatic seizing of power after Mazarin's death in March 1661 as an absolute and originary foundation of the greatness to come is itself a myth, a constitutive part of the dream of absolutism, cultivated in the stories the king told himself and his successor (in his *Mémoires*; see 57–59, 75–76) and to the world (as seen in the Hall of Mirrors). The story seemingly has a solid textual foundation in the *Mémoires* of Louis-Henri de Loménie, Comte de Brienne and secretary of state at the time, reporting from the dramatic March 9 meeting where the king announced his surprising decision, and on which modern retellings of the story tend to rely closely (as is the case for Rossellini). However, Brienne wrote this account much later, well after the decoration of the Hall of Mirrors, which means that rather than merely documenting the event, it was itself shaped by the myth. Brienne's own administrative record written shortly after the March 9 meeting is much more sober and matter-of-fact, without reference to any drastic announcement. Rather than a radical rupture, the scholarship suggests, what happened in 1661 was more of a reorganization, based on models and examples from the recent past.[76] What viewers encounter in the painting is therefore an origin of absolutism constructed *retrospectively*—as is often the case for points of origin.

The central painting contains another important retrospective pro-

---

76. In the words of Jérôme Janczukiewicz, "il n'y a pas trace d'annonce fracassante de la part du roi" (there is no trace of a sensational announcement from the king); hence the conclusion: "Tout cela apparaît plus comme une réorganisation [. . .] que comme une réforme véritable entraînant une rupture politique car le roi s'inspire de modèles et d'exemples donnés par les règnes précédents." (All of this seems more like a reorganization [. . .] than a true reform leading to a political rupture, for the king draws inspiration from models and examples given from previous reigns.) Janczukiewicz, "La prise du pouvoir par Louis XIV," 250, 263. Same position in Burke, *The Fabrication of Louis XIV* (in the section "The Myth of Personal Rule," 61–64); and in Chaline, *Le règne de Louis XIV*, 1:78–80. See also Dessert, *Louis XIV prend le pouvoir*.

jection. As I indicated earlier, the year 1661 was a period of relative calm, shortly after the Peace of the Pyrenees and the marriage between Louis XIV and his Spanish cousin, Maria Theresa. The lower left part of the painting evokes both the peace and the royal wedding, by an olive branch held in the right hand of the allegory of France (seated in the lower left-hand corner) and by Hymen (to the right of France), respectively. However, in 1661, "the charms that peace and favorable fortune offer" the king, according to the Latin inscription, are already counterbalanced by menacing signs from France's old enemies. The portrayal of the king seizing the helm of the state in 1661 is complemented on the opposite side of the vault by a representation of France's vainglorious neighboring powers—Germany, Spain, and Holland—harboring arrogant plans (*desseins*) that soon enough will provide the king with the occasion to display glorious exploits on the battlefield in a just war that France's enemies will have brought upon themselves (plate 7).[77]

Therefore, the conjuncture of "peace and favorable fortune" at this decisive juncture in 1661 not only offers the king its "charms" but also an occasion for him to engage in the pursuit of glory. In this painting, both Mars and Minerva encourage the king in this endeavor by visually prolonging the gesture of the king's left hand and directing both the king and the beholder toward the personification of glory on the cloud. These two allegorical figures reappear throughout the gallery as the principal qualities of the king's character—courage and wisdom—and thereby also represent the two sides of government: hard and soft power. In the painting discussed above, *Résolution prise de faire la guerre aux Hollandais, 1671* (plate 2), showing the king's decision to go to war with the Dutch, the two deities weigh on opposite sides of the balance. Here, however, they are in total agreement in their message to the king, suggesting that the king will need

---

77. According to Pierre Rainssant: "Dans l'autre partie du tableau l'on voit l'Allemagne, l'Espagne et la Hollande peintes sous la figure de trois femmes superbement vêtues, et avec une contenance fière et audacieuse, pour montrer l'orgueil et les desseins ambitieux de ces trois puissances voisines de la France." (In the other part of the picture we see Germany, Spain and Holland painted in the figure of three women haughtily dressed, and with a proud and audacious countenance, to show the vainglory and the arrogant plans [*desseins*] of these three neighboring powers of France.) Rainssant, *Explication des tableaux de la galerie de Versailles*, 6. Rather than the neighboring countries already scheming to bring down France, the early 1660s were marked by diplomatic incidents through which France and the young king sought the "symbolic assertion of the superiority of the French monarch." Burke, *The Fabrication of Louis XIV*, 64–65. Needless to say, these incidents are also commemorated in the vault of the Grande Galerie.

both wisdom and courage to reach glory.[78] It is significant that Minerva is closest to the king and his sublime decision: far from being motivated by the belligerent disposition of a young man wanting to prove himself, the pursuit of glory is the manifestation of his sovereign prudence.

Returning now to the representation of the king's body in the central painting, viewers encounter the same issues regarding royal expressivity and impassiveness as in section 4. To what extent is the crucial fact that the king is "burning with the love for glory" (as stated by the original Latin inscription) visible or legible in the painting? As discussed above, the general movement from the lower left to the upper right corner expresses this passion, accentuated by both the gesture and the gaze of the king himself. His attention is directed elsewhere than the court and even the helm of state. His absolutist intentions are being reshaped in this very moment. But is this fervor expressed on the king's face? Based on Le Brun's key to the expressions of the passions (see 125–27), the king's expression should be easily legible (see plates 3 and 4). However, the king's face in the painting undermines this simple decoding: his mouth, for example, is impassively closed, whereas the two drawings representing the expression of "L'amour simple" (simple love)[79] and of "Le désir" (desire) both suggest otherwise. Rather than love or desire, his facial expression seems closer to that of tranquility (plate 5).

This is of course not surprising in light of my earlier discussion concerning the expression of royal emotions. The king's face remains impassive and majestic, as a royal face had to be at all times. However, such a reading of the way in which the king's face appears in this painting seems to directly contradict how Rainssant describes it in the official *explication*:

[L]'on remarque [. . .] sur son visage et dans toute son action la noble ardeur dont il est transporté à l'aspect de la Gloire, qui se présente à lui dans le ciel.[80]

(One notices [. . .] on his face and in all his action the noble ardor by which he is carried away at the sight of Glory, which appears to him in the heavens.)

---

78. In the words of Rainssant, together Mars and Minerva "font entendre qu'elle [la Gloire] ne peut être le prix que de sa sagesse et de son courage" (make it understood that Glory can only be the reward of his wisdom and his courage). Rainssant, *Explication des tableaux de la galerie de Versailles*, 5.

79. According to Le Brun's taxonomy, love is either simple or composite.

80. Rainssant, *Explication des tableaux de la galerie de Versailles*, 4.

The king's noble passion certainly leads to "all his action" in the painting, but is it also expressed on his face? How would that be possible without contradicting his royal dignity? And why can viewers not see what Rainssant claims is there, when Le Brun's own taxonomy tells them exactly what to look for? This apparent paradox allows me to draw one last conclusion that furthers my argument about the function of allegory in the decorative program in the Hall of Mirrors. Once viewers can decode them, the group of allegorical figures not only tell a wider story, but they underscore the only non-allegorical element of the painting—namely, the king. Or better yet: through the allegory, the painting teaches viewers (including the king) what to see. As such, portraiture is non-allegorical; portraits communicate through similarity, not the otherness (*allos*) of allegory. Therefore, within the wider canvas whose only function is to fill in what the king's face cannot express, the royal face *both is and is not* expressive; it *both is and is not* a mirror of the king's soul. This is exactly the insight that made the king proclaim: "You have made me see things that I felt"—seeing now from the outside, from outside himself, what he had only felt on the inside back then.

In such an interpretation (and, I would add, in *any* interpretation making a serious attempt at deciding what the allegorical framework adds to the portrait of the absolutist king), the representation of the royal body becomes an overdetermined locus for visualizing and embodying what this new brand of absolutism is all about. Importantly, this painting is *not* propaganda, except in the etymological sense of "what should be propagated," and conflating royal panegyrics and propaganda risks obfuscating an understanding of the gallery's decorative program. The gallery is not making a claim to dynastic legitimacy but rather confirming a God-given right, propagated through a collective dream of magnificence and glory. Within this framework, it becomes all the more important to observe both what the official depiction of the originary moment of absolutism at the center of the Hall of Mirrors highlights and what it obfuscates.

I have already studied in detail the representation of the royal body, quite literally stretched between present government (his right hand on the helm) and future glory (the allegorical figure his other hand points to). What is entirely absent in this constellation in particular and from the gallery in general is any reference to the past: not only to Louis XIV's dynastic predecessors, starting with his father and grandfather (his grandfather, Henry IV, at the time was himself known as Henry the Great), and to the ancient roots of his dynastic line (including Charlemagne, literally Charles the Great), but even to *any* example from the past. The paintings are certainly hiding this absence through the way they dress up both abstract concepts and the king himself: the latter in Roman garb and the former as allegories from Roman mythology. But there is no reference to any person, event, or example predating 1661. Even the Roman deities are only there to better express the king's own inherent virtues. And the king's Roman outfit serves to locate him outside time rather than in a remote past. What the painting depicts is a moment of royal self-creation. This is the exact sense in which, as the French historian François Hartog has poignantly expressed in a different context, "absolutism is a presentism."[81] Neither absolutism nor the mirror have any past. It is not without interest to point out that as a palindrome, "1661" is a (nearly) perfect mirror number, closed onto itself, as if its own origin. Similarly, the self-image of the absolutist king on display in the Grande Galerie is as self-enclosed, flat, and devoid of historical depth as the surface of the mirror.

The logic of the mirror is everywhere in this central painting, ensconcing the representation of an actual mirror. To the right of the king's body suspended between government and glory, Louis's face is reflected in the shield of Minerva. Unlike the mirrors that give the gallery its modern name, this mirror is hidden in at least two different ways: first, within the painting, where it is visible only to the king and none of the other figures; second, because scholars have ignored it in interpretations of the gallery. However, the mirror is *not* hidden from the visitor of the gallery, but, on the contrary, clearly visible from the ground.[82] The lack of attention given to this mirror at the center of what Cornette calls "the image the king had of himself" is perhaps due to the fact that it was nearly imperceptible until the gallery's recent renovations. Two contemporary descriptions of the gallery, however, mention the mirror. First, the official description by Rainssant reminds us of Minerva's meaning: "Minerve, c'est-à-dire la Prudence, est à côté du trône avec son bouclier de cristal, où réfléchit l'image de ce Prince."[83] (Minerve, that is to say Prudence, is next to the Throne with her crystal shield, which reflects the image of this Prince.) Second, Claude Nivelon's description of the gallery provides the most extensive account of the mirror:

81. Hartog, *Anciens, modernes, sauvages*, 259. I will discuss Hartog's assertion in more depth in chapter 3 (158, 169–70).

82. After the recent restorations, this is also the case for the details I am commenting on in what follows.

83. Rainssant, *Explication des tableaux de la galerie de Versailles*, 4–5.

Minerve est représentée un peu assise sur un nuage, au côté du prince, tenant un bouclier luisant qui en reçoit l'image pour signifier que la Prudence royale, réfléchissant sur les sujets dignes des grands rois, a toujours eu la gloire en vue.[84]

(Minerva is represented lightly seated on a cloud, beside the prince, holding a shiny shield receiving his image in order to signify that royal Prudence, reflecting on topics worthy of great kings, has always had glory in sight.)

Although Nivelon claims to decode the mirror's meaning—stating that it is there "in order to signify that . . ."—its signification is in no way fully exhausted. Visual reflection does certainly evoke intellectual reflection, especially when it is the divinity of prudence and wisdom who is holding the mirror. It seems, however, that Nivelon's sentence slightly displaces the object of the king's reflection, which is less "topics [sujets] worthy of great kings" in general than one specific and very worthy subject: the king himself. If the shield that Minerva presents to the king "receives his image" ("en reçoit l'image"), as stated by Nivelon, isn't it rather in order to signify the sovereign's prudent introspection?

Through this question I am adopting the perspective of one of the only two commentaries I have been able to identify in modern scholarship that venture beyond a mere repetition of the brief descriptions quoted above. In the wonderful online iconographic catalogue of the gallery, Nicolas Milovanovic ends his description of the figure of Minerva in the central painting with the following observation:

It should be noted that the face of the king is reflected in Minerva's shield: it is a very competent evocation of Prudence, whose main symbol is the mirror, for the prudent man observes himself in order to know himself well, according to the precept adopted by Socrates and which was inscribed on the front of the temple of Apollo in Delphi: Know thy-self.[85]

---

84. Nivelon, *Vie de Charles le Brun*, 492.

85. "Il faut remarquer que le visage du souverain se réfléchit dans le bouclier de Minerve: c'est une très habile évocation de la Prudence dont le symbole principal est le miroir, car le prudent s'observe pour bien se connaître selon le précepte adopté par Socrate, et qui était inscrit au fronton du temple d'Apollon à Delphes: 'Connais-toi toi-même.'" Milovanovic, *Versailles, la galerie des Glaces*.

The only other substantial commentary on this motif by a modern scholar appears in a recent article by Sandra Bazin-Henry on Le Brun's mirror décors. After following Milovanovic's interpretation closely, Bazin-Henry ends on a more speculative note, with the following intriguing question that ventures far beyond the perspective in the period descriptions mentioned above:

> But this shield transformed into a mirror, which shows the reflection of the king's portrait, is it not also symbolic of the décor of the walls of Louis XIV's gallery, all adorned with mirrors, which the king traversed every day and in which the reflection of his person was offered in its entirety? [...] From the hidden mirror, painted in the central compartment of the vault, to the real and ostentatious ones of the mural decoration, there is perhaps a subtle dialogue set up by Le Brun between painting and mirror, where each staged the image of the king.[86]

Surprisingly, this suggestion of a "dialogue between mirrors and paintings" (which is also the title of the last part of the article where Bazin-Henry makes this case: "Dialogue entre glaces et peintures") is the *only* serious attempt at integrating the physical mirrors into an interpretation of the paintings that I have come across. And these observations are all the more important in the context of her discussion, which demonstrates the extent to which Le Brun himself had been involved in the design of mirror décors in the decades before the Hall of Mirrors was constructed.[87] However, although the quoted passage presents a rich and promising intuition, the author is quite timid in the way she pursues it. For what would the implications of this discreet connection between the shield and the actual mirrors be? Does it only conceal a self-conscious (if not self-congratulatory) nod by the painter, or is there an inherent claim about representation and kingship being made here? Bazin-Henry seems to be opting for the latter, by emphasizing the dual "m[ise] en scène [de] l'image du roi" (stag[ing of] the image of the king), but without actually pursuing

---

86. "Mais ce bouclier transformé en miroir, qui montre le reflet du portrait du roi, n'est-il pas également symbolique du décor mural de la galerie de Louis XIV, tout ornée de miroirs, que le roi traversait chaque jour et dans laquelle s'offrait tout entier le reflet de sa personne? [...] Du miroir caché, peint dans le compartiment central de la voûte, à ceux véritables et ostentatoires du décor mural, il y a peut-être là un dialogue subtil mis en place par Le Brun entre la peinture et le miroir, où chacun mettait en scène l'image du roi." Bazin-Henry, "Charles Le Brun et les décors de miroirs," para. 29.

87. See the earlier part of Bazin-Henry's article, as discussed above (100).

this insight. Upon further reflection, one might also wonder whether the passage really points to a "subtle dialogue" rather than establishing a one-way relation from the hidden painted mirror to the wall mirrors, where the former is "symbolic" of the latter. How do we know that the painted mirror is symbolic of the wall mirrors and not the other way around; or rather, that both are not part of the higher symbolism produced by the whole gallery? Bazin-Henry's proposition is certainly intriguing, but it can be explored more forcefully by situating the shield within the wider interpretation of the whole gallery that I propose here. For, as I argue below, if we approach the mirror within a framework that highlights the mirror quality of the whole decorative project, the shield will appear as a "mise-en-abîme"-like (or fractal-like) reflection that points to—or dialogues with—the other paintings as much as the actual mirrors.

However, before fully interpreting this hidden mirror scene at the core of the self-representation of French absolutism, there is one more aspect of the shield that merits attention: a crucial detail that, to my knowledge, has not received any attention in the scholarship. Actually, it is not exactly an aspect or detail of the shield itself, but rather of the relation between the reflection in the shield and the representation of the king next to the shield. Close visual scrutiny of this part of the painting reveals that even Milovanovic's and Bazin-Henry's descriptions are not totally exact (plate 6). Although Minerva's shield reflects the image of the king, as pointed out by Rainssant and Nivelon, this does not strictly imply that "the face of the king is reflected there [in the shield]," as stated by Milovanovic. Surprisingly, the shield does not present the king with a mirror image but with an image of himself with *another expression*, a face that clearly expresses the royal desire for glory, while the king's actual face, outside the mirror, remains impassive. The image of the king in the shield is the only royal face of the whole gallery that is not impassive and majestic, the only face filled with emotion. This point becomes visually quite striking in the juxtaposition of the detail in question with Le Brun's own mapping of the passions, with, on the one hand, simple love and desire, and, on the other, tranquility (see plates 3–6). In the painting in its present state, the image of the king on the shield is distinctly different from the face the shield reflects: the mouth is half-open instead of closed, the nose more prominent, the lips fuller, the forehead more prominent; in general, the traits of the reflected face seem less delicate and more virile, more passionate, even more carried away than those of the face outside the mirror.[88]

88. The analysis of the minute details of this painting based on what we see today needs to be done with care. As Alexandre Thuillier stresses, "This picture of *The King*

What does the singular presence of this emotional royal face mean? Why this division between the face and its reflection? And why here at the symbolic center of Versailles, itself decorated with the most impressive display of mirrors that humankind had ever seen? Taken together, these questions formulate the exact context inside which I turn to the wider question about the way the function of this mirror seems to reflect the function of the physical mirrors and the mirroring of the vault in general, but now with the added complexity of the dissimilarity captured in the hidden mirror scene at the heart of absolutism.

Before addressing these questions head-on, I would like to recall the mirror shield's symbolic density and iconographic richness, which is not necessarily exhausted by the quick decoding provided by the period descriptions and repeated by present-day commentators, who see it as nothing more than a mirror of prudence. First of all, the shield is obviously there as an allegorical object alongside all the other allegorical objects and figures surrounding the king, and a particularly important one at that, through its proximity to the focal point of the painting. As the shield of Minerva, it *is* a mirror of royal prudence. But the mirror is a liminal object that requires all the prudence the king can muster to keep it in check, connoting not only wisdom and prudence, but also its opposite: vanity. This surprising "Janus-like" quality of the mirror as allegorical object[89] should normally be controlled in the case of Minerva's shield, but the reflection's strange dissimilarity here opens up a wider range of significations, by drawing attention to the functioning of the allegory itself. Furthermore, in addition to serving as an allegory, the mirror shield is in an important sense the *opposite* of allegory. As a reflected image, the mirror is a symbol of faithful portraiture and, by extension of painting in

---

Governs for Himself is today difficult to judge. We know that towards the end of the 18th century it came partly loose from the vault and fell to the floor. It seems to have been frequently repainted. Despite its last particularly careful and sensitive restoration it has doubtless lost much of its prime freshness." Thuillier, "Charles Le Brun and the Hall of Mirrors," 27. However, although the precision of the facial details I mention above are open to discussion, the difference between the two faces seems incontestable. The preservation of the difference through successive restorations is in itself highly significant, since, in case of doubt, the obvious decision would have been to make the face on the shield an exact image of the one in front of the mirror. It is also worth observing that the passionate face is already depicted in the drawing that Jean-Baptiste Massé made of the painting *Le Roi gouverne par lui-même* (sometime between 1723 and 1731), although less so in the engraving based on this drawing (between 1731 and 1752) for the publication of his book *La Grande Galerie de Versailles*.

89. Frelick, *The Mirror in Medieval and Early Modern Culture*, 2.

general, working through similarity rather than difference. As such, its inclusion in this painting is a meta-reflective device that invites the beholder to ponder the kind of questions about the function of the gallery's decorative program addressed in this chapter. But if this is the case, what are the implications of the mirror reflection's seeming lack of faithfulness in this specific case? What does this peculiar mirror scene, the strange juxtaposition of two dissimilar royal faces at the symbolic center of Versailles, mean?

To present-day beholders, it may be tempting to see the distorted image of the king as a sign of subversion.[90] Within such an interpretation, the mirror shield would be the artist's secret critique of his patron, making visible, discreetly yet defiantly, that which should remain hidden. Whether the presumed content of this dark secret is related to despotism, lechery, vainglory, or another sovereign flaw, the identification hinges on the assumption that the shield functions as a mirror to the king's true soul, making visible the ugly decay of his body personal (so different from the splendor of his body politic), if not already his death mask. In a less lacerating version, the message would be a warning to the young king himself, a memento mori, in which case the truth of the mirror is at the same time an allegory of vanity. The distinction between warning and indictment might, however, be moot, since what were sins to be avoided in 1661 obviously were already sins of the past when Le Brun made the painting in the early 1680s. In any case, the mirror shield would be a receptacle for—or register of—the sins of absolutism, written into the reflection of the king's face; a hidden portrait of his true face; in other words, some version of the picture of Dorian Gray avant la lettre.

As attractive as such an interpretation may seem to us today, it is quite implausible for the period, for several reasons. First of all, it is important to notice that a major part of its attraction *for us* stems from an anachronistic idea about artistic authenticity: the Romantic conception of the great artist who, imprisoned in the official patronage system, suffers from a lack of liberty that prevents him from freely expressing his genius but has found a subtle way to voice his dissent. There is no reason to believe that the tension between complete artistic freedom, on the one hand, and official commissions, on the other, would have been lived at the time as the raw existential dilemma it could very well be for a post-Romantic artist seeking to express his genius. Paradoxically, then, the fact that we're

90. This paragraph, based on numerous discussions with colleagues and students of what *we* see in the painting, does not pretend to be exhaustive. It is a synthesis of the reactions of a large set of intrigued and interested modern beholders.

drawn to such an interpretation expresses our own discomfort about their lack of discomfort. The trajectory of Racine and Boileau is a case in point, given the ease (which, to us, seems conspicuous) with which they gave up on their own literary projects when they were promoted to official historiographers of the king. Le Brun, more than anybody else, would have known—and would have experienced—that artistic glory was to be found within the royal patronage system.[91] Now, this general argument obviously does not entirely preclude the inclusion of a secret subversive detail in this specific painting (for reasons other than the post-Romantic ones). However, the detail I have described is not *that* secret; after the recent restoration of the gallery, the dissimilarity between the two faces in our mirror scene is clearly visible from the ground for anyone who knows where to look. Therefore, it would be quite a surprising risk for the king's first painter to introduce this detail at the heart of the central painting in the Grande Galerie at Versailles (in what is certainly the politically, if not artistically, most important work of his career) in order to convey a secret subversive message regarding his royal patron. Le Brun's position became increasingly vulnerable toward the end of the period when the gallery was being constructed, even without the envoi of subversive messages. After the death of Colbert in 1683, his successor, Louvois, marginalized Le Brun in favor of his longtime rival Pierre Mignard, although Le Brun retained the king's support up to his death in 1690.

So what does the mirror shield show us, then? The shape and status of the shield give us a clue: on the one hand, it is not a flat surface, but a convex one, which produces a distorted image; on the other hand, it is Minerva's shield, connoting wisdom and prudence. The result is a distortion toward truth: royal desire is indeed real. As the painting's original Latin inscription reads: "gloriæ amore incenditur" (he is burning with love for glory). If this shield doesn't present a reflection of the king's real face, it does somehow present him with a face that is truer than the visible reality: the image in the shield shows him the royal passions ordinarily hidden under the serene appearance of his face. This recognition evokes the surprising sentence from Rainssant's official description of the gallery, which states, despite the visual evidence, that these emotions are visible on the king's face: "l'on remarque [...] sur son visage [...] la noble ardeur dont il est transporté" (one notices [...] on his face [...] the

91. See the introduction for a wider discussion of the modern inclination to reduce cultural expressions under absolutism to the dichotomy of subversive critique or empty propaganda.

noble ardor by which he is carried away).[92] As argued above (138–39), this statement pinpoints the collective work of all the allegorical figures and objects in the painting and their ambition to shape how viewers see the king, and particularly his face, which *both is and is not* expressive; *both is and is not* a mirror of his soul; is *both* the impassive face in the painting *and* the passionate reflection in the shield.

This mirror image thus runs counter to the speculum from the "mirror for princes" tradition: it is not an aspirational model for the king to emulate, but an image that is truer than the one his face presents to the world. The mirror of prudence presents the king with an image of his interiority, but the king doesn't really need it; he already is aware of it, as he is aware of the division between the mirror image and his face. Master of his passions as he is master of his face, Louis can turn his gaze away from the shield toward the object of his desire. The discrepancy in the painting between his face and its reflection is then a sign of the king's strength, not of weakness; it is yet another sign of his glorious mastery.

At the same time, the shield discreetly stresses the mastery of the painter. The private mirror constituted by the shield prefigures the king's encounter with the overall *œuvre* of the gallery. Within the painting, the shield of Minerva shows the king what art may bring him outside the painting. These paintings provide him with an image of things the king has felt (*choses que le roi a ressenties*), an image that in some way is truer than the visible reality.

This observation can be pushed one step further by taking into consideration the polyvalence of Minerva's shield from an iconographic point of view. For what appears here as a mirror of prudence serves elsewhere as a defensive weapon. Minerva is the Roman goddess who lent her shield to Perseus in order to contain and conquer the Gorgon Medusa. Interestingly, the absolutist artisans of glory explored this episode from ancient mythology in many different media. In Versailles alone, the motif of Perseus killing Medusa appears in several paintings and in a plan for a fountain. At the exact same time that Le Brun was in charge of the decoration of the Hall of Mirrors, two other key figures who shaped the cultural production of the time, Jean-Baptiste Lully and Philippe Quinault, were busy bringing the same episode to life on stage, in the opera *Persée*. In light of this fascination with the myth, it is perhaps not surprising that the iconography of the time normally shows the head of Medusa in Minerva's shield, rather than that of the sovereign, and this is also the case in

92. Rainssant, *Explication des tableaux de la galerie de Versailles*, 4.

FIGURE 10. Charles Le Brun, Study for *Le Roi gouverne par lui-même, 1661* (The King governs on his own, 1661) (ca. 1680). Black chalk, black China ink, wash with China ink, on paper. Château de Versailles, France. Photograph © RMN-Grand Palais / Art Resource, New York. Photograph: Gérard Blot.

many paintings in the Grande Galerie. For example, returning to *Résolution prise de faire la guerre aux Hollandais, 1671*, the shield is located in the open space in front of the king and Minerva, displaying the head of the Gorgon (plate 2).[93] Moreover, the shield's polyvalence was a factor even in the conception of the painting *Le Roi gouverne par lui-même, 1661*. An early sketch by Le Brun himself shows Minerva's shield at her side, representing the head of Medusa, instead of being directed toward the king as a mirror and representing the head of Louis (figure 10).

In the final version of the painting, the head of Medusa has a less prominent place; it is present on Minerva's brooch, but is so small that it's difficult to capture in reproductions. However, this iconographic proxim-

93. For two occurrences of the shield with the head of Medusa prominently displayed in battle scenes in the Grande Galerie, see *Le Passage du Rhin en présence des ennemis, 1672* and *La Franche-Comté conquise pour la seconde fois, 1674*.

ity of Medusa, even in the final version of the painting, adds a level of meaning to the shield. The presence of Medusa on the shield evokes a violent threat, but a threat that has been contained with Minerva's help. Therefore, in the Grande Galerie's immense exteriorization of the things the king had felt, the things he now knows, he is the master of his violent emotions, the master of his mortal body. In this way, the presence of Medusa only serves to highlight the king's prudence and valor. The painting thus recalls the final line of Giambattista Marino's famous poem in praise of the parade shield bearing Caravaggio's painting of the Medusa: "La vera Medusa è il valor vostro." (The real Medusa is your valor.) In this case, the real Medusa is the king's own valor. In the Hall of Mirrors, the weapon of this valor is deployed not only in the mirror of the king's soul on the painted ceiling, but also through the mirrors along the wall, through the mastery of new mirror technology. The hidden central mirror is visible only to the king, who doesn't need to look, because he already knows, because he already has seen, because he is not Narcissus enthralled by his image but Perseus who wields image-making for glory rather than vanity.

6. In Lieu of Conclusion: Mirrors for a Future without a Past

The Hall of Mirrors remains at once remote and close, and there are many roads leading from there to here, from them to us, invoking many different modernities. Most important of all these modernities is the mirror as an emblem for superficiality without any depth, for pure presence, which makes it an instrument for forgetting the past. It stands for a new glory with no need of analogies, radiating its own splendor. In this way, the Hall of Mirrors also embodies a change in the symbolism of the mirror itself, from "a model or example [to be followed]," the first meaning of the term given in the *Oxford English Dictionary*, to "an object having a smooth, flat [...] surface and intended to reflect a clear image," which emphasizes the object's purpose rather than the object itself.[94]

This clear mirror image becomes an instrument for moving beyond, for moving on. Mirrors, devoid of any past, any tradition, are today an expression of the auto-exemplarity on display everywhere, a modern auto-exemplarity that *is* display and nothing else. They reflect the triumph of the moderns, of a presentism that easily survived well beyond the end of absolutism. In this way, they are mirrors of modernity; as suggested by Baudrillard, that great theoretician of the simulacrum, the Versailles mir-

94. *OED*, "mirror."

rors are already proto-bourgeois.[95] Versailles is a brave new world, reflecting the birth of bourgeois values through the emergence of the mirror as the opulent object of bourgeois self-indulgence—with the same essential focus on superficiality, on a surface with no depth or history, not emerging from a tradition, the illusion of timelessness, which is really an eternal present.

Fast-forward to twenty-first-century Versailles and the first Dior video, a 2012 short by Inez van Lamsweerde and Vinoodh Matadin, featuring the Russian model Daria Strokous as carefree beauty personified. Although the short film is titled "Secret Garden—Versailles," the opening shots move from the outside to the interior, revealing the secret hidden behind the château's façade, in a primal scene in front of the large mirrors of the Hall of Mirrors. The model's expression is no longer one of awe, but rather of impassive intensity, as if transfixed. The most arresting shots show her with raised arms, back toward the camera, palms pressed against the mirror, lips close to the glass surface, eyes scrutinizing her own reflection, while descending, as if beauty were making love to beauty. This is also the first moment of color in the film, and the first time we actually see the garden, behind the camera, reflected in the mirrors surrounding the women. From this point on, there is a *dédoublement* taking place, as if beauty gave birth to beauty, through the appearance of other women who are clearly not Strokous, but who are all "the same," mirroring her actions, her poise, her awe. The secret of the garden is the promise of participation in this *dédoublement*: as they are created in the reflection of the magical mirrors of an absolutism that now speaks to us from the dreamlike realm of mythology, we are created in their reflection. But in the process, we become part of the circulation of awe and glory through which they are constituted and which somehow seem to overlap with the ever-widening circles of splendor and awe that constituted the dream of absolutism of yesteryear. To be sure, the mirror image itself has no past, it is indeed an image of pastlessness, but here the backdrop, the framing, the slightly darkened reflective surfaces all seem to add an otherworldly depth to the flatness of the glass. Beauty is a mirror, the film seems to tell us, but a mirror that not only holds forth the promise of impending carefree happiness, but which does so, somehow, by refracting our present in the already pastless present of the glorious mirrors of absolutism.

95. Baudrillard, *The System of Objects*, 21, following Melchior-Bonnet's reading of this passage in *The Mirror*, 96.

CHAPTER 3

Absolutist Absurdities

Let's imagine a scene of reading. Not the Dauphin reading the *Mémoires* left behind by his prematurely deceased father, as in chapter 1, but rather a modern scholar happening upon a peculiar little volume written in praise of Louis XIV. The volume was published in 1685, by which time the French court was firmly installed at Versailles and the Hall of Mirrors had finally been completed the year before. The War of the Reunions (1683–84) had ended with new territorial gains for France and the calamitous War of the League of Augsburg (1688–97) was still a few years away. However, our modern scholar is familiar with more recent revisionary historical work that considers 1685 as somewhat of a turning point in the king's reign, due to the passing of two royal decrees which will certainly be high on any list of its darkest moments, as two dark stains or self-inflicted wounds. It was the year of the Revocation of the Edict of Nantes, which had ensured a situation of relative civil unity and tolerance for the Protestant minority in France since the end of the French Wars of Religion. The Revocation led to the departure of close to a million Huguenots in a short period of time, resulting in a major brain drain in addition to immense human costs. The year 1685 also marked the establishment of the Code Noir, which regulated slavery in the French colonies, a document that one leading scholar has characterized as "the most monstrous juridical text of modern history."[1] In this context, the title of the little volume is initially puzzling to our modern scholar: *Parallèle de Louis le Grand avec les princes qui ont été surnommés grands* (Parallel of Louis the Great with [other] princes who have been called great). The importance of the enterprise is highlighted by the author's position of authority: the title page states that the author, the now-obscure Claude-Charles Guyonnet de Vertron, is an

---

1. "[L]e texte juridique le plus monstrueux de l'histoire moderne." Sala-Molins; quoted here from Cornette, "Chronique de l'État Classique," 470.

official royal historiographer. That is why the modern scholar decides to open the book at a random page, happening upon the following exclamation that lies two-thirds into the volume:

> Prodige de Grandeur! Louis ressemble à tous les Grands, toutefois aucun de ces Grands ne lui ressemble, parce qu'il est seul semblable à lui-même, et le Grand par excellence; En un mot l'Incomparable.[2]

> (Prodigy of Greatness! Louis resembles all the Great princes, although none of these Greats resemble him, because only he is similar to himself, and the Great prince par excellence. In one word the Incomparable.)

What is the modern scholar, what is *any* modern reader, to make of such a passage? To most of us, it will for sure sound like nothing but logical acrobatics: a tendentious use of specious reasoning and fallacious arguments—that is, if what is going on here should be called reasoning and argumentative activity at all. The passage is in fact the most-quoted— normally, the only quoted—passage from the book. And scholars always quote it without commentary, as if it spoke for itself and for the whole book: a privileged testimony to the outlandish and over-the-top nature of the most extravagant discourse surrounding Louis the Great.

Vertron's little book—condensed into this passage—together with the 1698 fairy tale "Sans Parangon" (Without equal) by another author who has remained marginal in scholarship, Jean de Préchac, constitute the epitome of what has been evoked somewhat flippantly in the chapter title as "absolutist absurdities." What I want to get at with this label is the peculiar challenge my corpus extends to our forbearance as modern readers. These are artifacts that seem so hyperbolic as to border on parody, if not outright subversion, and that are outright revolting or painful to our present-day sensibility. Although we know that we should not be surprised by the Eurocentrism of the enterprise of Vertron's *Parallèle*, we still balk at the idea of excluding a priori certain great Asian rulers from the project for being too cruel and barbarian to merit even being paralleled with somebody "as generous" as Louis XIV. Then there are the repeated allusions to the violent religious repression of the Protestant minority leading up to the Revocation, always brought up as a cause of celebration, if not as proof of the king's greatness. Turning to Préchac's fairy tale,

---

2. Vertron, *Parallèle*, 50. In what follows, references to the *Parallèle* will follow parenthetically in the main body of the text.

a similar logic operates as it celebrates the suffering of war—not in the abstract and not even referring to enemy suffering, but suffering on the French side—as merely an occasion for the king to further prove his heroic valiance. Importantly, these moments are not exceptions. It would not be an exaggeration to say that these texts are baffling to us as modern readers not only in the occasional over-the-top detail, but in their aim, in their structure, in the enthusiastic doggedness of their execution. It is as if they asked us to approach them as a source of ridicule (praise gone wrong), if not possible mockery (critique passing for praise).

My corpus here—and even my project—may seem far removed from the earlier inquiries in this book. Until now, I have explored the dream of absolutism from the vantage point of the sublime center of the reign, inward-facing in the *Mémoires* (chapter 1), and outward-facing in the Hall of Mirrors (chapter 2). What could I possibly add by turning to a corpus that modern scholars normally only approach in terms of marginality, banality, eccentricity, or even absurdity? And yet, my close examination of these two texts shows that they operate very self-consciously according to the same logic that is at work at the heart of absolutism, as I have delineated in the two preceding chapters. If they seem excessive and absurd to us, it is by pushing to the limit a logic that was everywhere at the time. In all their exuberance and outlandishness, they enact the same thrust toward a constitutive excess that I have shown at work in the king's own *Mémoires* and in the Hall of Mirrors at Versailles. While modern readers see them as a critique of the royal exuberance, I argue that they express a strain or fracture inscribed in the dream of absolutism itself. Therefore, what might look like "absolutist absurdities" to us in effect provide us with a clear window into the workings of the logic of absolutism.

More specifically, since both texts belong to well-known genres, the parallel and the fairy tale, an important part of my analysis will consist in observing how the demands of the absolutist occasion push the genres' conventions and expectations to the limit—and beyond. As I show, there are two challenges of particular importance in this regard: on the one hand, the way in which the texts tackle—and reflect on—the problem of expression (how to express the absolute?); on the other, the problem of ending, both for these specific texts and regarding the temporality of absolutism itself. By attending to the way in which an absolutist excess is legible in the very texture and structure of the artifacts, I demonstrate that these seeming "absolutist absurdities" are grappling with the paradoxes and impasses of the dream of absolutism itself.

Exhibit A: The Royal Historiographer and the
Unparalleled Greatness of Louis XIV

My first artifact is Vertron's 1685 *Parallèle de Louis le Grand avec les princes qui ont été surnommés grands*, the duodecimo volume with which the chapter opens. Although modern scholars normally deem this little book too excessive and exuberant, too over-the-top, to be taken seriously, it seems to have been a success at the time. A favorable review appeared in the *Journal des savants* and the *Mercure galant* in May 1685, and Pierre Bayle mentioned it in the *Nouvelles de la république des lettres* a few months later.[3] According to Vertron himself, the book was also received "with much pleasure" by the king.[4]

The title page supports several observations about the project (fig. 11). First of all regarding the position and authority of the author, who is invoked as "M. de Vertron, Historiographe du Roi, et de l'Académie Royale d'Arles." Although he is rarely read today, Vertron was named by Louis XIV as one of his official royal historiographers, one of only six to be named in a twenty-year period.[5] It is difficult for us to assess the importance of this position, but a first indication can be gleaned from the fact that when Jean Racine and Nicolas Boileau, two of the most celebrated writers of the age, were named to the same position a few years earlier, they immediately put aside their other projects. Unlike Boileau and Racine, however, Vertron was not a member of the French Academy, although his candidature had been considered and he was a very active member of the Royal Academy of Arles. As Vertron explains in an "Avertissement au Lecteur" (Notice to the reader), he originally wrote the manuscript of *Parallèle* as a speech to be delivered to the French Academy, but a matter of great urgency to "l'Empire des Lettres" (the Empire of Letters) obligated him to make another speech there, and this one ended up being pronounced

3. *Journal des savants*, May 14, 1685, 198–99; *Mercure galant*, May 1685, 8–9; *Nouvelles de la république des lettres*, September 1685, 1031–32. According to the brief notice in the latter by Bayle, "Son *Parallèle* a eu beaucoup de succès à la Cour, dont on sait que le jugement entraîne celui du Public" (His *Parallel* had a lot of success at the Court, whose judgment is known to influence that of the Public) (1032).

4. Vertron writes in a letter to Bayle, alongside the envoi of his book: "Le Roi, mon auguste maître, dont la modestie est égale à la grandeur, a eu la bonté de me dire qu'il l'avait lu *avec beaucoup de plaisir*, qu'il me remerciait, et qu'il me louerait davantage si je ne louais pas tant." (The King, my august master, whose modesty equals his greatness, was kind enough to tell me that he had read it *with much pleasure*, that he thanked me, and that he would praise me more if I had not praised him so much.) "Lettre 421: Claude-Charles Guyonnet de Vertron à Pierre Bayle"; my emphasis.

5. Cf. Grell, "L'histoire au service d'ambitions hégémoniques," 283.

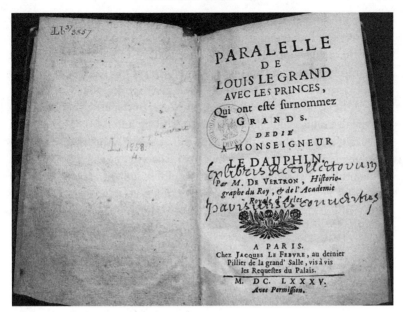

FIGURE 11. Claude-Charles Guyonnet de Vertron, *Parallèle de Louis le Grand avec les princes qui ont été surnommés grands* (Paris: J. Le Febvre, 1685), title page.

in front of the Royal Academy of Arles shortly before its publication. The polemic that stopped Vertron from presenting his *Parallèle* in front of the French Academy involved the identity of the so-called "Statue of Arles," an ancient sculpture of a female figure thought to be either Diane or Venus, which was found in Arles in 1651 and given to Louis XIV in the early 1680s for the decoration of the Hall of Mirrors at Versailles. Vertron was chosen to be the "Avocat de Diane" (Diane's advocate) in the decisive debate about the statue's identity in the French Academy. Although Vertron's side lost the debate, when Louis XIV as sovereign judge opted for Venus, this episode reveals his standing as an orator and a man of letters at the time. Vertron was both entrepreneurial and very productive, and he reached a wide circle of readers.[6]

But well before establishing Vertron's authority, the title page loudly announces the superlative position of the book's subject: this will be a work about the king, though not just any king, but Louis *le Grand*, Louis *the Great*. This epithet fulfills the expectations placed on Louis since birth. His parents, Louis XIII (with the epithet "the Just") and Anne of Austria, had been married for twenty-three years without children, with

6. See Vertron, "Avertissement au Lecteur," *Parallèle*, n.p.

Anne suffering several miscarriages. The unexpected birth in 1638 was considered a divine gift, if not a miracle of God, and the newborn was given the name Louis Dieudonné (Louis the God-given). However, it was not until after he had proven his worth on the battlefield that the young king finally delivered on his God-given promise and in 1671 first earned the highest epithet a king could have, one stating that he had finally realized his exemplary potential, elevating him beyond his place in the succession of the many Louis: *Louis le Grand*. And as discussed in chapter 2 (109), it wasn't until the early 1680s that its celebration became a constitutive part of French absolutist culture. In light of this dynamic, I argue that Vertron's comparative project functions as an inquiry into the nature of greatness itself and its exemplary function. Put differently, in the form of a question: if the king's epithet marks a triumphant zenith, may this crowning title also signal a breaking point, the possibility that this Louis may in fact be *the greatest*?

This leads to yet another important observation from the title page: the addressee. Vertron dedicates the book to "Monseigneur le Dauphin," the king's oldest son, crown prince Louis of France, destined to occupy the throne at the death of his father but who never became king. As discussed at length in chapter 1, questions of royal exemplarity are most pressing for the Dauphin. For if his father's superlative example were indeed an example to end all examples, which aspirations would be left for the next in line to the throne?

However, Vertron's book is of course not an objective, disinterested comparative analysis in any modern sense. Most of the king's official historiographers are in no direct way precursors of modern historiography. Few of them belonged to the relatively recent "tradition of empirical history." Instead, their works were self-consciously situated within the age-old tradition of the historical panegyric, whose understanding of history was rhetorical-literary, not empirical-analytical.[7] This distinction makes sense of the election of Vertron as well as of authors like Racine and Boileau for the position of royal historiographer, which otherwise seems absurd to modern historians in search of precursors and predecessors.[8]

7. For the distinction between the "tradition of empirical history," on the one hand, and rhetorical-literary historical panegyrics, on the other, see Soll, "Empirical History," esp. 297–99, 316.

8. For two examples, see the articles by Grell and Soll referred to in the preceding notes, which both react viscerally against "[c]ette imbrication entre la politique et l'histoire, étroitement liée à la glorification monarchique" (this imbrication of politics and history, closely tied to the glorification of the monarchy). Grell, "L'histoire au service d'ambitions hégémoniques," 295. Orest Ranum helps us make sense of the

For modern readers to appreciate these historians' work as the serious academic endeavor that it was, we must understand their activity as part of the rhetorical tradition inside which they operated. Their task was to *praise* and *glorify, not* to describe, explain, or analyze (however we might understand these three activities). The royal historiographers write the king's history to celebrate his exploits. The project is, in other words, about royal exemplarity, and it emerges from within a wider culture of exemplarity. It therefore comes as no surprise that Vertron affirms already in the introductory dedication to the Dauphin that the book is "le portrait de votre Auguste Père, et celui d'un héros achevé, que vous imitez, si parfaitement" (the portrait of your majestic father, and of a perfect hero, whom you imitate so flawlessly).[9]

Much of what I just said emerges through the first word of the book's title. The genre of the parallel has its roots in antiquity, theorized by Quintilian among others and best exemplified by Plutarch's *Parallel Lives.*[10] The early modern French reception of Plutarch's *Parallel Lives* owes a lot to Amyot's translation and the place it holds for Montaigne,[11] but perhaps even more to its central place in Jesuit education, where the parallel remained an indispensable pedagogical exercise well into the eighteenth century. Scholars have identified more than sixty parallels written in French, from Sully's *Parallèles de César et de Henry le Grand* published in 1615 all the way up to the Revolution. Two well-known examples published in the years after Vertron's book are Longepierre, *Parallèle de monsieur Corneille et de monsieur Racine* (1686), and, most famously, Perrault, *Parallèle des Anciens et des Modernes* (1688–97). This genre joins epideictic and agonistic writing, praise and criticism, ideally with a subtlety that leaves the final judgment to the reader, through "une manière dubitatrice et ambiguë" (a doubtful and ambiguous manner), as Montaigne notably wrote about Plutarch.[12]

---

discomfort of modern historians confronted with earlier historiographers' production of "an almost immutable structure of moral-political principles that had been developed and attributed permanently to various French kings": "This makes us uneasy. We search for the exceptions and the differences; in fact, we exaggerate them in order to preserve our sense of what it means to be a writer of history." Ranum, *Artisans of Glory*, 15, 16.

9. Vertron, Épître [dédicatoire], *Parallèle*, n.p.

10. What follows is indebted to Bernier, ed., *Parallèle des Anciens et des Modernes*, especially the first two chapters: Belleguic and Bernier, "Le siècle des Lumières et la communauté des Anciens"; Gicquiaud, "La balance de Clio."

11. See in this regard, Calhoun, *Montaigne and the Lives of the Philosophers*.

12. Montaigne, *Les essais*, 2:12, 556.

As the French historian François Hartog has shown, the genre of the parallel became a powerful weapon for the Moderns' side in the "Querelle des Anciens et des Modernes." Analyzing Perrault's *Parallèle*, Hartog identifies a peculiar obsession with "[la] dernière perfection" (the ultimate perfection). There is a relativization or historicization of the perfection of the Ancients, who had reached as far as they could—in other words, to their point of perfection—while this gesture is strangely missing in regard to the perfection of the Moderns. Hartog's conclusion runs as follows:

> This way of representing perfection (for the Ancients, rather as a point; levels and summit for the Moderns), indicates a difficulty with, or even a blindness regarding the present. [. . .] Why does the reflection stop en route? To each his own perfection, but ours is nearly the ultimate perfection! Why the devil? Through a blockage in the present. As if Perrault, even beyond the expected praise of the reigning sovereign, were not able to think beyond the present, beyond the "age of Louis the Great," which amounts to a formidable operation of valorization of the present. *Absolutism is a presentism.*[13]

As I argue, this presentism is manifest in its purest form in Vertron's *Parallel*. Returning to it one last time, the title page of his book announces yet another paradox of his project: the tension between *parallel* and *greatness*. In principle, the adjective "great" is of course in itself already a term of comparison, and as such very much within the logic of the parallel. Here, however, the horizontal comparative thrust of the parallel is threatened by the vertical thrust toward ultimate greatness: a greatness that threatens to undermine the whole enterprise of the genre of the parallel.

How, then, does Vertron actually perform the task of comparing all the great kings? Although, as I just stressed, this is not an objective comparison in any modern sense, Vertron's approach is at once comprehen-

---

13. "Cette façon de représenter la perfection (pour les Anciens, plutôt le point; les degrés et le sommet pour les Modernes) indique une difficulté avec voire un aveuglement sur le présent. [. . .] Pourquoi la réflexion s'arrête-t-elle en chemin? À chacun sa perfection, mais la nôtre est quasiment la dernière perfection! Pourquoi diable? Par un blocage sur le présent. Comme si Perrault, au-delà même de l'éloge obligé du souverain régnant, ne pouvait penser au-delà du présent, au-delà du 'siècle de Louis le Grand,' qui traduit en effet une formidable opération de valorisation du présent. *L'absolutisme est un présentisme.*" Hartog, *Anciens, modernes, sauvages,* 259; my emphasis.

sive and systematic. As the serious academician that he is, Vertron shows the basis and sources for his comparison in two appendices at the end of this little book: first, in a succinct "table chronologique" establishing the primary events in the lives of all the "princes qui ont porté le nom de GRAND" (princes who have carried the name GREAT) (60–66); second, in a short bibliography listing for each great prince the names of the authors consulted (67–72). The problem of synchronization in the chronological table highlights the erudition of the enterprise: Vertron cites all events before the birth of Christ not only in reference to this event, but also in relation to the founding of the city of Rome. Modern readers' surprise at seeing this scholarly scrupulousness coincide with unabashed bias[14] betrays our misconception regarding the nature of the enterprise. The book is itself the celebration of a conclusion given in advance; there is no question for which the book does not already have the answer. The mode is therefore not *first* deliberative and only *then* epideictic, but celebratory throughout. The goal of the exercise is not to identify *who* is the greatest, but to express through the comparison how Louis's greatness is superior. That Vertron sees this as his task is clear. However, as he stresses from the beginning, it is also that of all the royal academies: their only goal is "la gloire de leur FONDATEUR" (the glory of their FOUNDER). They are assembled only "pour mieux parler de LOUIS LE GRAND, dont le caractère auguste surpasse toutes les louanges" (in order to better speak about LOUIS THE GREAT, whose august character surpasses all praise) (5). But how to praise what is beyond praise, how to express what is beyond expression?

In light of this consideration, it is less surprising to encounter, already at the outset of Vertron's actual parallel of the great kings, a definition of royal greatness that refers to Louis the Great as a measure of perfection:

> Vous savez que pour mériter ce titre, il faut avoir comme Louis toutes les vertus au suprême degré, et que ce surnom est pour ainsi dire l'abrégé des qualités Héroïques et Royales. (10)

> (You know that to deserve this title, one must have as Louis all the virtues to a supreme degree, and that the epithet is, so to speak, the epitome of Heroic and Royal qualities.)

---

14. This partiality is even visible in the space accorded to each prince in the chronological table. While the other great princes only are allowed 3–9 lines each, with the higher number reserved for Cyrus and Alexander, and an exceptional 13 lines for Charlemagne, Louis is granted a full 20 lines.

The members of the royal academy of Arles to whom Vertron speaks are well aware of the nature of the challenge presented here. The greater greatness of Louis the Great is the premise of the inquiry. Therefore, their approach to royal greatness relies on the structure of Louis's greatness as evidence of the definition's pertinence, rather than the other way around. For Louis is greatness incarnated; he is the epitome of the wonders of the world in the same way that the epithet "the Great" is the epitome of all his beautiful heroic and royal virtues. In other words, the present great king has set a new standard for greatness against which Vertron and his colleagues can measure the great from the past. How do they hold up?

First of all, Vertron observes that many a sovereign was called "the Great" without actually meriting it, as a result of flattery, vanity, inflated heroic deeds, or complacent patriotism, if not a combination of these characteristics (11–15). The result is a claim to greatness that is—at best—local. Since these kings were only considered as great in their own country, by their own subjects, the memory of these kings' greatness is preserved only in "leur Histoires particulières" (their particular Histories) (14). This is the case, according to Vertron, on the one hand, for King Cnut the Great of Denmark and, on the other, for kings Alfonso the Great of León and Sancho the Great of Navarra, the reputation of the former having "hardly gone beyond the Baltic Sea" and of the two latter ones "beyond the Pyrenees."[15] In fact, Alfonso owed a large part of his conquests to the help he received from the French.

Then there is a select group of sovereigns whose claim to greatness reaches beyond the particular, both in terms of time and space. Not only were they "universellement appelés GRANDS" (universally called GREAT), but their renown speaks as strongly today as in their own time. Yet Vertron is quick to add, "mais cependant d'une manière bien différente de celle dont elle parle de LOUIS LE GRAND" (but nevertheless in a quite different manner from the manner in which it speaks about LOUIS LE GRAND) (15).

Over the next twenty pages (15–35), Vertron works out this difference in great detail, when he first lauds each member of the series of truly great sovereigns from history for his virtues and deeds and then pinpoints his flaws, before he favorably brings up Louis, lacking in flaws but never in greatness. Alexander the Great is an important case in point, since his example had been such a crucial aspirational comparison for Louis up to

---

15. "La réputation de celui-ci à peine a-t-elle passé la Mer Baltique, et celle des deux autres les Pyrenées" (14–15).

the 1670s.[16] Vertron stresses that while everybody knows that Alexander was a great conqueror, they are equally aware that his temerity often got the best of him—unlike Louis the Great, another great conqueror, who always acts with prudence (17–19). Likewise, Vertron praises the Roman emperor Theodosius the Great for having upheld the empire's dignity during barbarian attacks but reproaches him for his wrath, which sets him decisively apart from the present king (24–27). Drawing on the etymology of the name of the emperor and the way it echoes Louis's early epithet "Dieudonné," Vertron elegantly concludes that Louis "[. . .] c'est un THEODOSE, puisque Dieu nous l'a donné, [. . .] mais c'est un THEODOSE sans emportement" ([. . .] is a THEODOSIUS, since God gave him to us, [. . .] but a THEODOSIUS who is never carried away) (25).

In addition to Alexander and Theodosius, Vertron deemed worthy of the epithet "the Great," among others, Cyrus of Persia; Pompey (for his military conquests, although he was not properly a sovereign); the Roman emperors Constantine, Valentinian, and Justinian; the Holy Roman Emperor Otto; Gustav II Adolf of Sweden; and Osman, founder of the Ottoman dynasty (15–34). While he characterized fourteenth-century Osman as "ce superbe empereur" (this superb emperor) (32), he disqualifies two further Asian rulers known as "Great" for the horrible "cruautés dont ils ont déshonoré leur Règne" (cruelty with which they dishonored their Reign) (33), namely, sixteenth-century Sultan Suleiman of the Ottoman Empire and Tamerlane, late fourteenth-century founder of the Timurid Empire.[17] According to Vertron, these two Asian Greats are so different in their greatness that they need to be excluded from the genre itself: "ces Barbares, quoique surnommés Grands, ne peuvent entrer dans le Parallèle d'un Prince ennemi du sang, et dont l'âme est si généreuse" (these Barbarians, although called Great, cannot enter into the Parallel of a Prince who is the enemy of blood and whose soul is so generous) (33). They are literally *incomparable*. However, this exclusion establishes a surprising relation to Louis XIV, since, as I shall soon discuss, this is exactly the qualification Vertron will end up assigning to the king himself.[18]

16. For the changing fortune of Alexander the Great as example and model for Louis XIV, see Grell and Michel, *L'École des princes*.

17. Some of the identifications of the Greats through history are not completely obvious from the main body of the text, but assured after consultation of the "Chronological Table" at the end of the volume.

18. Further exclusions encompass titles of greatness where the epithet is not earned but part of the title itself, as for "ces noms héréditaires du GRAND SEIGNEUR, du GRAND KAM, du GRAND SOPHI, du GRAND CZAR, et de GRAND DUC DE TOSCANE" (these hereditary names of GREAT LORD, GREAT KAM, GREAT SOPHI,

Among the kings who actually deserved to be called "the Great," there is, according to Vertron, perhaps unsurprisingly, an essential difference between French and non-French kings. The great foreign kings on Vertron's exclusive list certainly all deserve their epithet, but Clovis, Charlemagne, and Henry IV, although not entirely flawless, deserve it even more. They are quite simply more exemplary. Vertron's transition from a final review of the great kings of foreign lands to the French Greats points forward both to Louis XIV and also to the book's climax, the crowning argument of Vertron's book ten pages later. This passage is the author's first mention of the three French sovereigns, before he looks more closely at each of their greatness in the subsequent pages (37–43):

> [S]i la Perse a fourni un CYRUS, si la Macédoine a donné un ALEXANDRE, si [. . .] [etc.]; LA FRANCE se peut vanter d'avoir eu des CLOVIS, des CHARLES, des HENRIS, qui sans flatterie ont mérité le titre de GRAND, par préférence aux autres, avec autant de justice que LOUIS XIV l'emporte au-dessus de ses Prédécesseurs. Ces Rois [. . .] revivent tous aujourd'hui dans la personne Auguste de LOUIS LE GRAND leur successeur. (35–37)

> ([W]hile Persia provided a CYRUS, Macedonia gave an ALEXANDER, [. . .] [etc.]; FRANCE can boast of having had CLOVIS, CHARLES, HENRIS, who without flattery have merited the title of GREAT, in preference to the others, with as much justice as LOUIS XIV wins over his Predecessors. These Kings [. . .] all live again today in the August person of LOUIS THE GREAT, their successor.)

France can rightfully boast of its kings' greatness—and that's exactly what France is in the process of doing here through the service of its most faithful royal historiographer. This crucial passage makes its point through a bold analogy followed by a surprising metaphor. First, Vertron establishes the following hierarchy of merit: the other French kings surpass the foreign kings in their claim to greatness to the same degree that Louis XIV surpasses his French predecessors. Consequently, the logic of the sentence seems to move from "the Great" (foreign kings) via "the Greater" (French kings) to "the Greatest" (the current French king), taking the reader chronologically toward the present and geographically toward Versailles. But, as I have shown, the comparison never really left Louis XIV's

---

GREAT CZAR, and GREAT DUKE OF TUSCANY) (34–35). Of interest here is the exclusion of the Great Mogul from this list of exclusions.

Versailles in the first place, since Vertron has already compared each element of the series of great kings with Louis—and found them inferior.

Vertron pushes this alternative logic one step further in the redirection of what at first glance looks like a straightforward model of revival. This insistence on a seemingly unidirectional passage from predecessor to successor recalls the metaphor of the king's two bodies. *Le roi ne meurt jamais*: the greatness of past kings lives on through the dynastic bloodline. His body natural is invested with their dignity in a way that evokes, in this specifically royal "revivre," an idea of progress, even a progress that continues beyond the present with future kings, as in the concern for "celui qui doit régner après nous" (he who shall reign after us) expressed by Louis XIV to his son in the opening of his *Mémoires* (see 55–56). However, whereas the two-body metaphor evokes dynastic continuation and permanence, Vertron imagines a culmination in the present. The great kings from the past "live again *today*" in Louis the Great; the great kings from the past all have a future, but importantly no further than the present; the parallel has no room for any future beyond Louis's own posterity.

At the same time, the passage gives a much wider understanding of greatness, for Louis had inherited not only the throne but also the virtues of his greatest predecessors. The more detailed parallel with Clovis and Charlemagne in the subsequent pages gives Vertron the occasion to more directly address a slight discomfort that had been lingering in his earlier comparisons. By the 1680s, Louis certainly had heroic conquests under his belt, but did he really rival all of the earlier sovereigns in this regard, starting with Cyrus and Alexander? Previously, Vertron had bypassed this uncomfortable point by stressing, at times, the quality and manner of his conquests rather than their quantity and magnitude. Contemporary readers who might have feared that this was a sign of weakness or at least a relative absence of greatness would have been reassured by hearing from Vertron that it is rather the other way around. If Louis had fewer victories on the battlefield than the greatest French conquerors before him, it was certainly not because he was wanting in heroic virtue. Rather, in the comparison with Clovis (37–39), Vertron asserts that the terror sparked by Louis's name—itself an expression of his heroic virtue—is such that there quite simply had not been more enemy kings to vanquish: "LOUIS LE GRAND a cherché souvent des Rois à combattre; et s'il n'en a pas trouvé, c'est que leur faiblesse, ou la terreur de son nom, les a empêché de paraître." (LOUIS THE GREAT often looked for Kings to combat; and if he didn't find any, it's because their weakness or fear of his name, prevented them from coming forward) (38).[19] And as the case of Charlemagne makes clear (39–43), if Louis presently rules over a smaller realm than that of his great predecessor, it is because Louis's other, subtler royal qualities have kept in check his more primal heroic impulses. It was in fact his virtuous moderation that had limited his conquests. The king himself had concluded that moderation was more heroic:

> Si LOUIS LE GRAND ne possède pas présentement tant de Pays, *sa modération* pour être grande, comme toutes ses qualités, a mis des bornes a ses Conquêtes. Il a jugé qu'il était plus héroïque d'imposer des Lois, et de donner la Paix aux autres Princes, que de soumettre une infinité de Peuples, quand il les trouvait hors d'état de résister. (41–42; my emphasis)

> (While LOUIS THE GREAT does not currently possess as many countries, *his moderation* in its greatness, like all his qualities, placed limits on his Conquests. He judged that it was more heroic to impose Laws and to give Peace to the other Princes than to defeat an infinity of Peoples, when he found them unable to resist.)

One can certainly wonder whether Vertron is not only praising the king for his heroic moderation, but also attempting to convince him of the virtues of this less-celebrated branch of heroism. Not surprisingly, this is a recurrent topic in academic praise of the period, and indeed in royal panegyrics through the ages: offering the sovereign ways of imagining a peace that is as heroic, glorious, and exemplary as war.[20] Within the specific context of Vertron's project, this consideration allows not only for a more complex model of royal greatness, but, as will soon become clear, one that is more appropriate for the time period. Louis is certainly a glorious conqueror, but his greatness also comprises less bellicose virtues often lacking in his predecessors and that are better suited to more peaceful and sophisticated times: justice, clemency, moderation, goodness. His is a refined greatness for whom "la Paix [...] [est] la véritable Victoire" (Peace [...] [is] the true Victory) (42); an invincible

---

19. For the importance of terror as a central feature of early modern kingship, see Schechter, *A Genealogy of Terror*, esp. chap. 1, "Holy Terror and Divine Majesty."

20. For a prominent example of such a celebration of glorious peace and its exemplary royal peacemaker in the French Academy immediately predating Vertron, see Tallemant, "Panégyrique du Roi sur la paix" (1679), in *Les panégyriques du roi*, ed. Zoberman, 171–75.

hero who "après avoir vaincu les autres, ne songe plus qu'à se vaincre lui-même" (after having vanquished the others, only thinks of vanquishing himself) (43).

It might be surprising for modern readers to see Vertron include the violent repression of France's Protestant minority among the many recent achievements evoked as expressions of the king's greatness beyond the battlefield. As mentioned in the opening of the chapter, Vertron's *Parallel* was published early in 1685, the year that saw the Revocation of the Edict of Nantes. The violent process of which the Revocation was the culmination allows for the following comparison between Clovis, as the first king known both as "the Great" and "Premier Christian King," and Louis XIV: "Nous voyons aujourd'hui, comme du temps de Clovis, la véritable Religion triomphante: mais nous voyons quelque chose de plus, l'Hérésie expirante, et l'Impiété sans crédit." (We see today, as in the time of Clovis, the true Religion triumphant; but we see something more: Heresy expiring, Impiety discredited) (38–39). A later list of glorious achievements includes "des Idolâtres éclairés, des Temples démolis, des Sectes confondues" (Idolaters enlightened, Protestant Churches demolished, Sects confounded) (53).[21] The ease with which Vertron included these elements in the general celebration of the king strongly suggests that the dissonance modern readers feel was not there for the audience of Vertron's speech. On the contrary, despite the immense human (and ultimately also financial) costs of these repressive politics, they were seen—and celebrated—as an absolutist confirmation of the adage of "une foi, une loi, un roi" (one faith, one law, one king), and thus an expression of unity and perfection.

Two brief synthetic moments a few pages apart sum up the whole comparative development of the book, with the expression "[e]n un mot" (in one word) in each case highlighting the density of the formulation. First, when Vertron emphatically concludes: "En un mot tout est grand, tout est parfait dans sa personne." (In one word, everything is great, everything is perfect in his person) (48). Second, when he draws the consequence of this conclusion for the wider comparative project of the *Parallèle* two pages later. This brings me back to the seeming "absolutist absurdity" from the opening of the chapter. This statement, I consider, represents the culmination not only of this specific book but also of a way of thinking about heroism, greatness, and exemplarity as such:

21. See p. 21 for a third mention of the king's anti-Protestant initiatives: "ses soins pour rappeler les Hérétiques dans le sein de l'Église" (his concern to bring back the Heretics to the bosom of the Church).

Prodige de Grandeur! Louis ressemble à tous les Grands, toutefois aucun de ces Grands ne lui ressemble, parce qu'il est seul semblable à lui-même, et le Grand par excellence; En un mot l'Incomparable. (50)

(Prodigy of Greatness! Louis resembles all the Great princes, although none of these Greats resemble him, because only he is similar to himself, and the Great prince par excellence. In one word the Incomparable.)

As the conclusion of a comparative project, this passage is baffling. Already the syntax obstructs the discursive progression of the argument, sandwiching it between an exclamation and a condensation into "one word." The same is the case for the vocabulary, with terms like *prodige, excellence, incomparable* refusing to remain within the paradigm of likeness established by the parallel. Or rather, these terms erect a vertical dimension over the horizontal plane of the parallel, which, paradoxically, turns likeness into a one-way relation.

This celebratory outburst will for sure ring hollow to many modern readers. As already mentioned at the beginning of the chapter, it is the most-quoted—often the *only* quoted—passage from the book, and scholars normally cite it without further comments, as if its message to readers were obvious. Without entering into the logical intricacies and acrobatics, it serves as an evident testimony of celebratory discourse having run amok. It is the epitome of what I have labeled "absolutist absurdities."

It is worth stressing, however, that the basic logic at work in this passage is not necessarily unsound or even paradoxical. First of all, this conclusion does not in any way contest the greatness of the other kings with that epithet. In this, it is well aligned with the implicit definition of greatness that Vertron has used throughout the comparative section of the book. The basic premise seems to be that greatness requires the possession of at least one great-making quality. It is only greatness par excellence that consists in the possession of the whole set of great-making qualities. However, it is not until the appearance of Louis and his level of perfection that the world realizes the richness of the concept. Louis will resemble this or that great prince in the latter's claim to greatness, since he also possesses the properties that allow them to be qualified as great. Conversely, the other great princes do not resemble Louis in his greatness, since they are lacking at least one—and often several if not many—of the great-making qualities. The greatness of the other kings becomes the springboard for the confirmation of Louis's even greater (that is: more *excellent*, more outstanding) greatness, as if the goal were to lead the reader to ask whether the present king were nothing less than

Louis the Greatest. As strained as it may seem to us, such a way of reasoning would have been familiar to those contemporary readers with any sustained exposure to theology, through the scholastic negotiation of the thorny relation between imperfect human creatures and a creator who, according to Thomas Aquinas's canonical expression, "contains within Himself the whole perfection of being."[22] It is therefore not the logic as such but rather the extension of its domain of application that is astounding, bringing it down to earth, as it were, from the theological distinction between creator and creature to the politico-theological distinction between perfect and imperfect sovereigns.

Or not exactly down to earth. For as I have already observed, in the process—a process that establishes Louis the Great as not only unparalleled but inherently "un-parallelable"—a vertical dimension is erected over the horizontal plane of the parallel. Alexander Gelley's differentiation between a horizontal and vertical dimension in the workings of exemplarity (as discussed above, 31–32) explains here the distinction between empirical examples of greatness that can be studied in parallel and the exemplary unparalleled one—"the Great prince par excellence," in Vertron's words. This is the place in the text where the inherent excess of the logic of exemplarity becomes most clearly visible. The exemplarity of the royal exemplar becomes so extraordinary, so outstanding, so incomparable that it can only resemble itself. The king has become his own example in an *auto-exemplarity* that threatens to bring the panegyric system to an end. Since Louis is his own origin and end, the praise must therefore end before the king and his image, the king mirroring himself in the image of his own superlative example, which lies at the heart of the dream of absolutism but which also threatens to be the example to end all examples.

For what is left to say? The question is pressing, particularly for the various addressees of the text, starting with its dedicatee, the Dauphin, but also for the academicians to whom Vertron speaks.

The title page of the book promises the Dauphin a comparison, but the conclusion is that Louis the Great is radically beyond parallel: He is "the Great prince par excellence. In one word the Incomparable." As I have already examined, in the dedication to the Dauphin, Vertron refers to his book as "a portrait [. . .] of a perfect hero, whom you imitate so

---

22. Aquinas, *Summa theologiae*, Ia 4.2. I would like to thank Steven Nadler and Giorgio Pini for having worked out this logic with me at the occasion of a presentation of this material at the Institute for Research in the Humanities at University of Wisconsin–Madison in 2019.

flawlessly." But is such a perfect imitation of the incomparable himself, of incomparability incarnate, really possible? How can the Crown Prince encounter the crowning argument of the text, this absolute crowning example? What can he hope for? The tenuous—if not untenable—position in which Vertron's panegyric performance situates the Dauphin recalls the surprising figures of royal imitation discussed in chapter 1 (70–72). These figures emerged in a corpus of poems written by some of the nation's most promising pens as submissions for the 1677 poetry competition of the French Academy, in praise of the king's educational enterprise in his (otherwise secret) *Mémoires*. Although the poems envision the son imitating the father in his actions, his exploits, and even his motivating fire, the perspective always remains that of the present king rather than that of his future successor. Even within an assignment as open and future-oriented as the consideration of the king's own preparation of his successor, it proved difficult and delicate to assign the Dauphin any agency or autonomy. Here, in the context of Vertron's *Parallèle*, the intense focus on the present king's unparalleled greatness leaves the author even less latitude to incorporate any meaningful place for the Dauphin. His celebration of the absolute perfection of Louis the Great brings out the full impact of Fontenelle's exclamation in his submission for the 1677 poetry competition: "Que le Sceptre est *pénible* après qu'il l'a porté!"[23] The scepter is certainly *heavy* after Louis has carried it, but the adjective *pénible* has even darker connotations that resonate with the situation of the Dauphin in 1685, at the mature royal age of twenty-three, living at a Versailles designed as a permanent celebration of the glorious exploits of his father: not only heavy, but awkward, uncomfortable, painful, excruciating, and unbearable.

Within Vertron's framework, it is radically *unthinkable* to carry the scepter after Louis the Great, *unthinkable* to carry on the dynastic bloodline beyond the present apex. The problem is therefore not exactly one of a future where the son does not measure up, the prospect of a trivial return to an ordinary, non-great Louis, a "Louis the Next," which inevitably would have meant "Louis the Not So Great." Rather, the only future that is imaginable within the perspective of the *Parallèle* is one of commemoration, a future that is nothing but the posterity of Louis the Great. Generally speaking, the offspring is the figure of the future, yet here there is room for neither offspring nor future. Despite Vertron's gesture toward the offspring in the dedication, the Dauphin is the inevitable and nec-

23. My emphasis. See the discussion of Fontenelle's poem in chapter 1, 70–71, esp. 70n33 for the bibliographical reference and the assignment of the authorship.

essary collateral damage in the construction of a present greatness that knows no tomorrow.

The argument seems to have reached a dead end. Again, it would be tempting to use the strange and self-undermining nature of these conclusions as a reason for ridiculing Vertron's project and not taking his book seriously. I claim, however, that the dead end is inscribed in the logic of royal exemplarity itself. Vertron's text brings into sharp focus a constitutive excess in the absolutist construction of royal authority. The royal auto-exemplarity of Louis the Great ("only he is similar to himself") and the impossibility of thinking of a future beyond the superlative present perfect that he represents are two sides of the same coin. For as Vertron makes clear, "In one word[, he is] the Incomparable" (50). This, I argue, is the precise sense in which *absolutism is a presentism*, to return to Hartog's striking formulation (see above, 158). The temporal "blockage" evoked by Hartog resides in the royal incarnation of ultimate perfection, as captured by the mirror of incomparability.

At this point, I would like to take a step back and recall the context of Hartog's observation. It emerges in an analysis of Perrault's *Parallèle* of the Ancients and the Moderns, which represented the major expression of the Modern side of the *Querelle* during the early 1690s.[24] Set against this background, Vertron's *Parallèle* served to display the most radical implications of the Moderns' position a few years prior to Perrault and well before the *Querelle* was properly launched.[25] Vertron's general argument about incomparability was in no way new, but it had never been formulated with such panache and with such relentless insistence. Vertron's text thus casts the emerging *Querelle* in a different light by accentuating the possibility that the heart of the *Querelle* was political rather than poetical. Or at the very least, that the modern side could triumph by recasting the discussion in political terms.

Somewhat unexpectedly, this issue returns the discussion to Peter Burke's reductive approach to absolutism, first explored in the introduction (14–16). Burke seems to preclude such an interpretation as the one suggested above, when, in his consideration of the way in which writers "made use of the idea that Rome had been surpassed in order to glorify Louis XIV," he observes: "It would of course be absurd to reduce the famous 'battle of the books' between the Ancients and the Moderns to a

---

24. The four dialogues constituting Perrault's *Parallèle* were published in 1688, 1690, 1692, and 1697.

25. In this, I follow Blanchard, "Ménestrier and the 'Querelle des Monuments,'" esp. 511.

means of propaganda for Louis XIV."[26] But then he goes on to add that "[a]ll the same, there was a political element in the literary commonplace that Louis was a new Augustus," invoking a specific case from 1682 when Louis XIV is characterized as "more august than Augustus."[27] The concessive "all the same" points to a blind spot in Burke's analytical framework: if the presence of a "political element" in a cultural artifact or practice necessarily implies a reduction to propaganda, it becomes complicated, to say the least, to deal adequately with the unquestionable political dimension of even "highbrow" cultural production devoted to the glory of Louis XIV. It is therefore tempting to see Burke's blind spot as an inability to see *their* blind spot—the blind spot of absolutism—as identified by Hartog. For the temporal blockage that Hartog pinpoints in absolutism is occasioned by "un aveuglement sur le present" (a blindness regarding the present): not a blindness *to* the present, but *in* the present; an inability to escape from the presentism that absolutism is. Within the context of my analysis here, this is a blindness that is constitutive of the dream of absolutism.

Returning now to the question about what is left to say, this question is pressing not only for the Dauphin but also for the writers working to glorify the king—as much those for whom Vertron originally wrote his speech (the French Academy) as those in front of whom he eventually delivered it (the Royal Academy of Arles). Again, what is left to be said? How to avoid turning praise of the king into mere idling? As has already been discussed, this question was on Vertron's mind from the outset of his speech, when he stressed, in a formulation that highlights the paradoxical nature of the enterprise, that the only reason that these academies exist is "pour mieux parler de LOUIS LE GRAND, dont le caractère auguste surpasse toutes les louanges" (in order to speak better about LOUIS THE GREAT, whose august character surpasses all praise) (5). The keyword here is obviously "surpasses," which already hints at the impossibility of the mission. The following page goes on to elaborate on this impossibility, but this time from the cognitive perspective of the academicians in front of their object of description. The task leads, on the one hand, to

---

26. Burke, *The Fabrication of Louis XIV*, 195.

27. The full sentence runs as follows: "All the same, there was a political element in the literary commonplace that Louis was a new Augustus, or even, according to an inscription on the king's bust at the convent of the Mathurins, 'more august than Augustus' [*Augusto augustior*]." Burke, 195; the quote is from *Mercure galant*, September 1682, 52. The quotation is followed by an erudite and nuanced comparison of the cultural context of Augustus and Louis (195–97), but without ever returning to the "political element."

an intellectual recognition of radical disproportion and, on the other, to an affective reaction of bedazzlement. For who could possibly have "des pensées et des expressions proportionnées au mérite du sujet" (thoughts and expressions proportionate to the worth of the subject), rather than being "ébloui de l'éclat de ses vertus" (bedazzled by the splendor of his virtues) (6)?

Vertron never explicitly evokes the concept of the sublime, neither here nor later in his short book, but these introductory passages come close to outlining the contours of what I would like to call a "royal sublime," which will be operative in the last part of his text. It first occurs in a thought experiment evoked in passing at the end of the text's comparative part, immediately after the conclusion of the comparison with the last of the other sovereigns called "the Great" (outlining the ways in which Louis is greater than his last great predecessor, Henry IV). What if, Vertron asks, the Heavens had granted us the wish for a king of our choice? In that case, "nous eût-il été possible d'en souhaiter, et même d'en imaginer un plus accompli que le nôtre?" (Would it have been possible for us to wish for one—indeed, even to imagine one—more accomplished than our king?) (46). A similar idea reappears five pages later, although it stresses the cognitive incapacity of the Ancients rather than that of Vertron himself and his contemporaries. Considering the ideals of human perfection according to Stoics, Lacedemonians, and Aristotle, Vertron observes that the living model provided by Louis the Great surpasses everything the Ancients could invent: "leur imagination n'a jamais pu tant inventer de perfections en faveur de leur Héros, que le Nôtre en possède effectivement" (their imagination never managed to invent as much perfection in favor of their hero as ours actually possesses) (51–52). In other words, unlike Voltaire's notorious quip about God ("Si Dieu n'existait pas, il faudrait l'inventer"[28]), if Louis le Grand didn't exist, nobody would have been able to invent him.

Between these two moments highlighting how unimaginable, how inconceivable, how unthinkable Louis's greatness is, the passage above culminates in the unparalleled auto-exemplarity of "only he is similar to himself." This ultimate formulation of what absolutism *is* (its ontology) needed to be framed by a reflection on its paradoxical epistemological status. If such an absolutism existed, how could its subjects grasp it, where would it have emerged from, and where would it lead to? And yet, once they are there, in the superlative presence of the current king, they realize that these are quite simply the wrong questions, asked from *outside* the

28. Voltaire, "Epître à l'auteur," 403.

dream that absolutism is: the sublime dream about an unimaginable and incomparable perfection, here and now.

From within that dream, Vertron arrives at the following conclusion, which clarifies once and for all the implicit temporality of such an absolutism and its consequences for the logic of exemplarity, by way of a long-standing question and its crude answer:

> [P]ourquoi donc chercher dans la fable les travaux d'un Hercule, et dans l'histoire ceux d'un Alexandre, si LOUIS LE GRAND donne des exemples de toutes les vertus? En effet personne ne doute que ses actions ne surpassent celles des Césars: Elles font l'admiration de notre âge, la honte du passé, et elles feront l'étonnement, pour ne pas dire le désespoir, des Héros des siècles à venir. (52–53)

> (Why then look for the work of a Hercules in fables, and that of an Alexander in history, if LOUIS THE GREAT gives examples of all the virtues? Indeed, no one doubts that his actions surpass those of the Caesars: They bring about the admiration of our era, the shame of the past, and will cause the amazement, if not to say the hopelessness, of Heroes for centuries to come.)

Absolutism is indeed a presentism: Louis XIV's greatness confounds not only the future (starting with the Dauphin) but also the past (starting with its greatest heroes and kings). And because this absolute supremacy of the present is itself a dream—or rather, a constitutive feature of the dream of absolutism—it is hard to reject it without stepping outside that collective dream altogether. Therefore, versions of this argument were to become the most trenchant weapon of the modern side in the *Querelle* between Ancients and Moderns over the next decade. It was quite simply impossible to argue forcefully enough against it, without criticizing the supposed perfection of the current monarchy itself in the process.

Interestingly, without ever actually using the term "sublime," what Vertron does here comes very close to turning the Ancients' most formidable weapon against them.[29] As showed a moment ago, the "royal sublime" is operative in Vertron's text. Vertron approaches his task of describing the king's greatness through, on the one hand, an intellectual recognition of radical disproportion and, on the other, an affective sense of bedazzlement. This approach (and the specific language in which it is voiced) is

---

29. For the importance of the notion of the sublime within the *Querelle*, see Norman, *The Shock of the Ancient*, 4–6, and the final chapter "The Ineffable Effect."

informed by and indebted to a reflection on the sublime running through the seventeenth century and accentuated in particular by the publication of Boileau's influential 1674 translation of pseudo-Longinus's treatise on the sublime. But isn't it a sacrilege and debasement to turn the highest aesthetical category into a political one? It is important to notice the degree to which a question like this is anachronistic, fueled by our own post-Romantic sensibility. While it is true that the discussion of the sublime in the aftermath of the *Querelle* contributed decisively to the development of an autonomous aesthetical philosophy in the following century,[30] this does not in any way preclude the possibility that the category of the sublime had an earlier political resonance. In fact, the tradition of the sublime is replete with politico-theological examples, and theories of the sublime are from the outset entangled in a language of majesty. Lofty, elevated, great, magnificent, extraordinary, marvelous, majestic: the category of the sublime evokes a similar vertical thrust as the one at work in the logic of royal glory and exemplarity. The reflection on the "merveilleux dans le discours" (the marvelous in discourse), to repeat the subtitle of Boileau's translation of Longinus, can certainly take other directions than the political encomium of the "royal sublime," but Vertron's mobilization of the language used in theories of the sublime to describe the perfection of the king is still very much prepared by the tradition. Is Vertron's *Parallèle* itself sublime? The comparative part of the book is too unconcerned with style for that even to be a question, but as I argue below, after the past has once and for all been reduced to silence, there is a shift in the text from a descriptive mode to an unabashed appeal to the affective register of the sublime.[31]

However, I want to return one last time to the conclusion of Vertron's comparative project, in order to observe that the very argument which establishes the incomparable supremacy of the Moderns gains its force from a way of thinking based on precedent, tradition, and past authority. Vertron's conclusion undermines the foundation upon which the culture of exemplarity is built by invalidating the principle of *historia magistra vitae* (literally, history as teacher of life): when the example of Louis is all that is needed, the archive of the past loses its function as a storehouse of examples to live by. History is shamed into silence.

Surprisingly, Vertron's book does not end here, but continues for another six to seven pages. What could possibly be left to say at this point?

---

30. See Norman, chap. 11.

31. For a systematic exploration of the notion of the "royal sublime," see Vredenburgh and Bjørnstad, "Un discours 'de majesté.'"

The perpetuation of his speech only makes sense as a performance of a certain absolutist affect rather than as a continuation (or further culmination) of the comparative project itself. As argued in the preceding chapter's analysis of the portrayal of the royal body in the Hall of Mirrors at Versailles, when it comes to the sovereign himself, absolutism is characterized by an *absence* of affect, beyond that of majestic impassivity. Vertron makes a similar point repeatedly when he stresses the way in which the great king vanquishes not only his enemies (on the battlefield) and predecessors (through the parallel) but also himself; unlike emperor Theodosius, Louis triumphs "sans emportement" (without getting carried away) (25). The affect of absolutism is most succinctly expressed by juxtaposing two expressions used by Vertron: *l'emporter sans s'emporter*. The affect of he who always wins, who always carries the day ("l'emporter") without ever himself being carried away or losing control of his emotions ("s'emporter").[32] This is radically different from the situation of those praising these unparalleled royal achievements. Confronted with the royal sublime, Vertron seems to imply, the artist can only attempt to grasp the impossible, while bearing witness to his own *emportement*, his own bedazzlement and transport, of himself having been carried away by this excess of royal greatness. This at least is what I take Vertron to do during the last few pages of the book. The continuation of his praise takes the form of a series of outbursts, where the *emportement* itself becomes a sign of *éblouissement* and sublime excess: Vertron thus calls on poetry to help his eloquence (55, 57), apostrophizes the king himself as the only worthy recipient of "ces nobles tranports" (these noble transports) (57), evokes him as "LOUIS le très-GRAND" (LOUIS the very GREAT) (57), and flirts with idolatry (55, 58), before twice switching to Latin (58, 59)—all in a form that is difficult to grasp and even more to follow, and in that sense reflective of the "transports" it is carried by. It is still an open question whether Vertron's style itself reaches the sublime, but at the very least it offers itself as an example for readers by modeling for them the appropriate affect of absolutism.

In concluding the discussion of Vertron's 1685 *Parallèle*, I return to the question of what can possibly come after such a radical exercise of royal exemplarity by indicating the direction Vertron's own encomiastic production took next. The year 1686 saw the publication of two related projects. First an expansion of the pool of great heroes of the past in *Le*

---

32. For "emportement," see Vertron, *Parallèle*, 25 (as quoted here, 161). The verbal expression "l'emporter" (to win) is used by Vertron throughout (e.g., 36; as quoted above, 162), and twice in the very last paragraph of the text (58–59).

Nouveau panthéon, ou Le Rapport des divinités du paganisme, des héros de l'Antiquité et des princes surnommés grands aux vertus et aux actions de Louis le Grand (The new pantheon, or the relation between the divinities of paganism, the heroes of antiquity and the princes called great, and the virtues and actions of Louis the Great), from which I will only quote a sentence from the dedication to the king, where the problem of how to speak about the king is itself turned into a figure of praise:

> [P]our parler dignement de l'exemple des Rois, du vrai modèle des Héros, du Prince des Conquérants (je dis plus) pour représenter au naturel le Conquérant des Princes, le Grand des Grands, et le chef-d'œuvre des Cieux, il faudrait savoir parfaitement le langage divin.[33]

> (In order to speak with dignity about the example of Kings, the true model of Heroes, the Prince of Conquerors (I say more) to represent true to nature the Conqueror of Princes, the Great of the Great, and the masterpiece of the Heavens, one would need to know perfectly the divine language.)

Again, what is left to be said? Who can claim to know a divine language able to express the ultimate perfection of this example transcending all examples? Vertron approaches the enunciative situation of negative theology, where all that can be expressed is what the king is not, in a pure *via negativa*. For what is left to be said in face of the royal sublime?

And yet, at the same time as the task of praising the king adequately is rendered impossible and the encomiastic project is closed, in what seems to be a more and more narrow exclusivity, it is also opened up. In a situation where discursive language is powerless and has to yield to exclamation, condensation, and inspired outbursts, *poetry* might be the only possible way forward. This is the direction Vertron takes in a fascinating companion project from 1686, of which the main publication has a title nearly identical to the book discussed above: *Parallèle poétique de Louis le Grand avec les princes surnommés grands* (Poetic parallel between Louis the Great and [other] princes called great). It consists of sonnets and other poems submitted by eager poets and rhymesters from all over France in an open competition to write poems to glorify the king, with Vertron and other members of his circle as judges.[34] This is an interest-

33. Vertron, *Le Nouveau panthéon*, épitre, s.p.
34. For a description of the ways the call for submissions was diffused and the geographical distribution of the actual published poems, see Luciani, "La Province

ing democratization of the genre of royal encomium. Suddenly it is not historiographers and academies that praise the king, but a large public of aspiring panegyric poets who are given the occasion to follow the model offered by Vertron in his first *Parallèle*. The more than one hundred sonnets in the book—and the many more that can be found in smaller booklets that were often bound together with the main book in one volume—are of varying quality, to say the least. However, for my context, it is the omnipresence of the same exemplarity of excess that is the most striking. Together, these poems constitute a unique corpus for a further exploration of the participatory bottom-up aspect of what recent scholarship has termed "the royal sublime" and "absolutist attachments."[35] But most of all, they add an important dimension to the idea of absolutism as a collective dream, by providing an archive documenting how this dream was also dreamt from below.

I will end my discussion of Vertron with a brief quotation from one of these sonnets, yet another text dedicated to the Dauphin, published under the pseudonym Euterpe (the muse of lyric poetry) and based on rhymes assigned by the editor (so-called "bouts rimés"), where we find the following two lines:

Du grand art de régner qu'on apprend de l'histoire
Louis seul est l'Exemple et sa Vie en fait Foi.[36]

(Of the great art of ruling which history teaches us,
Louis alone is the Example and his Life the Proof.)

These two lines provide a terse version of the logic of the *Parallèle*: history is called upon as a reservoir of learning in the mold of the Ciceronian *historia magistra vitae* (history as teacher of life), but only to be sent away as redundant. The glorious example constituted by the life of Louis is all that is needed.

It is now time to turn to the second case I present for consideration under the heading of "absolutist absurdities." After the exploration of

---

poétique au XVIIe siècle," 559–60.

35. Vredenburgh and Bjørnstad, "Un discours 'de majesté'"; Hogg, *Absolutist Attachments*.

36. Saint-Aignan, Vertron et al., *Recueil de sonnets*, 30. In the copy of the *Parallèle poétique* that I consulted at the Bibliothèque Nationale in Paris, this booklet and several others were included at the end of the volume.

Vertron's absolutist inflection of the age-old genre of the parallel, I will examine a surprising absolutist instantiation of the much more recent genre of the literary fairy tale.

Exhibit B: Absolutism from the Cabinet of Fairies to the Cabinet of the King

An anonymous early eighteenth-century engraving shows a pensive young man seated by a table. To his left, a radiant woman delicately holds the reins of two barely restrained eagles pulling her majestic chariot; the whole ensemble appears to float on a turbulent cloud (fig. 12). The man's high standing is obvious from his wig and fashionable outfit. On the table next to him we see the attributes of power: a crown and a scepter. The young man is a king, but a king observed in private, away from the splendor of the throne. He is leaning back in a tall armchair, with an inattentive expression on his face, as if he were alone. Where is his mind? Is he haunted by royal melancholy, by the solitude of power? What is *on* his mind?

The young king is clearly in the foreground in the image. However, through an effect of relative size, turbulent movement, and radiance, the viewer's gaze is drawn toward the woman in the upper right corner. She is enveloped by light, although it is unclear whether she is herself the source of the beams that form a halo around her, or whether she is the recipient of the sun's rays just behind her. In any case, her presence represents an intrusion in an otherwise orderly scene. By looking closely at the far right of the image, between the cloud of the other world and the parallel planks of the parquet, which ground the image in our perspectival space, the viewer can see that there is yet another space represented. The room opens toward what looks like a garden setting: a roundish basin with fountains, in front of a tight row of columns or trees. The distinction between interior and exterior is troubled by the radiant presence of the woman and the eagles on the cloud. How is the viewer to understand the juxtaposition of realistic and marvelous elements? What is going on? Who are the man and the woman?

The engraving illustrates the second edition (1717) of Jean de Préchac's fairy tale "Sans Parangon" (Without equal).[37] The tale had originally been published in 1698 as the first of two tales by Préchac, the other being "La

---

37. In the eight-volume collection *Le Cabinet des fees*, 2:151. The same illustration was used when this collection was reissued in 1731, 2:149.

FIGURE 12. Jean de Préchac, "Sans Parangon." Opening page and detail of the engraving of Sans Parangon and Belle Gloire. From *Le Cabinet des fées: Contenant tous leurs Ouvrages*, 8 vols. (Amsterdam: Eshenne Roger, 1717), vol. 2, 151. Photograph: Courtesy of Cotsen Children's Library, Department of Special Collections, Princeton University Library.

Reine des fées" (Queen of the fairies), in a volume titled *Contes moins contes que les autres* (Tales less tale-like than the others).[38] Both tales were collected alongside texts by other writers and published in 1717 as part of an eight-volume *Cabinet des fées* (Cabinet of the fairies) printed in duodecimo format. Their original dedicatory letter (to which I return below) is missing in this edition, but each fairy tale is preceded by an illustration. The copper-plate engraving appears above the title printed in bold letters, itself followed by "Il y avait une fois un Roi et une Reine . . ." (Once upon a time there was a king and a queen . . .).

The engraving thus portrays a scene from a fairy tale, and what the reader sees indeed corresponds to the expectations of the genre. First of all, the image stages the encounter between natural and supernatural planes of reality, with the marvelous intruding into an otherwise orderly, recognizable world. Furthermore, both the engraving and the opening

38. This collection was reissued twenty-six years later, between the two publications of "Sans Parangon" mentioned in the preceding footnote.

words of the tale remind us about the privileged proximity of fairies and kings, or, more precisely, of the preoccupations of fairy tales with royalty. The two realms are represented in tension. We see a king, a palace, a royal garden. Somehow, the realm of royalty is more worthy of the attention of the supernatural. The reader is in the domain of the extraordinary and incomparable, as stressed by the title of the tale. The subsequent sentences explicitly refer to the privileged link between royalty and the fairies, but they describe furious fairies and a king who abhors their enchantments, and a mediating queen who consults the fairies without informing her royal mate. Already at the threshold of the text, in word and image, a secret magic world aligns with positive executive power.

The tale's opening draws aptly on a genre and its conventions, but important differences emerge, as well. Préchac had been a prolific writer of popular novels, publishing between 1677 and 1690 more than thirty *historiettes* (small stories), as he himself called them on one occasion,[39] alongside a successful career as secretary, private teacher, and high bureaucrat for the great of the age. As pointed out by Tony Gheeraert, whose modern edition of "Sans Parangon" I will quote from in what follows, Préchac's two careers, at once novelist and favorite of princes, were inseparable: "he wrote only in order to better flatter the great and to make his way in the world."[40] When he picked up his pen again after eight years and published his only two fairy tales in 1698, he did so at the height of the vogue of fairy tales in late seventeenth-century French salons. In fact, the two most widely read writers of fairy tales both published their most popular collections the year before Préchac's book came out, namely, *Les Contes des fées* by Madame d'Aulnoy (who thereby coined the term "fairy tale") and *Histoires ou contes du temps passé* (Histories or tales of past times) by Charles Perrault. But when Préchac turns to this new, fashionable genre, his writing is still encomiastic. He certainly writes to please his readers, leading them through a charming oscillation between suspense and marvels, but he also does so to please and celebrate his patrons. The result is a new way of weaving actual historical events into the texture of the tale through thinly veiled allegories, which would have an important afterlife in the following century. In the words of Lewis Seifert, "Préchac is the first French writer of fairy tales to make such explicit and sustained al-

---

39. Namely, in the dedicatory letter of *Le Prince esclave*, quoted here from Gheeraert, "Introduction," 668.

40. "[I]l ne fut auteur que pour flatter les grands et ainsi mieux faire sa cour." Gheeraert, 667–68. When I quote from Gheeraert's 2005 edition of "Sans Parangon" in what follows, the references will be given parenthetically in the text.

lusions to historical reality, a technique frequently employed during the 18th century (albeit more often in the satirical mode)."[41] In the case of "Sans Parangon," the story allegorically retells the decisive moments of the reign of Louis XIV as a series of events structured according to the whims of an enchanted Chinese princess named Belle Gloire (Beautiful Glory) and the challenging tasks she gives King Sans Parangon (Without Equal).[42]

The king in the engraving is thus not only a fairy-tale character but also a specific king. But how does the position and function of the princess in the cloud relate to this king? What do the engraving and the corresponding scene in the fairy tale reveal about the royal agency of King Sans Parangon and, through him, of Louis XIV? How is the reader to interpret the absentminded expression on the king's face? The engraving was published in 1717, two years after the death of Louis XIV. Would it have been thinkable to include this illustration in an earlier publication? Where is the line that distinguishes praise from critique? In what follows, I unpack the relation between the king and the princess within the tale, on the one hand, and between the real-life king and his fairy-tale avatar, on the other, by looking more closely at certain key scenes in the fairy tale. This is an extraordinary fairy tale that might easily baffle modern readers. However, as I demonstrate, the element of the story that many scholars have found the most puzzling, indeed the most subversive—namely, the dynamic between the king and the princess as portrayed in the engraving—leads to the very heart of the symbolic universe of absolutism, and to what I call the dream of absolutism. Préchac's peculiar casting of the lead couple of the tale stages nothing less than the dynamic encounter between the two central concepts in my exploration of the dream of absolutism: King Without Equal (who is thereby also, Without Example) courting Princess Beautiful Glory. This is a tale that glorifies the king by presenting him

41. Seifert, "Jean de Préchac," 400.

42. The translation of the name of the eponymous hero of "Sans Parangon" as King Without Equal is not completely obvious. According to the primary definition in Furetière's dictionary, "parangon" is a "[v]ieux mot qui signifiait autrefois une chose excellente et hors de comparaison" (an old word that used to mean an excellent thing beyond comparison), with the first example given as "Cela est sans *parangon*" (This is without *parangon*). Furetière, *Dictionnaire universel*, "parangon." Within the tale, we learn that the reason the prince was given this name by the good fairy at the outset was "parce que jamais prince ne pourra lui être comparé" (because never [any] prince could be compared to him) (696). Therefore, a bolder translation of the name of the eponymous hero of the tale would have been: King Incomparable. A more pedantic choice would have been King Without Paragon, and it wouldn't have been completely far-fetched to go with King Without Example.

with an image of the marvelous workings of absolutism. But such a grand enterprise is not without its complications and surprises.

First of all, a few more remarks regarding the threshold that marks the entry into the fairy tale proper are in order. Integrating a thinly veiled allegory of the glorious exploits of Louis XIV into a fairy tale is a delicate business: such a low genre, without precedent in the canon from antiquity and associated with women and children, could tarnish instead of adding to the glory of the king. The titles of both the fairy tale and the book where it was first published already betray an acute awareness of this risk by claiming a special status for our story: Prince Sans Parangon may be a fairy-tale prince, but a fairy-tale prince like no other; similarly, the title of the 1698 book declares itself a volume of fairy tales, but from the outset these are tales less tale-like than the others.[43] Because it is so close to the glorious exploits and the marvelous and fabulous reality of the actual and even more incomparable King Louis, the story is at once more marvelous and more real than other fairy tales.

The same preoccupation fills the dedicatory letter of the original volume. For to whom should an author dedicate a celebration of the king written in a genre too low to merit being dedicated to the king himself? Préchac sidesteps the problem in a curious fashion by addressing the dedicatory letter not to the King Without Equal nor to any other person but rather to what he calls "la Sans Parangon des cascades" (the cascade Without Equal), that is, to "la très haute, très magnifique, et excellentissime cascade de Marly" (the most high, the most magnificent, and most excellent cascade of Marly) (687).

The cascade of Marly was the most recent and impressive architectural-technological wonder at the time Préchac wrote his tales. Situated at the Marly estate—the king's leisure residence, close to Versailles, but in a more private, less formal, yet also more exclusive setting—it consisted of sixty-three basins made from colored marble leading a vast and richly ornamented artificial river down a steep hill (fig. 13). It was the greatest cascade of the age, and the sense of wonder it evoked was increased by the contraption that supplied the water from the nearby river Seine, the so-called Marly machine, itself considered a marvel of hydraulic

---

43. The title of the original collection is completely absent in the 1717 volume of the *Cabinet des fées*, where the engraving first occurs with "Sans Parangon." Interestingly, the title reappears when this volume is reissued in 1731. In both tales by Préchac, a version of the original title, although singular rather than plural, is inserted between the opening illustration and the title of the tale: "conte moins conte que les autres" (tale less tale-like than the others).

FIGURE 13. J. Rigaud, *Vue de la cascade de Marly* (eighteenth century). From *Recueil choisi des plus belles vues des palais, châteaux et maisons royales de Paris et des environs* (Paris: J. Fr. Chereau, n.d.). Photograph: Courtesy of Marquand Library of Art and Archaeology, Princeton University.

engineering. So impressive were the size and beauty of the cascade that its workings were attributed to fairies.[44] The hyperbole is therefore less excessive than we might at first think when Préchac opens his dedication:

CHARMANTE CASCADE,

Le rapport qu'il y a de vous aux ouvrages des fées, m'engage à vous dédier ces contes, qui paraîtront moins fabuleux toutes les fois qu'on examinera avec attention votre surprenante beauté, et tous les autres prodiges dont vous êtes environnée, cet agréable château où l'on trouve toutes choses sans y rien apporter, ces jardins délicieux, ce superbe bocage, qui sans s'assujettir à l'ordre des saisons, ni sans attendre le secours des siècles, est devenu une vaste forêt; toutes ces merveilles justifient mes contes. (687)

(CHARMING CASCADE,

The relation that exists between you and the works of the fairies brings me to dedicate to you these tales, which appear less fabulous every time one

44. See Gheeraert, "Introduction," 671–72; and Thacker, *The History of Gardens*, 157–58, for further details.

attentively examines your surprising beauty, and all the other prodigies surrounding you, this pleasant palace where one finds all things without bringing any, these delicious gardens, this superb bocage, which without surrendering to the order of the seasons or waiting for the help of the centuries has become a vast forest: all these marvels justify my tales.)

The very first line establishes a juxtaposition between the works of the king (namely, the cascade, the palace, the gardens), on the one hand, and the works of the fairies, on the other. In fact, the mobilization of a vocabulary of the extraordinary ("your *surprising* beauty," "all the other *prodigies*," and so on) evokes a royal reality that surpasses the world of fairies. Therefore, as I suggested in my interpretation of the title of the original 1698 volume, "these tales [. . .] appear less fabulous"—that is, less tale-like—for two precise reasons. First, on a general level, the stories are less fantastic because the works of the fairies are less fabulous than those of the king in the real world. Second, in this specific case, the allegoric tale we are about to read actually recounts the real exploits of the king.

There is a tight connection between the sense of marvel at the king's exploits and the perception of an increased human mastery over nature. The royal gardens at Versailles and Marly had elevated the ability of humans to impose order on the chaos of nature to a new level. Even the seasons and growth cycles were losing their control over humankind. In the case of the cascade, what visitors see is even more against nature, if not to say above nature, supernatural. Its "surprising beauty" points directly to the feeling of being in the presence of a prodigy or marvel. As the rest of the dedicatory letter makes clear, water had never moved in this way before; certainly there had been jets of water, but "vous seule, admirable Cascade, êtes remontée jusqu'au faîte des montagnes" (you alone, admirable Cascade, have risen up to the height of mountains). Indeed, novelty, beauty, and abundance seem to merge when the cascade meets the sun. Not only does the cascade "distribu[e] [ses] belles eaux avec une abondance prestigieuse" (distribute [its] beautiful waters with a prodigious abundance), but "la lumière de [ses] eaux éclaire tous les lieux des environs" (the light from [its] waters illuminates all the surrounding places) (687). Very much like the sun and the monarch who is known to us as the Sun King, the cascade is not only a beautiful object in itself, but also a force that enables further beauty in its surroundings.

In the very last sentence of the dedicatory letter, the author exhorts that "la Sans Parangon des cascades [. . .] merit[e] toutes les louanges et tous les applaudissements qu'on saurait [lui] donner" (the cascade without equal [. . .] deserve[s] all the praise and all the applause we are able to give [it]) (687). The same is obviously true for the king without equal. In this way, at its threshold, the book reminds the reader of the glorification due to the king, while the tale that follows glorifies him by presenting him with an image of the anatomy of this glory. The challenge facing the writer of such an encomiastic fairy tale is not entirely unlike the task of those who were writing the actual history of Louis XIV's reign. In the remarkable statement from the early years of his personal reign first quoted in the introduction, the king himself declares to the members of the Petite Académie in charge of overseeing that vast project:

> Vous pouvez, Messieurs, juger de l'estime que je fais de vous, puisque je vous confie la chose du monde qui m'est la plus précieuse, qui est *ma gloire*: je suis sûr que vous *ferez des merveilles*; je tâcherai de ma part de vous fournir de la matière qui mérite d'être *mise en œuvre* par des gens aussi habiles que vous êtes.[45]

> (You may, Gentlemen, judge the appreciation I have for you, since I entrust you with the thing in the world which is the most precious to me, namely, *my glory*. I am sure you will *do marvels*; I will try on my side to provide you with matter which deserves to be *given form* by people as competent as you are.)

As formulated in this authoritative statement, the function of the official encomiastic literature is to find a *form* that can accommodate the glorious *matter* provided by the king. The academicians will do marvels (earning their own glory in the process) by conveying the glorious marvels done by the king. This intent is also the justification of Préchac's project: "all these marvels"—that is, cascade, palace, garden, all provided by the king—"justify my tales."

These same elements highlighted by the dedicatory letter are also present in the engraving—palace, garden, cascade—but only in the background. The threshold of the tale redirects the reader's attention away from the public splendor of the expressions of absolutism and toward its inner, private core or principle. Indeed, as I shall return to soon, the cabinet of the king portrayed in the engraving is the only space where the actual reign of Sans Parangon intersects with that of the fairies—but even then, only in an ambiguous manner in this least tale-like of tales. Instead, the influence of the fairies occurs *before* the birth of the prince

---

45. Perrault, *Mémoires*, xxv–xxvi; my emphasis. See above, 22–23, for a first discussion of the statement.

as an enabling and empowering force. Returning now to the opening of the tale, the uninitiated reader will first of all be struck by the very slow staging of its eponymous hero. The king and the queen from the "Once upon a time" sentence quoted above are in fact his maternal grandparents (corresponding to Philip III of Spain and Margaret of Austria), and Prince Sans Parangon is not born until a third of the way into the tale. At that moment, much is already decided. The mother of Sans Parangon (corresponding to Anne of Austria) has managed to enlist a good fairy, Clairance, to counteract the nefarious influence of the furious, evil fairy Ligourde. The young prince's future is shaped by the spells and counter-spells cast by the two fairies. In fact, the long delay before his birth is the work of Clairance, who abducts him after a first, invisible birth and keeps him for twenty-one years in an enchanted world to protect him against the violent intentions of Ligourde. This interval has the advantage of explaining not only the long sterility of Anne before the birth of Louis XIV (it lasted twenty-one years, making his birth a miracle and him Louis Dieudonné, the God-given), but also the political precocity of the young Prince Sans Parangon.

The good fairy makes sure that he receives a solid education in the art of government, the art of war, the fine arts, and so on. In other words, the prince receives a pre-education that he remembers when his real education begins after his second birth. The same is the case when it comes to his love of Belle Gloire, who is presented as "la princesse de la Chine, qui était sans contredit la plus belle et à même temps la plus fière princesse de la terre, et qui était enchantée pour plusieurs siècles" (the princess of China who was without question at once the most beautiful and the proudest princess of the world, and who had been enchanted for several centuries) (696–97). From the first days of his prenatal abduction, the prince is as if enchanted by her songs. Soon "Belle Gloire s'acquit un si furieux ascendant sur son esprit, qu'il s'ennuyait toujours partout où il ne la voyait pas; [. . .] ne se proposant en toutes choses que de plaire à Belle Gloire." (Belle Gloire got such a fierce grip on his mind that he was always distraught wherever he did not see her [. . .] and all he wanted was to please Belle Gloire) (698). In this way, the prologue becomes a long prolepsis: the amorous game of challenges given by the proud princess and their realization by the brave prince, which structures the last two-thirds of the tale recounting the life of Sans Parangon *after* his birth (and which thus represents the fairy-tale version of the real exploits of Louis XIV), is only reenacting a similar pattern from *before* his birth.

Or so it seems. From an encomiastic point of view, there is an obvious danger if *too* much is decided before the birth of the prince. However

efficient the educational prolepsis is as a narrative device, it still risks seriously limiting the heroic potential of the prince by subjecting his power
to that of the fairies. Or worse, perhaps this narrative efficacy itself causes
a problem by limiting the absolute liberty of the hero. Before considering the narration of the "real" life of Sans Parangon, I will look at two
key moments from his prenatal existence where the narration seems to
undermine the sovereignty of the fairies in their own enchanted world.

This is how Préchac describes the taking of the prince by the good
fairy: "Clairance enleva Sans Parangon; et comme son art lui apprenait
les grandes choses que ce prince opérerait à l'avenir, elle se fit un grand
plaisir de le bien élever." (Clairance abducted Sans Parangon; and since
her art informed her about the great deeds the prince would bring about
in the future, she took great pleasure in raising him well) (696). The logic
of this passage becomes opaque once the reader realizes that the "art" of
Clairance evoked here is her psychic capacity. The fact that the prince has
been raised so well by Clairance seems to explain his precocity and his
victorious life in general (that is the apparent function of the prolepsis),
but the reader now realizes that the fairy undertakes her educational project only *because* of the luminous future of the prince. It is as if his future
preexisted the education he receives from Clairance, or at least existed
independently of it, without really needing it.

A couple of pages later, this displacement in the hierarchy of powers
has its most striking example. What is at stake here is neither the description by the narrator nor the imagination of the reader (two scenarios envisioned in the discussion of Vertron above), but the power of imagination of the prince himself. Equipped by the good fairy with "une baguette
dont il n'avait qu'à frapper trois fois pour faire paraître tout ce qu'il ima-
ginait" (a magic wand with which he just had to hit thrice to make all
he imagined appear), Sans Parangon starts practicing his mastery of the
fine arts by constructing and decorating a "superb palace" that has some
resemblance to Versailles. After a description of the stairways and the
apartments, and before that of the garden, the tale leads the reader into

> une grande galerie ornée de glaces et de belles statues de marbre et de
> bronze, avec des peintures merveilleuses, où l'on remarquait des actions
> d'un héros si prodigieuses, qu'on ne voyait rien de pareil même dans la
> fable. (699)

> (a large hall decorated with mirrors and beautiful statues of marble and
> bronze, with marvelous paintings where one noticed such prodigious ac-
> tions by a hero, that one could not find anything similar even in myth.)

The allegorical description of Versailles here is even more easily deci-
pherable than elsewhere, since the Hall of Mirrors in the seventeenth
century was called precisely "la Grande Galerie." Whose work is this
enchanted gallery? The execution of the palace is certainly the result of
fairy magic and owes more specifically to the wand offered by Clairance
to Sans Parangon; but the imagination, the conception, belongs to the
future king, who anticipates the work of his architects, of his artists,
and, above all, of his painter—a fictionalized Charles Le Brun—as well
as his own heroic actions depicted in the work of the painter. In fact,
this passage reiterates the distinction drawn by Louis XIV to the Petite
Académie: there, it was a question of the matter provided by the king
and the marvels made by the academicians; here, the order is inversed,
and the representation precedes the action, with the prince playing
the role of the future hero as well as that of the present artist. If the enchanted hall of mirrors depicts actions so extraordinary that "one could
not find anything similar even in myth," the experience owes less to the
executive power of the fairy (after all, myths frequently contain marvels) and more to the power of imagination and anticipation of the future king. The images of the heroic actions yet to come transcend even
myth, and these are the actions that the rest of Préchac's tale narrates. In
his prenatal existence, the prince thereby produces his own prolepsis in
"these marvelous paintings," which readers are invited to see as surpassing even the amazing events of the fairy tale that they are in the process
of reading.

It is worth pausing for a moment here, in order to compare this surprising version of the phantasm of a radically autonomous, absolutist
conception with other instantiations of the same dream discussed earlier
in this book. In chapter 1, I explored the king's own dream about writing the one and only book necessary for the instruction of the Dauphin,
a dream resurfacing in the submissions to the French Academy's award
competition inviting the nation's poets to envision that enterprise: heroic exploits from the past finding their glorious expression in the present when the hand that wielded the sword now holds the pen, as if the
sublimity of the deed could only be properly captured in language by he
who originally conceived the deed. Earlier in this chapter, I showed how
Vertron upped the ante further, when he stressed that neither the Ancients nor his contemporaries could possibly conceive of Louis le Grand
if he didn't already exist (which explains the superiority of the Moderns
over the Ancients); his incomparability is such that he is properly un-
inventable. This is where the structure of Préchac's encomiastic fairy tale
seems to go one step further in imagining a sublime act of prenatal self-

invention: Prince Sans Parangon had it all in him from the beginning, indeed from *before* the beginning.

To further ponder the anatomy of this self-invention, I return to chapter 2 and my analysis of the actual paintings by Charles Le Brun in the Hall of Mirrors at Versailles. There is, in fact, one more layer of anticipation in the passage from Préchac quoted above. In the real-life counterpart to what Préchac calls, inside the allegory of his tale, "marvelous paintings where one noticed such prodigious actions by a hero," there is an intriguing echo of the key scene of the tale. As demonstrated in chapter 2, the most glorious of these "prodigious actions" did not occur on the battlefield or even in the deliberation of wars to come, although these actions constitute the subject of nearly all the large-scale paintings of the gallery. Rather, it is the scene depicted in the central painting, which, according to the official contemporary description by Pierre Rainssant, "on doit regarder comme le premier, puisqu'il renferme ce qui a été, pour ainsi dire, l'*origine* de toutes les belles actions, qui sont représentées dans les autres" (should be considered as the first, since it encloses what was, as it were, the *origin* of all the beautiful actions which are represented in the others).[46] What is at stake here is the nature of this origin. It is in the middle of the central painting, literally at the symbolic center of Versailles, that the key constellation from the fairy tale reappears: the young king who is amorously turned toward a personification of glory (see chapter 2 and plate 1). The present-day inscription of this painting plays down the importance of the amorous constellation through a myopic focus on the right hand of the absolute king who had just seized full power, represented by the helm of a ship, after the death of first minister Cardinal Mazarin: "Le Roi gouverne par lui-même, 1661" (The King governs on his own, 1661). However, the rest of the royal body, and especially the gesture of his left arm and the direction of his eyes (which are *not* looking at the state he is governing), says more about the logic of this newly inaugurated absolutism. As discussed in detail in chapter 2, this unexpectedly expressive royal body corresponds better with the original tripartite Latin inscription of the painting: "INTER PACIS ET FORTUNÆ FLORENTIS ILLECEBRAS / LUDOVICUS MAGNUS AD GUBERNACULA IMPERII ACCEDENS / GLORIÆ AMORE INCENDITUR" (Amidst the charms that peace and favorable fortune offer him / The king taking the government of his state / He is burning with love for glory).[47] If this painting

---

46. Rainssant, *Explication des tableaux de la galerie de Versailles*, 2; my emphasis.

47. See above, 135–49; for the quotation, 135n75; and Bjørnstad, "'Plus d'éclaircissement touchant la grande galerie de Versailles,'" 336–38.

FIGURE 14. Jean Baudoin, "Gloire" and "Gloire des princes." From *Iconologie, ou, Explication nouvelle de plusieurs images, emblèmes, et autres figures hiéroglyphiques des Vertus, des Vices, des Arts, des Sciences* . . . (Paris: Chez Mathieu Guillemot, 1644), 79. Photograph: Courtesy of Rare Book Division, Department of Special Collections, Princeton University Library.

shows the origin of "all the beautiful actions" that followed, it does so not only by depicting Louis's decision to "govern on his own," but above all by reminding the viewer of his reasons for doing so. The founding moment is when Louis seizes sole power; the founding motivation is his pursuit of glory.

The constellation of the amorous king and female personification of glory is an iconological commonplace, and Le Brun's depiction of glory both here and elsewhere in the gallery is clearly indebted to the plates that Jean Baudoin commissioned for his 1644 translation/adaptation of Cesare Ripa's *Iconologia* (fig. 14).[48] It is important to notice, however, that this constellation is much more than an iconological device, much more than an efficient instrument for transmitting a certain message. Rather, the commonplace is a constitutive part of the period's way of thinking about royal glory.

Within the structure of the fairy tale, these observations make for an even richer prolepsis. Before his birth, Prince Sans Parangon anticipates several of his future skills and exploits, including the actual construction of a Versailles-like palace. He also conceives of other, even more glorious accomplishments and their representations that will decorate the walls of the central gallery of this palace. And at the heart of these "marvel-

48. Cf. the entries entitled "Gloire" and "Gloire des princes" in the first part of Baudoin's *Iconologie*, 81–82.

ous paintings where one noticed such prodigious actions by a hero, that one could not find anything similar even in myth," the visitor to the enchanted palace will find inscribed the motivation for the whole glorious enterprise, which is also the structuring device of the fairy tale itself. Like the gallery, the tale turns out to be a hall of mirrors.

This focus on the core constellation of the king and the female personification of glory reveals the striking similarities between the 1717 engraving from the second edition of "Sans Parangon" and the central painting of the Hall of Mirrors. There are certainly some intriguing differences, too, mainly related to the pose of the king in the engraving, and I will return to these below. But first, a further mapping of the similarities is in order. Members of the Petite Académie in fact consider the personification of glory in great detail in their descriptions of Le Brun's painting. I find particularly fascinating the great lengths to which André Félibien goes to evoke her beauty, as if to justify the enthrallment of the king:

> [. . .] une belle femme assise sur les nuées, et dont les traits du visage ont beaucoup de douceur, de grâce et de majesté. Sur ses cheveux blonds brille une couronne d'or, et sa tête est toute environnée de lumière. Elle a la gorge et les bras découverts. Une espèce de tunique blanche qui lui couvre le reste du corps est serrée d'une ceinture d'or, et par-dessus est un grand manteau bleu rehaussé d'or. Cette figure représente la gloire.[49]

> ([. . .] a beautiful woman sitting on the clouds and whose facial traits are filled with sweetness, grace and majesty. On her blond hair shines a crown of gold, and her head is entirely surrounded by light. Her chest and arms are bare. A sort of white tunic covering the rest of her body is fastened with a belt of gold, and on top is a great overcoat in blue enhanced with gold. This figure represents glory.)

The engraving echoes an emphasis on the clouds, her majestic pose, and radiance. It is obvious that the anonymous engraver, like Préchac himself, was well versed in the iconological tradition. It is also likely that the engraving responds to the passage from the tale analyzed here by referring directly to the central painting at Versailles. In fact, considering one last time the passage of the fairy tale referring to the Hall of Mirrors, it

---

49. For this quotation, see Bjørnstad, "'Plus d'éclaircissement touchant la grande galerie de Versailles,'" 325. Other members of the Petite Académie who stress the same constellation in their description of this painting are Tallemant, François Charpentier, and Rainssant.

is notable that the very next sentence evokes the space that corresponds to the third plane of the engraving: "le magnifique jardin où l'on entrait en sortant du palais; on rencontrait de grands bassins de marbre blanc, avec des jets d'eau" (the magnificent garden that one entered while exiting the palace; there one found large basins of white marble, with jets of water) (699).[50]

Returning now to the question of the relative autonomy of the fairies, on the one hand, and of the allegorized king, on the other, the preceding discussion has demonstrated that the sovereignty of the fairies is at times undermined inside their own enchanted world. This development anticipates a more radical displacement of the marvelous *after* the birth of the prince. The fairies are, in fact, nearly absent from Sans Parangon's kingdom, except for the regular visits of Princess Belle Gloire. The glorious exploits of Sans Parangon are all the more marvelous because they are achieved in a sovereign way without the magic participation of the fairies in a world that is as if disenchanted, except for the new magic of the king. In order to praise the actual king more forcefully, the fairy tale undermines the premises of the genre itself, with the final step being the peculiar ending (to which I return shortly), when Belle Gloire challenges Sans Parangon to "faire la guerre aux fées" (wage war against the fairies) (727). This is a tale less tale-like than the others because the true seat of power, including the magical power to perform real-life marvels, has shifted from the cabinet of the fairies to the cabinet of the king.

And yet, an enchanted Chinese princess remains present in this anti-fairy development, as its source and instigator, in a way that merits closer scrutiny. When Sans Parangon and Belle Gloire first meet outside the world of the fairies, Sans Parangon is already a young man. His father had died when he was very young (corresponding to Louis XIII's death in 1643, when Louis XIV was four years old), so Sans Parangon has been king for a long while, but he is not yet governing on his own; he still depends on the counsel of "un fameux druide" (a famous druid) (703) chosen by his mother (and corresponding to Mazarin). The good fairy Clairance has just made her first and only appearance in the actual life of Sans Parangon, explaining that Belle Gloire is in fact the embodiment of a spell cast by the evil fairy Ligourde, intended to give him "dangereux conseils" and "espérances chimériques" (dangerous advice [and] chimeric expectations) (705). However, filled with desire to see the princess again, the

---

50. Interestingly, the subsequent enumeration of aspects of the basins develops into a description of the Cascade of Marly, which was of course not in immediate sight but close by, recalling the dedicatory letter.

king pays no attention to the warnings of the good fairy and only notices her indication that Belle Gloire will appear to him once a month, following the movement of the sun through the zodiac.

> Enfin le changement du soleil si désiré arriva, et le même jour Belle Gloire parut dans le cabinet du roi, dans un char en forme de trône, parsemé d'émeraudes et de lauriers, et attelé de douze cygnes: je ne parlerai point de son ajustement, parce qu'il était effacé par son extrême beauté, et par l'éclat de ses yeux qui aurait ébloui tout le monde, si elle n'eut pas été invisible. (705)

> (Finally, the long-awaited passage of the sun happened, and the same day Belle Gloire appeared in the cabinet of the king in a chariot in the form of a throne, covered with emeralds and laurel leaves, and pulled by twelve swans: I will not speak of her finery because they were eclipsed by her extreme beauty and by the sparkle of her eyes, which would have dazzled everyone, if she had not been invisible.)

This passages echoes the scene from the 1717 engraving, with the difference that Belle Gloire's throne-shaped chariot for the time being is pulled by swans, not eagles.[51] Everything else in the engraving seems to respond perfectly to this passage, including the portrayal of the location: the cabinet of the king. According to Furetière, the primary meaning of the term "cabinet" at the time was "[l]e lieu le plus retiré dans le plus bel appartement des Palais, des grandes maisons" (the most withdrawn place in the most beautiful apartment of palaces, of great mansions).[52] Furetière goes on to point out a figurative meaning related to what happens in this space, a meaning that is spelled out most explicitly in the first edition of the French Academy's dictionary from 1694: "*Cabinet*, veut dire aussi, Les secrets, les mystères les plus cachés de la Cour" (*Cabinet*, also means, The most hidden secrets or mysteries of the Court).[53] It is from within the cabinet of the king that Belle Gloire dominates Sans Parangon, and this is

---

51. It is not until later in Sans Parangon's reign that Belle Gloire's swans are replaced by eagles, after a curious accident in which they are blinded by the splendors of the new Versailles-like palace and end up in the canal in the palace garden instead of in the king's cabinet ("Sans Parangon," 711). Traditionally, swans pull the chariot of Aphrodite/Venus, while Zeus/Jupiter holds the reins of eagles. Therefore, the switch from swans to eagles in the fairy tale discreetly displaces the emphasis from Venus to Jupiter, or from mastery in matters of love to sovereignty tout court.

52. Furetière, *Dictionnaire universel*, "cabinet."

53. *Dictionnaire de l'Académie française* (1694), "cabinet."

indeed the best-kept secret of the court, the most hidden mystery of the state. It is therefore only fitting that she is invisible to everybody except the king.

Belle Gloire's first visit to the king's cabinet sets up the dynamic between the two lovers of daring challenges and glorious exploits that will structure the rest of the tale. Just before departing, the princess questions whether the king has "assez de vertu pour me servir à ma mode, et pour me sacrifier toutes choses" (enough virtue to serve me as I require, and to sacrifice all things for me) (706). At the same moment during her second visit, she demands: "[I]l me faut des victimes mêlées de sang et de lauriers; en un mot, songe que tu es né pour Belle Gloire." (I need victims mixed with blood and laurel leaves; in one word, remember that you were born for Belle Gloire) (707). These visits make the king realize that the druid (alias Mazarin) has prevented him from following the natural instincts of his heart. It is this realization, in turn, that leads him to the decision to govern on his own when the druid passes away shortly thereafter. Without Belle Gloire's enabling intervention, the text seems to imply, there would be no royal seizure of full power and, consequently, no royal greatness, no Louis the Great. Inside the logic of the fairy tale, the scene from the 1717 engraving predates and prefigures the one in the central painting in the Hall of Mirrors.

The narration of King Sans Parangon's further heroic actions basically follows the same somewhat monotonous pattern: first a tricky challenge from the enchanted princess, then the disbelief of the king confronted with such an obstacle, and finally his success, which is as triumphant as it is surprising. Quite naturally, every new challenge from Belle Gloire leads Sans Parangon to a heroic exploit for which a counterpart in the life of Louis XIV is easily identifiable for the informed reader,[54] be it the military campaign in Franche-Comté in 1668, the work on the Canal des Deux Mers linking the Mediterranean and the Atlantic (1666–81), the crossing of the Rhine in 1672, the main construction of Versailles, or a series of specific victories in the War of the League of Augsburg (1688–97).

For an illustration of the dynamics directing the heroic life of Sans Parangon, it suffices to return to the construction of his royal residence, but

54. This identification would have been all the easier for contemporary readers since the various artifacts celebrating the heroic exploits of the king would revolve around the same relatively brief catalog of prodigious actions. There would already be a strong sense of familiarity, if not to say repetition, after visiting the Hall of Mirrors and then reading the texts by Vertron and Préchac. Luckily, modern editions of the fairy tale have helpful information for less-informed modern readers.

this time its non-enchanted, real-life version. Belle Gloire's first request for a beautiful palace where the king can welcome her had led Sans Parangon to construct one of the world's most beautiful palaces in the capital of his state. However, he was not even finished with this project (corresponding to the embellishment of the Louvre in Paris) when Belle Gloire let him know that she disliked city dwellings. In fact, she continued, "s'il voulait lui donner un témoignage bien véritable de son attachement, et de sa complaisance pour elle, il fallait lui bâtir à la campagne, un palais et des jardins semblables à ceux qu'il avait imaginés lui-même chez Clairance, par la vertu de sa baguette." ([I]f he wanted to give her a proper testimony of his affection and his complaisance for her, then he had to build in the countryside a palace and gardens similar to those he himself had imagined at Clairance's, with the help of his wand.) Sans Parangon is "épouvanté d'une proposition si extravagante" (excruciated by such an extravagant proposition); after all, he is painfully aware that "le palais de la fée n'était qu'une illusion" (the fairy palace was only an illusion) (710). However, instead of relenting, Belle Gloire heightens the challenge:

> Tu sais bien, reprit Belle Gloire, que les choses ordinaires ne m'accommodent point, et que je n'aime que celles qui approchent de l'impossible; je t'ai fait connaître ce que je désire, c'est à toi à te consulter, et à examiner si tu as, et assez de courage, et assez d'envie de me plaire, pour l'entreprendre. (710)

> (You are well aware, Belle Gloire continued, that ordinary deeds don't suit me at all, and that I only like deeds that approach the impossible; I have let you know what my desire is, now it is up to you to look into yourself and examine whether you have both enough courage and enough will to please me, for undertaking it.)

The challenge fills Sans Parangon with an embarrassment without equal,[55] because he is convinced of the impossibility of the task. And yet, to his own surprise, Sans Parangon is up to the challenge. In fact, "[il] n'eut jamais de repos que le palais et les jardins ne fussent dans leur perfection [. . .] et quoiqu'il ne tâchât qu'à imiter ce qu'il avait déjà fait chez la fée, il est constant qu'il surpassa le palais enchanté en beaucoup de choses." ([He] didn't relax at all until the palace and the garden had reached their perfection [. . .] and although he only tried to imitate what he had already

---

55. "Jamais il n'y eut d'embarras pareil à celui de ce Prince." Préchac, "Sans Parangon, " 711.

done during his stay with the fairy, it is a fact that he surpassed the enchanted palace in many ways) (711). The last line in this passage marks an important moment in the reorientation of the marvelous inside an encomiastic framework: it is the royal reality that supplants the illusion of the fairies, the real palace that surpasses the enchanted one. The true marvels are found not in fairy tales but at Versailles.

In this way, the appropriateness of the title of the volume where the fairy tale was first published is once and for all confirmed. This fairy tale is less of a tale than the others because all it does is present us with the allegorical truth about Versailles and its king. Furthermore, it is worth noticing that the enchanted palace already was the work of the king; all he does here is, as we just heard, "imitate what he had already done during his stay with the fairy." By surpassing the enchanted palace, it is his own example he goes beyond, thereby remaining faithful to his name to the highest degree. Sans Parangon outdoes even his own magical example. His is an absolutism without equal.

The logic at work here is *not* that of a movement toward rest, toward a satisfied state of peace, which would be reached once the challenges have been fulfilled—that is, in the present case, once Versailles has reached its definitive perfection, as one could imagine from the expression quoted above: "[il] n'eut jamais de *repos* que . . ." ([he] didn't *relax* at all until . . .) ([or more literally,] [he] never had any *rest* until . . .). Rather, the movement seems perpetual, insatiable, driven by a sense that what has been achieved is never enough. Therefore, the marvelous exploits of the king are only half the story of this glorious absolutism. To get the full picture, so to speak, we need to return to the primary scene in the cabinet of the king and to the dynamic between Sans Parangon and Belle Gloire, as portrayed in the 1717 engraving.

As the unfolding of the events in the fairy tale makes clear, the real-life marvelous exploits achieved by the king do not in any way rely on the magical power of the fairies. Moreover, their execution is not in any way dependent on the intervention of Belle Gloire. In this sense, his power is indeed absolute. And yet, although he *could* have done as much without the secret intervention of Belle Gloire, he would not have *wanted* to do it and so would not actually have done it without her. In this way, the agency of the king becomes highly ambiguous. Belle Gloire dominates him, but in an entirely hidden way, exercising her influence on his will outside the view of his subjects. While Sans Parangon may be an active king in the eyes of the world, his role in relation to Belle Gloire is one of passivity, if not submission. In fact, as reported in the tale, he acts and talks only in response to her challenges. The royal desire for glory has become the desire *of* glory, identical to Belle Gloire's own desire and subject to the whims of her logic.

This is the point where it becomes crucial to return to the way in which the 1717 engraving departs from the typical depiction of the constellation of the king and the incarnation of glory, both from the central painting in the Hall of Mirrors and from the text of the fairy tale. What is the reader to make of the fact that in the engraving the king looks absentmindedly ahead of him, without seeming to pay any attention to the presence of the object of his desires on the clouds above his left shoulder? The pose of the king is quite different from that in any official royal portrait. Seated in his cabinet, away from the gaze of his subjects, the majesty of the king is evoked through the attributes of power (crown, scepter) on the table next to him, but in a way that recalls the symbols of futility in a *vanitas* painting. At the same time, the majesty missing from the portrayal of the king seems to have been displaced to the princess on the clouds: her radiance, her vigorous pose, the reins in her hand, and her imposing chariot, which the tale explicitly calls a throne. We are in the cabinet of the king, in front of the inner, secret, invisible workings of absolutism, of which the king's exploits in the world outside the cabinet are only the expressions. What the reader sees in the engraving is therefore the merger of three different loci of interiority: first, the most withdrawn physical space of the castle; second, the inner principle of absolutism; third, the king's own interiority. If the king in the engraving looks like he is alone, it is because he is alone, lost in thought about his glorious exploits to come. And the similarity between the clouds in the engraving and thought bubbles in modern cartoons is more than incidental. Art historians argue that clouds in early modern art serve as markers of differentiation in the pictorial field, associated with an irruption of otherness, opening up to a different reality that can include dreams, visions, prophecies, and miracles.[56] This use is already obvious in the central painting in the Hall of Mirrors, where the king's glorious future is figured on similar clouds. And it is resonating in the words from Louis XIV to Charles Le Brun after the latter had escorted him around in the gallery for the first time, explaining the symbolism of the paintings, as analyzed at length in the preceding chapter: "Vous m'avez fait voir des choses que j'ai ressenties." (You have made me see things that I felt.)[57]

If the engraving shows the exterior expression of the king's feelings, the unfolding of the fairy tale shows the logic through which these feel-

56. Damisch, *A Theory of /Cloud/*, chaps. 2 and 3, esp. 41–44, 80, 108–9.
57. See section 4 of chapter 2.

ings are exteriorized: first, at the level of daring decisions, then, executed as glorious exploits. A close analysis of the implementation of this dynamic, in the way it structures the last two-thirds of the tale, reveals two characteristics that could at first be deemed accidental, but whose systematic recurrence indicates their constitutive function. First, a strong insistence from Belle Gloire on *dignity* or *worthiness*, both on her own worth and on that of Sans Parangon. Sans Parangon needs to make himself worthy of Belle Gloire (707, 712, 713, 723, 724), but also of himself, be it by honoring his name (707, 719, 726, 727) or by turning away from those who are not worthy of him, whether enemies (718) or mistresses (701). The second recurrent feature is related to an intermediary stage in the dynamic of the glorious challenges, separating their announcement and their fulfillment: a reaction of disbelief about the nature of the task expressed, most often either by the king himself or quite simply by the narrator. The princess only likes deeds "qui approchent de l'impossible" (that approach the impossible) (710). Beyond this insistence on their impossibility, there is another qualification that reappears repeatedly, pointing to the way in which these tasks are perceived as going against reason: "[c]e terrible discours" (this terrible discourse) (708); "une proposition si extravagante" (such an extravagant proposition) (710); "une entreprise si nouvelle et si hardie" (such an unprecedented and daring enterprise) (713); and finally "ce ridicule projet" (this ridiculous project) (725).

Impossible, terrible, extravagant, ridiculous: it is worth recalling that the challenges characterized in this way within the tale correspond to actual exploits ascribed to Louis XIV outside the allegory. Therefore, it may seem that we are not far from the charge of absurdity in the title of the chapter, but with the important distinction that there I evoke a common reaction from modern beholders with the term "absolutist absurdities," whereas here the allegation comes from within an absolutist setting. How are we as modern readers to make sense of this surprising feature? Does the fairy tale celebrate achievements while gesturing at them as "absurdities"? If so, how could this *not* be critique and subversion? Before concluding this chapter, I will address these questions by looking at two striking examples of the unfolding of this dynamic from the very end of the tale.

The first of these final challenges set by Belle Gloire for Sans Parangon brings us very close to the contemporary France of Préchac by way of recent military history. For the construction of the king's heroic glory to be efficient, the storytelling requires obstacles to overcome; to Belle Gloire, a political crisis only implies a potential for heroism. We encounter the most shocking instantiation of this dynamic in the description of the crisis corresponding to the beginning of the War of the League of Augsburg (1688–97), where Belle Gloire's reaction is described in the following way: "Belle Gloire qui apprit que tant de grandes puissances conspiraient contre Sans Parangon, et étaient prêtes à fondre sur ses États, l'en félicita au lieu de le plaindre." (Belle Gloire who learned that so many great powers were conspiring against Sans Parangon, and were ready to swoop in on his State, congratulated him on it, rather than pitying him) (721). The felicity at the heart of the congratulation (cf. the French verb *féliciter*) has the same source as the looming catastrophe, and without any concern for the inevitable suffering involved in the war. In effect, the princess is so untroubled that she doesn't dissimulate for a second the reason why the king's position is so precarious, but rather states openly that the crisis the king faces originated from his own pursuit of glory—in other words, in the wars he has waged, the palaces he has built, and so forth, in order to please the princess. Here are her chilling words to the king:

> [S]onge que tu as plusieurs puissances à combattre, c'est un[e] hydre qui a une infinité de têtes, *tes trésors sont épuisés par les complaisances que tu as eues pour moi,* au lieu que tes ennemis qui n'ont encore fait aucune dépense, ne manquent ni d'hommes ni d'argent. (722; my emphasis)

> (Ponder the fact that you have many powers to overcome, it is a hydra with an infinity of heads, *your treasures are exhausted by the complaisance you have had for me,* while your enemies who have not yet had any costs lack neither men nor money.)

Reading passages like this, where the demands of the extravagant dignity structuring the tale seem to run amok, it would be easy to forget that the text we are reading is written in praise of the king's pursuit of glory and not as its denunciation. Indeed, it may seem very natural to read these baffling words from the princess as a critique of the king: "your treasures are exhausted by the complaisance you have had for me." Modern scholars have seen a subversive message in passages like these,[58] and I would, in fact, claim that it is very difficult *not* to do so. How else could we understand such a hyperbolic emphasis on glory at the expense of royal rationality?

For any modern reader, such an interpretation would easily be further confirmed by the existence of contemporary documents from within

---

58. See, for example, the readings proposed by Defrance, "Le conte de fées," 62–65; and Gheeraert, "Introduction," 683–86.

the French court where the king's pursuit of glory is indeed denounced in the strongest possible terms. That is the case in the now-renowned anonymous 1694 *Lettre à Louis XIV* by François de Salignac de La Mothe-Fénelon. In one of many hard-hitting passages, Fénelon admonishes the king for having spent his whole life outside the path of truth and justice in the following terms: "Tant de troubles affreux qui ont désolé toute l'Europe depuis plus de vingt ans, tant de sang répandu, tant de scandales commis, tant de provinces saccagées, tant de villes et de villages mis en cendres, sont les funestes suites de cette guerre de 1672, entreprise pour votre gloire." (All the horrible troubles that have distressed the whole of Europe for more than twenty years—all the blood spilled, all the scandals committed, all the provinces ravaged, all the cities and towns burned to ashes—these are the disastrous consequences of this war of 1672, undertaken for your glory.)[59] Don't these words seem to anticipate Belle Gloire's challenge?

And yet, there is nothing indicating that the tale was intended as subversive or received in that vein. While scholars know very little about the reception of the book,[60] already the absence of scandal is significant. Préchac presents his tales as a celebration of the sovereign, and nothing indicates that it was not received as such. If we wanted to pursue speculations in this direction, we should rather ask, with Tony Gheeraert, whether "perhaps the charge of *maître de requêtes* that the author was entrusted with two years later is [. . .] linked to this encomiastic performance."[61]

More importantly still, the extravagant and excessive logic of glory at work here is *not* a satirical invention by Préchac. It can be found everywhere around him, in the diffusion of the official legend of Louis le Grand. Préchac's retelling of the history of Louis XIV is in fact very close to the official version of the story from the French Academy, which features the same focus on the marvelous and miraculous actions of the king, and the same concern with constructing obstacles that would allow his royal glory to shine. It is enough to return to the first part of the War

59. Fénelon, *Lettre à Louis XIV*, 50; Fénelon, *Letter to Louis XIV*, 110. I will return to Fénelon's admonishment in the closing of the chapter.

60. For the fullest discussion of the wider context inside which the book is published, in the heyday of the popularity of fairy tales, see Gevrey, "Introduction," xxiv–xxix, but without further indications about its reception.

61. "[P]eut-être la charge de maître de requêtes que le romancier se verra confier deux ans plus tard est [. . .] liée à cette performance encomiastique." Gheeraert, "Introduction," 670. Préchac furthermore received a reward in the sum of 2,000 livres from the king in person in 1706; see Gevrey, "Introduction," ix.

of the League of Augsburg in order to find the French Academy adopting the function of Belle Gloire. While the fairy-tale princess took delight in the fact that "so many great powers were conspiring against Sans Parangon and were ready to swoop in on his state," a very similar sentiment informs the following statement from Paul Tallemant in an official panegyric of the king in the French Academy in 1689, when France was in the midst of war:

En effet, Messieurs, notre auguste monarque sur la bonne foi des traités vivait dans une tranquillité profonde, cet ordre admirable établi dans tous ses états [. . .] ne lui laissai[t] presque plus de nouveaux sujets de gloire à espérer; et voilà que de toutes parts les ligues formées l'obligent à reprendre les armes, vont lui fournir de nouveaux sujets de victoire, et donner lieu à de nouveaux triomphes.⁶²

(Indeed, Gentlemen, our august monarch, on the good faith of treaties, lived in profound tranquility; this admirable order established in all of his states [. . .] almost left him with no more new subjects for glory to hope for; and then from every direction new alliances taking shape obliged him to take up arms once more and will provide him with new subjects for victory and give rise to new triumphs.)

We recognize from "Sans Parangon" the exhaustion of a reign already so glorious that there barely remain "plus de nouveaux sujets de gloire à espérer" (more new subjects for glory to hope for). Felicity in the face of an unexpected threat from abroad also appears in the panegyric, in its very last sentence: "applaudissons-nous sans cesse du bonheur que nous avons de vivre sous un règne si fécond en miracles" (let's ceaselessly rejoice at the good fortune we have to live under a reign so rich in miracles).⁶³ This discourse was the last panegyric of the king pronounced in the French Academy. But the acclamation continued elsewhere, as in Préchac's "Sans Parangon."⁶⁴

62. *Les panégyriques du roi*, ed. Zoberman, 243.

63. Tallemant, 246.

64. In his introduction to this last panegyric of the king, Zoberman reflects on the disappearance of the genre, evoking "une sorte d'épuisement" (a sort of exhaustion): "Le nombre de 'miracles' a-t-il diminué? Le discours a-t-il cessé de trouver dans la réalité royale l'air de fiction produit par le merveilleux? [. . .] Naturellement, le cérémonial académique continue de pourvoir à la production de l'éloge, mais plus sous cette forme directe et exclusive que constituait le panégyrique du Roi." (Did the number of "miracles" diminish? Did the discourse cease to find in the royal reality

Within Préchac's text, the celebration continues beyond the War of the League of Augsburg. The transition toward the tale's peculiar dénouement provides one last instance of the recurrent mixture of a language of excess and an emphasis on dignity, when Belle Gloire presents Sans Parangon with her final challenge, inviting him to "faire la guerre aux fées" (wage war against the fairies). The princess traces the origin of this challenge back to the king's heroic exploits by letting him know that "son grand courage et les choses extraordinaires qu'elle lui avait vu faire, lui avaient inspiré une pensée qui paraîtrait extravagante, mais qu'elle trouvait digne de Sans Parangon" (his great courage and the extraordinary deeds she had seen him do had inspired a thought which could seem extravagant, but which she found worthy of Sans Parangon) (727). In other words, the extraordinary actions of the prince give rise to a thought that may seem extravagant to others, but which the princess considers to be worthy of him, fitting for him. In fact, it is worthy precisely *because* it challenges common sense, *because* it defies any ordinary rational logic. Does the glorious dignity of this extravagant thought reside exactly in its appropriation of the art of making marvels? Are we here at the limits not only of the logic of Belle Gloire but of the logic of royal glory tout court, a logic that strives toward a heroic and perpetual effort at going beyond limits, toward the extreme, toward excess? Is it in order to remain faithful to this logic that the story ends before the battle between the king and the fairies? This lack of a proper dénouement has, of course, an obvious referential reason, since Louis XIV had not exhausted the field of glorious exploits at the time that Préchac wrote his story. In addition, there is a structural reason: the logic of glory does not allow for a satisfied "they lived happily ever after."

For modern readers, it may be difficult to read the curious and curiously extravagant tale about King Sans Parangon and Princess Belle Gloire without seeing a secret subversive message, a satirical denouncement of a hyperbolic emphasis on royal glory at the expense of sovereign rationality. However, as I have shown throughout this book, the absolutist logic of glory—with its excesses and seeming extravagance—is not a satirical invention by Préchac. It could be found everywhere around him in the diffusion of the official legend of Louis the Great, the real-life Sans Parangon, starting with the French Academy and the Petite Aca-

---

an air of fiction produced by the marvelous? [. . .] Naturally, the academic ceremony continued to provide for the production of praise, but no long under the direct and exclusive form that constituted the panegyric of the King). *Les Panégyriques du roi*, ed. Zoberman, 241.

démie—or in the center of the Hall of Mirrors at Versailles. In fact, the affirmation of this absolutist logic at the heart of Sans Parangon's reign may very well find its most precise formulation in a text whose purpose is precisely the transmission of that very logic. As we have seen, glory constitutes "the thing in the world which is the most precious" to the king. In the *Mémoires* for the instruction of the Dauphin, a personification of glory flaunts its extravagant dignity, while being presented as an insatiable mistress—a Belle Gloire as conceived by nobody else than her incomparable lover. It is in the final lines of the first part of the *Mémoires* for the year 1661 that Louis XIV states to his son

> [...] que la réputation ne se peut conserver sans en acquérir tous les jours davantage; que la gloire enfin n'est pas une maîtresse qu'on puisse jamais négliger, ni être digne de ses premières faveurs, si l'on n'en souhaite incessamment de nouvelles.

> ([...] that a reputation cannot be preserved without adding to it every day, that glory, finally, is not a mistress that one can ever neglect, nor be worthy of her first favors without always wishing for new ones.)[65]

In closing, I would like to return one last time to Belle Gloire's most astonishing statement to Sans Parangon. The scandal of this line resides in its truth, not only for the reign of the fairy-tale king within the text but also for his counterpart at Versailles outside the allegory: "your treasures are exhausted by the complaisance you have had for me." This is certainly the far end of the logic of glory. A point from which any modern observer could only envision the undoing of this logic: an occasion finally to address the human costs of royal glory, which are here so close to piercing through as the corollary of the financial costs evoked through the "exhaustion" of the royal treasures. However, we are here far away from Fénelon's perspective in the admonishment cited a few pages ago. The facts evoked are certainly similar, but the interpretive frameworks are incompatible. Unlike Préchac, Fénelon writes from outside the dream of absolutism; it is symptomatic in this respect that the letter most likely never reached Louis XIV.

In Préchac's encomiastic fairy tale, it is glory herself who pronounces the verdict. The perspective remains within "those webs of myths and facts spun by writers, webs that bound the prince to the pursuit of *gloire*,"

---

65. Louis XIV, *Mémoires, suivis de Manière de montrer les jardins*, 73; Louis XIV, *Mémoires for the Instruction of the Dauphin*, 37.

to return to a key formulation from Orest Ranum quoted in the intro-duction.[66] Belle Gloire's words, then, are a *promise* of further greatness to come—all the greater for being earned at the edge of the precipice in the hour of catastrophe.

Is this the point where the dream of absolutism turns into a night-mare? It would be more precise to say: It is the point where what is a dream for the dreamer resembles most a nightmare for the outsider. From within the dream, the scandal is an occasion for new victories, more glory, more greatness. From the outside, the view offers the grim realities of immense suffering and senseless loss, as voiced by Fénelon. Only the second of these perspectives, that of the nightmare, is easily available to us, as modern observers. And yet, by ignoring the dream for the nightmare, we not only risk failing to understand *their* predicament but perhaps also our own.

66. Ranum, *Artisans of Glory*, 337.

Seven Theses on the Dream of Absolutism

If, as I claimed in the very first sentence of the preface, this is *not* a book about Louis XIV, what is it about?

As I hope I have demonstrated throughout the book, the dream is a compelling framework both methodologically and ontologically. Methodological in the sense that it allows for a sustained close analysis of outlandish and exuberant materials without too quickly giving in to our modern demystifying impulses, present not only in Thackeray's "exact calculation" and the wider "propagandistic reduction" discussed in the introduction, but also in the very notion of absolutism. The dream has its logic, but one that is capable of integrating contradictions and assembling elements without needing them to cohere. As such, it allows for hermeneutic patience in the encounter with materials whose celebration of the glorious royal exemplar may appear otherwise alien and appalling.

At the same time, saying this much already implies an ontological foundation that undergirds the affective force of the dream. The dream of absolutism is a dream about a divinely invested ontological hierarchy, fueled by passions such as admiration and devotion, upheld by participatory cultural practices revolving around royal glory and royal exemplarity. Importantly, therefore, it is not a top-down enterprise, but a dream dreamt together collectively, from the king's erudite historiographers to the humble sonneteers who entered their work into competitions to praise Louis XIV. Together, they form an invested, imaginative totality, with ample room for tensions and contradictions.

The artifacts explored in each of the book's three chapters are very different in terms of media, genre, and the scene of enunciation. Nevertheless, discreetly guided by the framework of the dream, these three case studies have led to similar observations about the way in which absolutism operates through space (the priority of verticality), time (absolutism as presentism) and mood (celebration). Now, I turn to the framework proper, in order to articulate the following seven theses on the dream of absolutism, informed by the preceding analyses:

First, the dream is the opposite of demystification. It displaces our attention from the decoding and interpretation to the lived experience, which is what matters. The dream, therefore, allows us to see what the retrospective, demystifying gaze of many modern scholars—the *-ism* of absolut*ism*—has taken away from the historical phenomenon. Absolutism only existed *in, through,* and *as* dream and is only available to us as such.

Second, the dream knows only the present tense, here, now. Through effects of glory and exemplarity, the absolutist artifact induces a sense of a superlative presence, akin to the Augustinian *nunc stans,* a divine eternity breaking into and standing still in the present. A present that just is. Like the Cordouan Lighthouse, it emits royal glory without anybody watching.

Third, the dream is not communication but participation, not theory but practice. It is activity-oriented, accompanied sometimes by an uncomfortably triumphal energy, sometimes by a lighter atmosphere of pleasure, joy, festivity, celebration. Therefore, courtly pleasures (gallantry, civility, opera, rococo) are not necessarily the opposite of absolutism but rather an extension of the dream. A play-like absorption that is not false consciousness but rather a split consciousness: the dreamer knowing it is a dream, yet dreaming on, at once inside and outside of the dream.

Fourth, the dream implies a suspension of regular relations of agency, causality, and factuality. Within the radical verticality of absolutism, the obvious ontological top-down structure is complemented by a surprising bottom-up surge. A dream dreamt not by one but by many, collectively. Its mode of expression could take the form of Escher's lithograph depicting a self-drawing hand, as mentioned in chapter 1. From within the dream, the totality and coherence of absolutism emerge in the figure of the single hand of the sovereign master drawing its own portrait. From a distance, though, it is clear that this figuration itself is drawn by the many hands collaborating in the cultural production of sovereign single-handedness, as is the constitutive erasure of this collaboration. But the same dream—with a similar sovereign disregard for detached notions of agency, causality, and factuality—is expressed through the material gathered by Vertron, as analyzed in chapter 3, in a practice akin to early modern fan fiction.

Fifth, the dream is all display and ostentation. This may sound like a truism or pleonasm, but it is in reality the aspect most alien to a modern, post-Romantic perspective. The dream is exuberant, excessive, imposing.

Its collective sway emerges from the metonymic traces of the pleasure of taking part in greatness. It is at once display and the pleasure at displaying; it is the power of ostentation before it was deflated by the modern suspicion that reduced it to manipulation.

Sixth, the dream, in this sense, is real, powerful, and operative in the world. At the intersection of aesthetics and politics, it is the carrier of a force that emerges as a glorious image, a collective emotional reality that becomes real in the external world. It is Belle Gloire inspiring policy.

Seventh, this dream, latent in our collective political imaginary, can still be dreamt today. Scarcely hidden under an inch-deep democratic sensibility and a shallow post-Enlightenment mindset, it reemerges in the bottom-up surge carrying forward present-day potentates, in the collective dream of glory, of clarity, of greatness. Contemporary history amply demonstrates the extent to which we have radically underestimated the place of the premodern dream of absolutism within the logic of modernity. However, if the dream comes back to haunt us, it is not because it erupts from a deep irrational past in *them*, in their inability to think like us, but rather because it haunts *us* from within. A detailed inquiry into this persistence of the dream of absolutism within the logic of modernity is still to come, but I have developed some of the tools needed to take its measure in the book that ends here.

Acknowledgments

This book has its faraway origin in a postdoctoral project on "royal exemplarity" funded by the Research Council of Norway in the late 2000s. The way from there to here has been longer than expected, and it wasn't until a decade later that the pieces of the project fell into place with the realization that the book I hadn't been writing all these years was *not* exactly about royal exemplarity but rather about the dream of absolutism. The completion of the project was made possible by a sabbatical leave from Indiana University and the generous support from Indiana University's College of Arts and Humanities Institute and from the National Endowment for the Humanities. Equally decisive were the auspicious surroundings where the book was actually written: during a residency first at the Institute for Research in the Humanities at the University of Wisconsin–Madison and then at Indiana University's Institute for Advanced Study. I would like to thank these institutes and agencies, both in the abstract and as personified in their administrative staff, for their assistance throughout the process.

I am grateful for the occasion to present material from the project at different stages of the process at the following institutions: DePauw University, Stanford University, Sorbonne Nouvelle University, University of Chicago, University of Oslo, University of Illinois at Chicago, University of St. Gallen, University of Virginia, University of Wisconsin–Madison, Macalester College, and University of Kentucky. It is a pleasure to acknowledge the traces of the lively intellectual exchanges with colleagues and students alike on the pages of this book.

This project grew and took shape in dialogue with generous communities of scholars, at Indiana University, among fellow US early modernists, and among collaborators in France and Norway. Moving from Europe toward Bloomington, I would like to acknowledge my gratitude to Anne Eriksen, Karin Gundersen, Helge Jordheim, Kyrre Kverndokk,

Gro Bjørnerud Mo, and Roger Strand; to Alain Cantillon, Gérard Ferreyrolles, Éric Méchoulan, Hélène Merlin-Kajman, Anne Régent-Susini, Philippe Sellier, and Brice Tabeling; and to Saul Anton, Faith Beasley, Hélène Bilis, Andrew Billing, Chris Braider, Ann Delehanty, Dan Edelstein, Claire Goldstein, Katherine Ibbett, Radhika Koul, Ullrich Langer, John Lyons, Larry Norman, François Rigolot, Jennie Row, Volker Schröder, David Sedley, Matt Senior, Harriet Stone, Esther Van Dyke, Ellen Welch, and Barbara Whitehead. Juliette Cherbuliez, Ellen McClure and Jeff Peters are HEJJ!, most penetrating readers who made me rewrite my introduction, raise my ambitions, and broaden my scope. Late in the process Dalia Judovitz, Hélène Merlin-Kajman, Gro Bjørnerud Mo, Jane Newman, and Dror Wahrman all gave me decisive feedback that allowed me to rethink not only key arguments but also the structure of the book.

At Indiana University, I have had the good fortune of being part of several eminently generous interdisciplinarity communities, including Renaissance Studies, the Center for Eighteenth-Century Studies, and the Center for Theoretical Inquiry in the Humanities. This project has benefited from the generative feedback from numerous colleagues and friends, including Guillaume Ansart, Fritz Breithaupt, Alison Calhoun, Michel Chaouli, Andrea Ciccarelli, Aurelian Craiutu, Jonathan Elmer, Margot Gray, Oscar Kenshur, Sarah Knott, Giles Knox, Eric MacPhail, Richard Nash, Oana Panaïté, Bret Rothstein, Kaya Şahin, Massimo Scalabrini, Rob Schneider, Rebecca Spang, Johannes Türk, and Nicolas Valazza. The most transformative conversations happened within the team formerly known as IHSI and whose impact on the project I cannot even start to verbalize: Constance Furey, Patty Ingham, and Sonia Velázquez. Finally, thanks are due to the students in my various graduate seminars on absolutism and exemplarity in the last decade for their help in working through this project, in particular Kate Bastin, Nicole Burkholder, Jonathan Hall, Matt Hermane, Jake Ladyga, Katie Larson, Jade Liu, Sean Sidky, Jonathan Van Hecke, Amanda Vredenburgh, and David Wagner.

Beyond the scholarly communities mentioned above, the completion of this book owes a good deal to the support and solidarity of at least two communities of writers: at Indiana University, the new instantiations each semester of the CWG, with special thanks to Laura Plummer; and beyond Bloomington, even more crucially, to the unflinching FSP gang, Lorena Llosa and Sarita See.

Research assistants Amanda Vredenburgh, Jonathan Van Hecke, and Jonathan Hall brought not only diligence and discernment to the task, but also poise and grace, while the trenchant interventions of copy editor Clare Counihan helped give shape (and sometimes even swagger) to the shapeless so that a certain dream came better through.

I also want to thank Randy Petilos and Alan Thomas at the University of Chicago Press for their faith in the project and their perceptive guidance, the two anonymous readers for their insightful suggestions and criticism that allowed me to improve the final version of the manuscript, and copy editor Erin DeWitt and indexer June Sawyers for their adroit assistance at the editing and production stage.

The greatest thanks are due to SV, shrewdest reader, most incisive commentator, and most generous interlocutor, then, now, and always. This book is dedicated to her.

* * *

This book contains material from three previously published articles, as follows: in chapter 1, from "The Marginalization of the *Mémoires* of Louis XIV," *The European Legacy: Toward New Paradigms* 17, no. 6 (2012): 779–89, © Taylor and Francis, available online: http://www.tandfonline.com/ DOI: 10.1080/10848770.2012.715809; in chapter 2, from "'Vous m'avez fait voir des choses que j'ai ressenties': Le roi, son peintre et la question des émotions publiques," *Littératures classiques* 68, no. 1 (2009): 43–56 (DOI:10.3917/licla.068.0043); and in chapter 3, from "From the Cabinet of Fairies to the Cabinet of the King: The Marvelous Workings of Absolutism," *The Princeton University Library Chronicle* 76, nos. 1–2 (2015): 243–65 (DOI: 10.25290/prinunivlibrchro.76.1-2.0243).

Bibliography

Primary Texts before 1850

Aquinas, St. Thomas. *Summa theologiae.* Translated by Fathers of the English Dominican Province. Westminster, MD: Christian Classics, 1981.

Baudoin, Jean. *Iconologie, ou, Explication nouvelle de plusieurs images, emblèmes, et autres figures hiéroglyphiques des Vertus, des Vices, des Arts, des Sciences.* . . . Paris: Chez Mathieu Guillemot, 1644.

Bossuet, Jacques Bénigne. *Logique du Dauphin.* Paris: Éditions universitaires, 1990.

Corneille, Pierre. *Trois discours sur le poème dramatique.* Paris: Sedes, 1963.

Descartes, René. *Discours de la méthode / Discourse on the Method.* Translated by George Heffernan. South Bend, IN: University of Notre Dame Press, 1994.

Dictionnaire de l'Académie française, dédié au Roi. 2 vols. Paris: Jean Baptiste Coignard, 1694.

Les fastes de la Galerie des Glaces: Recueil d'articles du "Mercure Galant" (1681–1773). Edited by Stéphane Castelluccio. Paris: Payot, 2007.

Félibien, André. *Entretiens sur les vies et sur les ouvrages des plus excellents peintres anciens et modernes.* Trevoux: l'Imprimerie de S.A.S, 1725.

Félibien, André. *Le portrait du Roi.* 1663. In *Recueil de descriptions de peintures et d'autres ouvrages faits pour le Roi,* 69–94. Paris: Veuve de S. Mabre-Cramoisy, 1689.

Félibien, André. *Le Songe de Philomathe.* 1683. In *Recueil de descriptions de peinture et d'autres ouvrages faits pour le Roi,* 459–505. Paris: Veuve de S. Mabre-Cramoisy, 1689.

Fénelon. *Letter to Louis XIV.* In *Moral and Political Writings,* 108–14. Translated and edited by Ryan Patrick Hanley. Oxford: Oxford University Press, 2020.

Fénelon. *Lettre à Louis XIV et autres écrits politiques.* Edited by Pierre-Eugène Leroy. Paris: Bartillat, 2011.

Furetière, Antoine. *Dictionnaire universel.* 1690. Paris: S.N.L./Le Robert, 1978.

James I. *Basilikon Doron.* In *The Political Works of James I.* Edited by Charles Howard McIlwain. Cambridge, MA: Harvard University Press, 1918.

Louis XIV. *Mémoires de Louis XIV pour l'instruction du Dauphin.* 2 vols. Edited by Charles Dreyss. Paris: Didier, 1860.

Louis XIV. *Mémoires et réflexions.* Edited by Daniel Hamiche. Paris: Sicre, 2001.

Louis XIV. *Mémoires for the Instruction of the Dauphin.* Edited and translated by Paul Sonnino. New York: Free Press, 1970.

Louis XIV. *Mémoires pour l'instruction du Dauphin.* Edited by Pierre Goubert. Paris: Imprimerie Nationale, 1992.

Louis XIV. *Mémoires, suivis de Manière de montrer les jardins de Versailles.* Edited by Joël Cornette. Paris: Tallandier, 2007.

Louis XIV. *Œuvres de Louis XIV.* Edited by Grouvelle. Paris: Treuttel et Würtz, 1806.

Louis XIV. *Pensées de Louis XIV, extraites de ses ouvrages et de ses lettres manuscrites.* Paris: Didot, 1827.

Louis XIV. *Pensées de Louis XIV, ou maximes de gouvernement et réflexions sur le métier de roi, extraites des mémoires écrits par ce prince pour son fils le grand Dauphin.* Paris: C.-J. Trouvé, 1824.

Mabillon, Jean. *Traité des études monastiques.* Farnborough: Gregg Press, 1967.

Machiavelli. *The Prince.* Edited by Quentin Skinner and Russell Price. Cambridge: Cambridge University Press, 1988.

Massé, Jean-Baptiste. *La Grande Galerie de Versailles et les deux salons qui l'accompagnent, peints par Charles Le Brun, . . . dessinés par Jean-Baptiste Massé, . . . et gravés sous ses yeux par les meilleurs maîtres du temps.* Paris, 1753.

Ménard, Pierre. *L'Académie des princes, où les rois apprennent l'art de régner de la bouche des rois. Ouvrage tiré de l'histoire tant ancienne que nouvelle; et traduit par Pierre Ménard.* Paris: Sebastien Cramoisy and Gabriel Cramoisy, 1646.

Montaigne, Michel de. *Les essais.* 3 vols. Edited by Villey-Saulnier. Paris: Presses Universitaires de France, 1988.

Nivelon, Claude. *Vie de Charles le Brun et Description détaillée de ses ouvrages.* Edited by Lorenzo Pericolo. Genève: Droz, 2004.

Les panégyriques du roi prononcés dans l'Académie française. Edited by Pierre Zoberman. Paris: Presses de l'Université de Paris-Sorbonne, 1991.

Pascal, Blaise. *Pensées.* Edited by Philippe Sellier. Paris: Classiques Garnier, 1999.

Pascal, Blaise. *Pensées.* Translated by Roger Ariew, according to the Sellier edition. Indianapolis: Hackett, 2005.

Perrault, Charles. *Mémoires de Ch. Perrault. Œuvres choisies de Ch. Perrault, . . . avec les mémoires de l'auteur. . . .* Edited by Collin de Plancy. Paris: Brissot-Thivars, 1826.

Préchac, Jean de. "Sans Parangon." In *Contes merveilleux: Perrault, Fénelon, Mailly, Préchac, Choisy et anonymes.* Edited by Tony Gheeraert, 687–729. Paris: Champion, 2005.

Préchac, Jean de. "Sans Parangon." In *Contes moins contes que les autres: Sans Parangon et La Reine de fées.* Paris: Claude Barbin, 1698.

Préchac, Jean de. "Sans Parangon." In *Contes moins contes que les autres: Sans Parangon et La Reine de fées.* Paris: Compagnie de libraires associés, 1724.

Préchac, Jean de. "Sans Parangon." In *Le Cabinet des fées: Contenant tous leurs Ouvrages en huit volumes.* Amsterdam: Charles Le Cène, 1731.

Préchac, Jean de. "Sans Parangon." In *Le Cabinet des fées: Contenant tous leurs Ouvrages en huit volumes.* Amsterdam: Estienne Roger, 1717.

Racine, Jean. *Œuvres complètes.* Paris: Bibliothèque de la Pléiade, 1999.

Racine, Jean. *Phaedra.* Translated by Richard Wilbur. San Diego: Harcourt Brace Jovanovich, 1986.

Rainssant, Pierre. *Explication des tableaux de la galerie de Versailles, et de ses deux salons.* Versailles: F. Muguet, 1687.

Recueil de plusieurs pièces d'éloquence et de poésie présentées à l'Académie française pour le prix de l'année M.DC.LXXVII. Paris: Le Petit, 1677; reissued, Paris: Jean-Baptiste Coignard, 1695.

Richelet, P. *Dictionnaire français*. Genève: J. H. Widerhold, 1680.

Saint-Aignan, duc de, Monsieur de Vertron et al., eds. *Recueil de sonnets en bouts rimés à la Gloire du Roi, proposés en différent temps, pour des Prix considérables qui étaient des Médailles d'Or ou des Portrait de Sa Majesté*. Le Havre de Grace: Jacques Gruchet, 1686.

Thackeray, William Makepeace [Mr. Titmarsh, pseud.]. *The Paris Sketch Book: With numerous designs by the author, on copper and wood*. 2 vols. London: John Macrone, 1840.

Vertron, Claude-Charles Guyonnet de. "Lettre 421: Claude-Charles Guyonnet de Vertron à Pierre Bayle." *L'Édition électronique de la correspondance de Pierre Bayle*, May 24, 1685. http://bayle-correspondance.univ-st-etienne.fr/?Lettre-421-Claude-Charles-Guyonnet&lang=fr.

Vertron, Claude-Charles Guyonnet de. *Le Nouveau panthéon, ou Le Rapport des divinités du paganisme, des héros de l'Antiquité et des princes surnommés grands aux vertus et aux actions de Louis le Grand*. Paris: J. Morel, 1686.

Vertron, Claude-Charles Guyonnet de. *Parallèle de Louis le Grand avec les princes qui ont été surnommés grands*. Paris: J. Le Febvre, 1685.

Voltaire. "Épître à l'auteur du livre des trois imposteurs." *Œuvres complètes de Voltaire*. Edited by Louis Moland, vol. 10, 402–5. Paris: Garnier, 1877–85.

Studies (after 1850)

Ackerman, Simone. "De l'histoire à la première personne à la littérature au second degré: Réflexions sur les *Mémoires* de Louis XIV." In *Actes de Columbus: Racine, Fontenelle: "Entretiens sur la pluralité des mondes," histoire et littérature*, edited by Charles G. S. Williams, 259–70. Paris: Papers on French Seventeenth-Century Literature, 1990.

Agamben, Giorgio. *The Kingdom and the Glory: For a Theological Genealogy of Economy and Government*. Translated by Lorenzo Chiesa and Matteo Mandarini. Stanford, CA: Stanford University Press, 2011.

Althusser, Louis. "Ideology and Ideological State Apparatuses (Notes towards an Investigation)." In *Lenin and Philosophy and Other Essays*. Translated by Ben Brewster. New York: Monthly Review Press, 1971.

Apostolidès, Jean-Marie. *Le roi-machine: Spectacle et politique au temps de Louis XIV*. Paris: Minuit, 1981.

Baby, Hélène, and Josiane Rieu, eds. *La Douceur en littérature de l'Antiquité au XVIIe siècle*. Paris: Classiques Garnier, 2012.

Bar, Virginie. *La peinture allégorique au Grand siècle*. Paris: Faton, 2003.

Barbeito, José Manuel. *El Alcázar de Madrid*. Madrid: Colegio Oficial de Arquitectos de Madrid, 1992.

Baudrillard, Jean. *The System of Objects*. Translated by James Benedict. London: Verso, 2005.

Bazin-Henry, Sandra. "Charles Le Brun et les décors de miroirs." *Bulletin du Centre de recherche du château de Versailles*, December 22, 2017. https://doi.org/10.4000/crcv.14600.

Bazin-Henry, Sandra. "'Tromper les yeux': Les miroirs dans le grand décor en Europe (XVIIe–XVIIIe siècles)." PhD diss., Université Paris IV, 2016.

Beasley, Faith. *Versailles Meets the Taj Mahal: François Bernier, Marguerite de la*

Sablière and Enlightening Conversations in Seventeenth-Century France. Toronto: University of Toronto Press, 2018.

Belhoste, Jean-François. "La glace dans la galerie et le décor français." *La Galerie des glaces après sa restauration*, 145–66. Dijon: Faton, 2007.

Belleguic, Thierry, and Marc André Bernier. "Le siècle des Lumières et la communauté des Anciens: Rhétorique, histoire et esthétique." In *Parallèle des Anciens et des Modernes: Histoire, rhétorique et esthétique au siècle des Lumières*, edited by Marc André Bernier, 1–28. Québec: Presses de l'Université Laval, 2006.

Berger, Robert W. "Galerie des Glaces." In *Versailles: The Château of Louis XIV*, 51–58. University Park: Pennsylvania State University Press, 1985.

Bjørnstad, Hall. *Créature sans créateur: Pour une anthropologie baroque dans les "Pensées" de Pascal*. Paris: Hermann Éditeurs, 2013.

Bjørnstad, Hall. "'Plus d'éclaircissement touchant la grande galerie de Versailles': Du nouveau sur les inscriptions latines." *XVIIe siècle* 243, no. 2 (2009): 321–43.

Blanchard, Jean-Vincent. "Claude-François Ménestrier and the 'Querelle des Monuments.'" *Papers on French Seventeenth-Century Literature* 71, no. 36 (2009): 507–14.

Boulègue, Laurence, Margaret Jones-Davies, and Florence Malhomme, eds. *La Douceur dans la pensée moderne: Esthétique et philosophie d'une notion*. Paris: Classiques Garnier, 2017.

Brown, Jonathan. *Velázquez: Painter and Courtier*. New Haven, CT: Yale University Press, 1986.

Brown, Jonathan, and John H. Elliott. "The Hall of Princely Virtue." *A Palace for a King: The Buen Retiro and the Court of Phillip IV*, 156–63. New Haven, CT: Yale University Press, 2003.

Burke, Peter. *The Fabrication of Louis XIV*. New Haven, CT: Yale University Press, 1992.

Burke, Peter. *Louis XIV: Les stratégies de la gloire*. Translated by Paul Chemla. Paris: Seuil, 1995.

Calhoun, Alison. *Montaigne and the Lives of the Philosophers: Life Writing and Transversality in the Essais*. Newark: University of Delaware Press, 2015.

Canova-Green, Marie-Claude. "On ne naît pas roi, on le devient: Louis XIV au miroir de ses Mémoires." In *Louis XIV l'image et le mythe*, edited by Mathieu da Vinha, Alexandre Maraval, and Nicolas Milanovic, 33–44. Rennes: Presses Universitaires de Rennes, 2014.

Carruthers, Mary. "Sweetness." *Speculum* 81, no. 4 (2006): 999–1013.

Castaner Muñoz, Esteban. "L'exhaussement du phare de Cordouan: Un chantier des Lumières (1786–1789)." *Bulletin monumental* 164, no. 2 (2006): 187–94.

Chaimovich, Felipe. "Mirrors of Society: Versailles and the Use of Flat Reflected Images." *Visual Resources: An International Journal on Images and Their Uses* 24, no. 4 (2008): 353–67.

Chaline, Olivier. "De la gloire." *Littératures classiques*, no. 36 (Spring 1999): 95–108.

Chaline, Olivier, ed. "La gloire à l'époque moderne." Special issue of *Histoire, économie et société* 20, no. 2 (2001).

Chaline, Olivier. *Le règne de Louis XIV*. 2 vols. Paris: Flammarion, 2005.

Chartier, Roger. Introduction to *La société de cour*, by Norbert Elias, i–lxxvii. Translated by Pierre Kamnitzer and Jeanne Etoré. Paris: Flammarion, 1985.

Church, William F. "The Decline of French Jurists as Political Theorists." *French Historical Studies* 5 (1967): 1–40.

Colomer, José Luis. "Paz política, rivalidad suntuaria: Francia y España en la Isla de los Faisanes." In *Arte y diplomacia de la Monarquía Hispánica en el siglo XVII*, edited by José Luis Colomer, 61–88. Madrid: Fernando Villaverde Ediciones, 2003.

Cornette, Joël. "Chronique de l'État Classique (1652–1715)." In *L'État classique: Regards sur la pensée politique de la France dans le second XVIIe siècle*, edited by Joël Cornette and Henry Méchoulan, 431–500. Paris: Éditions Vrin, 1996.

Cornette, Joël. Introduction to *Mémoires, suivis de Manière de montrer les jardins de Versailles*, by Louis XIV, 11–46. Edited by Joël Cornette. Paris: Tallandier, 2007.

Cornette, Joël. *Le roi de guerre: Essai sur la souveraineté dans la France du Grand Siècle*. Paris: Payot, 2000.

Cosandey, Fanny, and Robert Descimon. *L'absolutisme en France: Histoire et historiographie*. Paris: Seuil, 2002.

Croix, Alain, and Jean Quéniart. *Histoire culturelle de la France: Tome 2, De la Renaissance à l'aube des Lumières*. Paris: Seuil, 1997.

Damisch, Hubert. *A Theory of /Cloud/: Toward a History of Painting*. 1972. Translated by Janet Lloyd. Stanford, CA: Stanford University Press, 2002.

da Vinha, Mathieu. "Monseigneur le Dauphin, fils de Louis XIV: Introduction." *Bulletin du Centre de recherche du château de Versailles*, April 14, 2014. https://doi.org/10.4000/crcv.12465.

Defrance, Anne. "Le conte de fées au risque de l'éloge politique: *La tyrannie des fées détruite* (Mme d'Auneuil) et autres contes de la première génération." *Le conte merveilleux au XVIIIe siècle: Une poétique expérimentale*, edited by Régine Jomand-Baudry and Jean-François Perrin, 55–73. Paris: Kimé, 2002.

DeJean, Joan. "Power Mirrors: Technology in the Service of Glamour." In *The Essence of Style: How the French Invented High Fashion, Fine Food, Chic Cafés, Style, Sophistication, and Glamour*, 177–200. New York: Free Press, 2005.

Démoris, René. "Le langage du corps et l'expression des passions de Félibien à Diderot." In *Des mots et des couleurs II*, edited by Jean-Pierre Guillerm, 39–67. Lille: Presses Universitaires de Lille, 1986.

Dessert, Daniel. *Louis XIV prend le pouvoir: Naissance d'un mythe?* Bruxelles: Éd Complexe, 1989.

Drevillon, Hervé. *Les rois absolus (1629–1715)*. Paris: Belin, 2011.

Dreyss, Charles. "Étude sur la composition des Mémoires de Louis XIV pour l'instruction du Dauphin." In *Mémoires de Louis XIV pour l'instruction du Dauphin*. 2 vols. Edited by Charles Dreyss, vol. 1, I–CCLI. Paris: Didier, 1860.

Dumora, Florence. *L'Œuvre nocturne: Songe et représentation au XVIIe siècle*. Paris: Champion, 2005.

Eliade, Mircea. *The Sacred and the Profane*. Translated by Willard R. Trask. New York: Harcourt, 1959.

Elias, Norbert. *The Civilizing Process*. Vol. 1: *The History of Manners*. Translated by Edmund Jephcott. Oxford: Blackwell, 1969.

Elias, Norbert. *The Court Society*. Translated by Edmund Jephcott. Oxford: Blackwell, 1983.

Elias, Norbert. *La société de cour*. Translated by Pierre Kamnitzer and Jeanne Etoré. Paris: Flammarion, 1985.

Emmens, J. A. "Les Menines de Velazquez: Miroir des princes pour Phillipe IV." *Nederlands Kunsthistorisch Jaarboek* 12 (1961): 50–79.

Ferrier-Caverivière, Nicole. *L'image de Louis XIV dans la littérature française, de 1660 à 1715*. Paris: Presses Universitaires de France, 1981.

Frelick, Nancy M., ed. *The Mirror in Medieval and Early Modern Culture: Specular Reflections*. Turnhout, Belgium: Brepols, 2016.

La Galerie des glaces: Histoire et restauration. Dijon: Faton, 2007.

Ganim, Russell. "Views of Kingship: *Britannicus* and Louis XIV's *Mémoires*." In *Classical Unities: Place, Time, Action*, edited by Erec R. Koch, 315–24. Tübingen: G. Narr, 2002.

Gelley, Alexander, ed. *Unruly Examples: On the Rhetoric of Exemplarity*. Stanford, CA: Stanford University Press, 1995.

Gevrey, Françoise. Introduction to *Contes moins contes que les autres, précédés de L'Illustre Parisienne*, i–xxxviii. Edited by Françoise Gevrey. Paris: STFM, 1993.

Gheeraert, Tony. Introduction to *Contes moins contes que les autres*. In *Contes merveilleux: Perrault, Fénelon, Mailly, Préchac, Choisy et anonymes*. Edited by Tony Gheeraert. Paris: Champion, 2005.

Giavarini, Laurence, ed. *Construire l'exemplarité. Pratiques littéraires et discours historiens (XVIe–XVIIIe siècles)*. Dijon: Éditions Universitaires de Dijon, 2008.

Gicquiaud, Grégory. "La balance de Clio: Réflexion sur la poétique et la rhétorique du parallèle." In *Parallèle des Anciens et des Modernes: Histoire, rhétorique et esthétique au siècle des Lumières*, edited by Marc André Bernier, 29–48. Québec: Presses de l'Université Laval, 2006.

Goldstein, Claire. *Vaux and Versailles: The Appropriations, Erasures, and Accidents That Made Modern France*. Philadelphia: University of Pennsylvania Press, 2007.

Goubert, Pierre. Introduction to *Mémoires pour l'instruction du Dauphin*, by Louis XIV, 1–39. Edited by Pierre Goubert. Paris: Imprimerie Nationale, 1992.

Le Grand Robert. grandrobert.lerobert.com.

Grell, Chantal. "L'histoire au service d'ambitions hégémoniques: La monarchie française et l'instrumentalisation du passé au XVIIe siècle." In *Les cours d'Espagne et de France au XVIIe siècle*, edited by Chantal Grell and Benoît Pellistrandi, 279–305. Madrid: Collection de la Casa de Velázquez, 2007.

Grell, Chantal, and Christian Michel. *L'École des princes ou Alexandre disgracié: Essai sur la mythologie monarchique de la France absolutiste*. Paris: Les Belles lettres, 1988.

Grenet-Delisle, Claude. *Louis de Foix: Horloger, ingénieur, architecte de quatre rois*. Bordeaux: Fédération historique du SudOuest, 1998.

Guillaume, Jean. "Le phare de Cordouan, 'merveille du monde' et monument monarchique." *Revue de l'art*, no. 8 (1970): 33–52.

Halévi, Ran. "Louis XIV: La religion de la gloire." *Le Débat*, no. 150 (2008): 175–92.

Halévi, Ran. "Savoir politique et 'mystère de l'état': Le sens caché des *Mémoires* de Louis XIV." *Histoire, économie et société* 19, no. 4 (2000): 451–68.

The Hall of Mirrors: History & Restoration. Translated by Ann Sautier-Greening. Dijon: Faton, 2007.

Hamon, Maurice. "Les commandes de glaces pour Versailles aux XVIIe et XVIIIe siècles." *Actes du colloque Verre et fenêtre pendant la période moderne*. Paris-La Défense, Versailles, October 13–15, 2005. http://www.mosquito.fr/demo/verrefenetre/pages/p402_01_hamon.html.

Hampton, Timothy. *Writing from History: The Rhetoric of Exemplarity in Renaissance Literature*. Ithaca, NY: Cornell University Press, 1990.

Hartog, François. *Anciens, modernes, sauvages*. Paris: Points, 2005.

Hochner, Nicole. "Against Propaganda: The Juxtaposition of Images in Early Modern France. Reflections on the Reign of Louis XII (1498–1515)." In *Exploring Cultural History: Essays in Honour of Peter Burke*, edited by Melissa Calaresu et al., 231–47. Farnham, UK: Ashgate, 2010.

Hoffmann, Kathryn A. "Sun-Eye and Medusa-Head: Louis XIV's *Mémoires*." In *Society of Pleasures: Interdisciplinary Readings in Pleasure and Power during the Reign of Louis XIV*, 13–39. New York: St. Martin's Press and Macmillan Press, 1997.

Hogg, Chloé. *Absolutist Attachments: Emotion, Media, and Absolutism in Seventeenth-Century France*. Evanston, IL: Northwestern University Press, 2019.

Janczukiewicz, Jérôme. "La prise du pouvoir par Louis XIV: La construction du mythe." *XVIIe siècle* 227, no. 2 (2005): 243–64.

Jouanna, Arlette. *Le Pouvoir absolu: Naissance de l'imaginaire politique de la royauté*. Paris, Gallimard, 2013.

Jouanna, Arlette. *Le Prince absolu: Apogée et déclin de l'imaginaire monarchique*. Paris, Gallimard, 2014.

Jouhaud, Christian. *Les Pouvoirs de la littérature: Histoire d'un paradoxe*. Paris: Gallimard, 2000.

Kisluk-Grosheide, Daniëlle, and Bertrand Rondot, eds. *Visiteurs de Versailles: Voyageurs, princes, ambassadeurs, 1682–1789*. Paris: Gallimard, 2017.

Klaits, Joseph. *Printed Propaganda under Louis XIV: Absolute Monarchy and Public Opinion*. Princeton, NJ: Princeton University Press, 1976.

Kleber, Hermann. "Louis XIV mémorialiste: La genèse des *Mémoires* de Louis XIV." In *Les princes et l'histoire du XIVe au XVIIIe siècle*, edited by Chantal Grell et al., 523–33. Bonn: Bouvier, 1998.

Koch, Ebba. *Mughal Architecture: An Outline of Its History and Development (1526–1858)*. New Delhi: Oxford University Press, 2002.

Kruger, Steven. *Dreaming in the Middle Ages*. Cambridge: Cambridge University Press, 1992.

Lahaye, Matthieu. *Le fils de Louis XIV: Monseigneur le Grand Dauphin, 1661–1711*. Seyssel: Champ Vallon, 2013.

Legge, Rosemary. "The Mirror and Manners: Watching, Being Watched, and Watching Oneself in Rococo Spaces." *Lumen* 37 (2018): 91–105.

Levy, Evonne. *Propaganda and the Jesuit Baroque*. Berkeley: University of California Press, 2004.

Lichtenstein, Jacqueline. *The Eloquence of Color: Rhetoric and Painting in the French Classical Age*. Translated by Emily McVarish. Berkeley: University of California Press, 1993.

Lignereux, Yann. *Les rois imaginaires: Une histoire visuelle de la monarchie de Charles VIII à Louis XIV*. Rennes: Presses Universitaires de Rennes, 2016.

Lockwood, Richard. "The 'I' of History in the *Mémoires* of Louis XIV." *Papers on French Seventeenth-Century Literature* 14, no. 2 (1987): 551–64.

Luciani, Isabelle. "La Province poétique au XVIIe siècle: Sociabilité distinctive et intégration culturelle." *Revue d'histoire moderne et contemporaine* 47, no. 3 (2000): 545–64.

Lyons, John D. *Exemplum: The Rhetoric of Example in Early Modern France and Italy.* Princeton, NJ: Princeton University Press, 1989.

Maral, Alexandre. "Architectural Work on the 'Grande Galerie.'" In *The Hall of Mirrors: History & Restoration*, 40–51. Translated by Ann Sautier-Greening. Dijon: Faton, 2007.

Maral, Alexandre. "La galerie: Une affaire d'architecte? L'exemple de la Grande Galerie de Versailles." In *Les Grandes galeries européennes, XVIIe–XIXe siècles*, edited by Claire Constans and Mathieu da Vinha, 51–64. Paris: Éditions de la Maison des sciences de l'homme, 2010.

Maral, Alexandre. "The Marbles and the Mirrors." In *The Hall of Mirrors: History & Restoration*, 52–53. Translated by Ann Sautier-Greening. Dijon: Faton, 2007.

Marin, Louis. *Le portrait du roi.* Paris: Editions de Minuit, 1981.

Marin, Louis. *Portrait of the King.* Translated by Martha M. Houle. Minneapolis: University of Minnesota Press, 1988.

McClure, Ellen M. "The Absolute Author: Louis XIV's *Mémoires pour l'instruction du dauphin.*" In *Sunspots and the Sun King: Sovereignty and Mediation in Seventeenth-Century France*, 68–102. Urbana: University of Illinois Press, 2006.

Méchoulan, Éric. "La douceur du politique." In *Le doux aux XVIe et XVIIe siècles: Écriture, esthétique, politique, spiritualité*, edited by Marie-Hélène Prat and Pierre Servet, 221–38. Lyon: Centre Jean Prévost, 2003.

Melchior-Bonnet, Sabine. *The Mirror: A History.* Translated by Katharine H. Jewett. New York: Routledge, 2001.

Meyer, Daniel. *L'histoire du Roy.* Paris: Editions de la Réunion des Musées Nationaux, 1980.

Milovanovic, Nicolas. *Du Louvre à Versailles: Lecture des grands décors monarchiques.* Paris: Les Belles Lettres, 2005.

Milovanovic, Nicolas. "Les inscriptions dans le décor de la galerie des Glaces à Versailles: Nouvelles découvertes." *Comptes rendus de l'Académie des Inscriptions et Belles-Lettres*, fasc. I (2005): 279–306.

Milovanovic, Nicolas. "The Portrait of the King: Louis XIV in the Decor of the Hall of Mirrors." In *The Hall of Mirrors: History & Restoration*, 142–53. Translated by Ann Sautier-Greening. Dijon: Faton, 2007.

Milovanovic, Nicolas. *Versailles, la galerie des Glaces, catalogue iconographique.* Co-production RMN-EPV, 2008. www.galeriedesglaces-versailles.fr.

Montagu, Jennifer. *The Expression of the Passions: The Origin and Influence of Charles Le Brun's "Conférence sur l'expression générale et particulière."* New Haven, CT: Yale University Press, 1994.

Mormiche, Pascale. *Devenir prince: L'école du pouvoir en France XVIIe–XVIIIe siècles.* Paris: CNRS Éditions, 2009.

Mormiche, Pascale. "Éduquer le Dauphin: Exempla, image du père, éducation exemplaire?" *Bulletin du Centre de recherche du château de Versailles*, 2014. https://doi.org/10.4000/crcv.12368.

Morrissey, Robert. *The Economy of Glory: From Ancien Régime France to the Fall of Napoleon.* Translated by Teresa Lavender Fagan. Chicago: University of Chicago Press, 2014.

Norman, Larry F. *The Public Mirror: Molière and the Social Commerce of Depiction.* Chicago: University of Chicago Press, 1999.

Norman, Larry F. *The Shock of the Ancient: Literature and History in Early Modern France.* Chicago: Chicago University Press, 2011.

Oxford English Dictionary [*OED*]. www.oed.com.

Orso, Steven N. *Philip IV and the Decoration of the Alcázar of Madrid.* Princeton, NJ: Princeton University Press, 1986.

Parish, Richard. "'Une vie douce, heureuse et amiable': A Christian *joie de vivre* in Saint François de Sales." In *Joie de vivre in French Literature and Culture,* edited by Susan Harrow and Timothy Unwin, 129–40. Amsterdam: Rodopi, 2009.

Pendergrast, Mark. *Mirror Mirror: A History of the Human Love Affair with Reflection.* New York: Basic Books, 2004.

Pepper, Thomas. "Kneel and You Will Believe." In *Yale French Studies. Depositions: Althusser, Balibar, Macherey, and the Labor of Reading,* edited by Jacques Lezra and Thomas Kavanaugh, 27–41. New Haven, CT: Yale University Press, 1995.

Perez, Stanis. "Les brouillons de l'absolutisme: Les 'mémoires' de Louis XIV en question." *XVII*e *siècle* 222, no. 1 (2004): 25–50.

Prat, Marie-Hélène, and Pierre Servet, eds. *Le doux aux XVI*e *et XVII*e *siècles: Écriture, esthétique, politique, spiritualité.* Lyon: Centre Jean Prévost, 2003.

Preyat, Fabrice. *Le Petit Concile de Bossuet et la christianisation des mœurs et des pratiques littéraires sous Louis XIV.* Berlin: LitVerlag, 2007.

Ranum, Orest. *Artisans of Glory: Writers and Historical Thought in Seventeenth-Century France.* Chapel Hill: University of North Carolina Press, 1980.

Revel, Jacques. "La cour." In *Les lieux de mémoire, tome III.* Vol. 2: *Les France.* Edited by Pierre Nora, 129–93. Paris: Gallimard, 1992.

Rigolot, François, ed. "The Renaissance Crisis of Exemplarity." Special issue of *Journal of the History of Ideas* 59, no. 4 (1998).

Rossholm Lagerlöf, Margaretha. "La Galerie des glaces at Versailles (1678–1684): Omnipotence in Reflection." In *Fate, Glory and Love in Early Modern Gallery Decoration: Visualizing Supreme Power,* 150–97. Farnham, UK: Ashgate, 2013.

Sabatier, Gérard. *Versailles ou la disgrâce d'Apollon.* Rennes: Presses Universitaires de Rennes, 2016.

Sabatier, Gérard. *Versailles, ou la figure du roi.* Paris: Albin Michel, 1999.

Sancho, José Luis. "L'espace du roi à la cour d'Espagne sous les Habsbourg." In *¿Louis XIV espagnol? Madrid et Versailles, images et modèles,* edited by Gérard Sabatier and Margarita Torrione, 119–36. Versailles: Centre de recherche du château de Versailles, 2009.

Saule, Béatrix. "The Hall of Mirrors during Louis XIV's Reign: From the Ordinary to the Extraordinary." In *The Hall of Mirrors: History & Restoration,* 54–73. Translated by Ann Sautier-Greening. Dijon: Faton, 2007.

Schechter, Ronald. *A Genealogy of Terror in Eighteenth-Century France.* Chicago: University of Chicago Press, 2018.

Schlüter, D. "Herrlichkeit. I." In *Historiches Wörterbuch der Philosophie,* III, 1079–80. Basel, Schwabe, 1976.

Seifert, Lewis C. "Jean de Préchac." In *The Oxford Companion to Fairy Tales.* Edited by Jack Zipes. Oxford: Oxford University Press, 2000.

Soll, Jacob. "Empirical History and the Transformation of Political Criticism in France from Bodin to Bayle." *Journal of the History of Ideas* 64, no. 2 (April 2003): 297–316.

Soll, Jacob. *The Information Master: Jean-Baptiste Colbert's Secret State Intelligence System.* Ann Arbor: University of Michigan Press, 2009.

Solomon, Howard M. *Public Welfare, Science, and Propaganda in Seventeenth-Century France: The Innovations of Théophraste Renaudot.* Princeton, NJ: Princeton University Press, 1972.

Sonnino, Paul. "The Dating and Authorship of Louis XIV's *Mémoires.*" *French Historical Studies* 3 (1964): 303–37.

Sonnino, Paul. Introduction to *Mémoires for the Instruction of the Dauphin,* by Louis XIV, 3–17. Edited and translated by Paul Sonnino. New York: Free Press, 1970.

Stollberg-Rilinger, Barbara. *The Emperor's Old Clothes: Constitutional History and the Symbolic Language of the Holy Roman Empire.* Translated by Thomas Dunlap. New York: Berghahn Books, 2015.

Stone, Harriet. *Crowning Glories: Netherlandish Realism and the French Imagination during the Reign of Louis XIV.* Toronto: University of Toronto Press, 2019.

Thacker, Christopher. *The History of Gardens.* Berkeley: University of California Press, 1985.

Trésor de la langue Française informatisé [*TLF*]. www.atilf.fr/tlfi.

van Lamsweerde, Inez, and Vinoodh Matadin. "Secret Garden: Versailles." Vimeo, 2012. https://vimeo.com/41499247.

Veyne, Paul. "Buts de l'art, propagande et faste monarchique." In *L'empire gréco-romain,* 379–418. Paris: Seuil, 2005.

Volle, Nathalie, and Nicolas Milovanovic, eds. *La galerie des Glaces après sa restauration—contexte et restitution: Actes du colloque École du Louvre–Musée national du château de Versailles—Centre de recherche et de restauration des musées de France, 16–17 octobre 2008.* Paris: Ecole du Louvre, 2013.

Vredenburgh, Amanda, and Hall Bjørnstad. "Un discours 'de majesté': Le sublime royal dans les expressions de l'absolutisme sous Louis XIV." *Romanic Review* 111, no. 2 (2020): 227–48.

Vuilleumier Laurens, Florence, and Pierre Laurens. *L'âge de l'inscription: La rhétorique du monument en Europe du XVe au XVIIe siècle.* Paris: Belles Lettres, 2010.

Weiss, Allen S. *Mirrors of Infinity: The French Formal Garden and 17th-Century Metaphysics.* New York: Princeton Architectural Press, 1995.

Welch, Ellen R. *A Theater of Diplomacy: International Relations and the Performing Arts in Early Modern France.* Philadelphia: University of Pennsylvania Press, 2017.

Wellington, Robert. *Antiquarianism and the Visual Histories of Louis XIV: Artifacts for a Future Past.* Farnham, UK: Ashgate, 2015.

Ziegler, Hendrik. "'His house at Versailles is something the foolishest in the world . . .': La Grande Galerie de Versailles à travers les récits de voyageurs et d'ambassadeurs étrangers autour de 1700." In *Europäische Galeriebauten / Galleries in a Comparative European Perspective (1400–1800),* edited by Christina Strunck and Elisabeth Kieven, 351–82. Munich: Hirmer Verlag, 2010.

Zoberman, Pierre. "Eloquence and Ideology: Between Image and Propaganda." *Rhetorica* 18, no. 3 (2000): 295–320.

Index